On Coaching
with The Birkman Method®

Robert T. De Filippis
April 2018

Published by BookLocker.com, Inc., St. Petersburg, Florida.

Printed on acid-free paper.

BookLocker.com, Inc.
2018

First Edition

Dedication

I dedicate this book to the memory of my sister Connie, who died suddenly at the age of 29. Pregnant with a son we lost the same day, she did not have the gift of long life that most of us take for granted.

Robert De Filippis

Author's Note

I left my career as a manufacturing executive in 1980, returned to school part-time while I built a consulting practice and supported a growing family. During those early years, I was introduced to The Birkman Method® as a client. I quickly decided to become certified as a practitioner and began my multi-decade involvement with the Birkman organization. Along the way, and I can't recall precisely when, I was fortunate enough to meet Dr. Birkman himself and a kinder, more gracious, and more professional man, I've never met.

By the mid-nineties, I was ready to begin my Ph.D. dissertation, and I submitted my proposal for candidacy. Life had other plans for me, and I dropped out with the hope that I could return one day and complete it. It didn't happen, so in early 2000 I used my original proposal and finished what I started. It would have been my dissertation but became the book titled, *You, Your SELF and the 21st Century: Coaching yourself and others in postmodern times featuring The Birkman Method*, published in 2003.

One day much later, Dr. Birkman was my guest of honor at a breakfast I co-sponsored with a colleague in Tyson's Corner, VA. The purpose of the event was to introduce The Birkman Method® to a select group of companies based in the Washington, DC metro area. I don't recall all the details of our conversations during that time together, but one, in particular, gave me a surprise and a delight.

As I was taking him to the airport, he told me that he carried my book with him for airplane reading and was learning more about his own work by reading it. As surprised and delighted as I was, I don't think I fully understood what he was saying. Then I re-read this testimonial:

One of the blessings of any creative person is witnessing other creative people discovering your ideas, valuing, and using them, then innovatively building upon them. Robert T. De Filippis' book is an excellent example of such an effort. While I developed The Birkman Method® on an empirical basis, almost since its creation, innovative consultants have expressed "theoretical" models for the results. Mr. De Filippis is the first to put his ideas down in written form. His application of The Method using neuro-cognitive science constructs is informative and forward thinking. His unique philosophical/psychological/scientific approach will no doubt be enlightening to many. I have always enjoyed being on the "cutting-edge" in my industry and recommend You, Your SELF and the 21st Century: Coaching yourself and others in postmodern times, in this spirit.

Roger Birkman, Ph.D.

As Dr. Birkman pointed out, his work was developed on an "empirical basis," mine is based on how our "neuro-cognitive processes" construct and maintain our personalities.

In my mind, this is the perfect marriage: 1. A valid, reliable, and comprehensive psychometric instrument to describe personality traits, and 2. A process that explains how our personalities are constructed and maintained. Together, this combination is custom made for the professional coach. The book you have in hand, takes this combination to the next level; it is expressly written with the certified Birkman practitioner in mind.

On Coaching with The Birkman Method®, is a derivative of *You, Your SELF and the 21st Century.* It brings the reader up to date on the most applicable neuro-cognitive science as it applies to The Birkman Method® and the latest changes to the method itself. Further, it is my hope that its *"philosophical - psychological"* background offers balance to the utility usually promoted in coaching books.

You will find it's not an easy read but rather a book to be studied in increments. Your efforts will be handsomely rewarded with a new level of understanding that will make your coaching efforts even more effective.

Finally, this book has taken over 30 years of practice and study to write. And the only regret as it is published is that Dr. Birkman didn't have a chance to read it because he, his lifelong work, and our friendship, inspired so much of it.

Robert De Filippis

Introduction

"The reality of life is that your perceptions—right or wrong—influence everything you do. When you get a proper perspective of your perceptions, you may be surprised how many other things fall into place."

Dr. Roger Birkman
1919-2014

This book is designed to help the professional Birkman practitioner use the Birkman Method ®, in Dr. Birkman's terms, to "get a proper perspective on their own perceptions" while assisting their clients to do the same.

"What is the proper perspective?" It starts with balancing the authentic and social selves of our personalities. It finishes with an operational awareness of our subconscious decision processes. The goal is to learn how to make more effective life decisions and enjoy "how many other things fall into place."

Why psychometrics?

Ninety five percent of our decision processing happens below our level of awareness. The other five is *conscious* and is only called on when there's a conflict in our *subconscious* decision making. This is like what German philosopher Martin Heidegger called a "breakdown in the transparency of living." He meant that much of life, like the subconscious decision processes are transparent to us and become apparent when they need a conscious overriding decision. Properly designed, psychometrics help us become conscious of our unconscious decision processes.

Although psychometrics concerns many areas of human psychology, in this book, our attention will focus on personality traits. The Birkman Method® is such an assessment technique. It focuses explicitly on personality traits and not personality types. This distinction is essential because personality types have fallen out of favor in modern psychological research as too reductive. They're still used by some to help crystallize people's understanding of themselves but would leave out too much vital information for the professional coach.

Even well-defined personality traits are not enough info.

The German American psychologist, Kurt Lewin, offered this formula referring to human behavior, B=f (P, E), meaning Behavior is a function of the interaction of Personality and Environment. While his formula gives us a basic understanding of human behavior, it leaves out the variables at work internal to the person doing the behaving. As coaches, we need to know so much more about these internal variables if we are to offer maximum value to our clients.

To that end, we go a bit deeper, P=f (AS, PS) + E, where Personality is a function of the Authentic Self and Public Self plus Environment. Of course, this begs the question, what is the Authentic Self and how does it function. Which brings us to needs and temperament, and then expectations, genetics, and our central nervous system. Very soon the whole scope of human personality, including our historical, cultural, and familial backgrounds, beg for consideration.

Human behavior is an emergent property, the observable action, resulting from an unobservable set of variables interacting in complex biological organisms—us. It is not a simple stimulus-response process.

What to expect in this book.

We will explore how the private, or authentic self, is shaped by our needs and how our temperament, influenced by our genetics, is structured into our biology. We'll see how needs are shaped by our expectations from early childhood interpretations of our experiences. We'll explore how our public self is shaped by our linguistic interpretations we learn from our native cultures, and how our perceptions are limited by our sensory systems. We'll see how our languaging is molded and shaped by our past experiences to become the cognitive maps we use to create and navigate our external worlds. We will study how our cognitive maps contain the scripts and rules of engagement we use to travel our lives' journeys. We will see how the history of our cultural, familial, and personal experiences shape our behavioral patterns as we keep re-applying what worked for the same or similar circumstances in the past.

Finally, we will see that behavioral patterns are formed by personality traits and how those traits are made up of many characteristics defined and explained by the nine Birkman components.

The Birkman Application.

As a qualified Birkman Method practitioner you know that Usual Behaviors (UBs) and Stress Behaviors (SBs) hinge on the client's needs being satisfied. You also know Needs are not observable or known without reflection and inquiry. You will learn how to uncover the subconscious scripts and rules hidden in Needs and examine the calculus that creates them in their decision processes (95 percent of which is subconscious).

A simple way of saying this is you will discover how the clients' cognitive maps often take them to the wrong places.

The key to Birkman Method coaching.

This book will provide a method of understanding the unobservable (95 percent) that shapes the observable (5 percent). Thus, it answers the question "why people continue to behave as they do even when they don't produce the results they say they want?" The Birkman Method® feedback reports lay out the map to this process with unsurpassed clarity. And the goal of this process was defined in Dr. Birkman's research when he made two crucial observations that apply directly to coaching:

"Behavior is not determined so much by objective facts as by the meanings the individual attaches to those facts."

and

"The perceptions of some individuals about "most people" and/or "self" may be illusory, irrational, or unreal. Nevertheless, these perceptions are real and reasonable to the individuals, and so, influential on their behaviors."

Therefore, the role of the coach is to create awareness of the unconscious processes, that is, the potential illusory, irrational, unreal, and erroneous interpretations of facts, that might be shaping the client's ineffective behavior. This way the coach helps clients avoid reflexively taking inferential leaps and wondering why they are not getting the results they want. They can then make the most effective conscious decisions to achieve their objectives.

By the end of this book, the coach will be able to act as another observer of the clients' circumstances thereby assisting them to stop, reflect and inquire into their own choices. And in the process, deconstruct and reconstruct the subconscious mechanisms of their decision processes, if they so choose.

The historical basis of this book.

We are not blank slates at birth. So, the Standard Social Science Model no longer provides a thorough foundation for understanding human behavior. Our behavior is a product of nature as well as nurture. But to understand the deeper foundations of how we are nurtured by our cultures as well as our families, I have provided an abridged overview of the Western Intellectual Tradition from the fundamental questions of the pre-Socratic philosophers to the most recent discoveries of our contemporary cognitive scientists. Their inquiry and research contain the evolution of our understanding of the nature of human experience and the world within which we live. This historical treatment is because to truly appreciate human behavior we need to understand how we have evolved to our current way of being.

Although each of us possesses a unique personal history, we also share a cultural history of intellectual traditions. By understanding these traditions, we can examine nurture as well as nature in the development of our unique personalities. When we explore shared history, we find common meanings. But each of us can interpret meaning to shape and fit our view of the world. So, we need to consider individual experience as well as historical circumstances if we are to understand the human beings with whom we interact. Our collective history is a practical roadmap to that understanding and can be found in our philosophical tradition.

Main premise.

All attempts to coach successfully begin with an understanding of how human beings come to be who they are. In other words, making a sincere and informed effort to understand and accept another's web of beliefs about themselves and the world within which they live. This understanding is the minimal requirement for connecting with others. And there is just no effective coaching without authentic connections to our clients. This connection starts with a need to understand that these webs of beliefs are expressed differently based on unique physiological makeup and culture-based interpretations of the circumstances within which we all find ourselves at any given time. This includes us—the coaches.

From my experience as a coach and consultant, I have come to believe that the inborn goal of all human beings is the full expression of the authentic self. This goal is increasingly more difficult to achieve as the pressures and challenges of postmodern times compound our lives.

In most instances of substantive and lasting human change where I have been privileged to assist, what appears to be change is in fact, the expression of the authentic self.

Finally, as I have learned more about evolutionary psychology, it has become apparent to me that I have begun to understand human behavior in new ways that offer more practical and lasting possibilities for us all.

Presuppositions

Our public identities are the manifestation of both our social and authentic selves. In other words, the persona that we coach, counsel, teach, and manage is made up of behavioral responses created by interactions between and among external social structures and internal cognitive structures.

The external social structures are:

- Historical categorical imperatives carried in our culture as fragments from past cultural norms.
- Familial categorical imperatives taught to us as children as rules.
- Present cultural categorical imperatives shaping the public rules of engagement that determine what is socially acceptable today.
- Common and reoccurring cultural frames of meaning that inform our social interactions (language games)

The internal cognitive structures are:

- Neurophysiological or the central nervous system [CNS] that comes with:
- A universal species cognitive ability [theory of mind] that allows us to recognize that other humans have self's like our own and are intentional agents that are driven by appetites, desires, and motivations to achieve their unique goals.
- Bio-programming of a sort. What some call "mentalese" or a kind of "deep neurological language" that comes with our neurophysiology and gives us the ability to learn a functional language to communicate and coordinate our actions with others.
- A functional language capability to fill our culturally based schema and create scripts.
- Scripts and rules for organizing our experience and actions
- Self and social perceptions upon which we base our rules.
- Personal rules of engagement, which are hypothetical and have been shaped by personal experience as we interact with our native culture's categorical rules.

As we create our identities and interpret our world, we are forming self-perceptions [based on internal structures] and social perceptions [based on our personal experiences] that govern our actions in life. Given how we interpret our self and the world, we form and maintain rules of engagement. These rules provide the basis for how we act in the world. These rules also promote and support our point of view. And humans, being intentional agents, are never very far from protecting our point of view as though if we allow another, ours will disintegrate.

In this regard, most all my coaching experience has revealed a consistent kind of resistance. This resistance is shaped by a robust effort to maintain our points of view even in the face of undeniable facts and irresistible forces to the contrary. So even when everything is pressuring us to change our perspective, we have a difficult time choosing to see our worlds or ourselves from another angle.

This difficulty is the precise opportunity that presents itself to a professional coach, consultant, manager, teacher, or counselor. It is also the precise challenge.

I attempted to meet the challenges in my coaching practice with a methodology based on an understanding of human behavior grounded in linguistic philosophy. It has been with this understanding that I have been able to assist in the deconstruction of the ineffective and the reconstruction of more effective ways of being with my clients.

It bears repeating.

"During his research, Dr. Roger Birkman found that individual perceptions of others were more critical to the accurate measurement of personality than any series of self-reported statements alone. The hypothesis implicit in this theoretical position is that a close relationship exists between an individual's motives, attitudes, and behaviors and how that same individual judges the motivations, beliefs, and actions of others.

Specifically, he found that:

Behavior is not determined so much by objective facts as by the personal meanings we attach to those facts.

Our perceptions about "most people" and/or "self" may actually be illusory, irrational, or unreal. Nevertheless, these perceptions are real and reasonable to us as individuals, and so, are influential on shaping our behaviors.

What he didn't mention.

These personal meanings and interpretations are happening below our level of consciousness. The good news is that The Birkman Method® makes our subconscious perceptions unmistakably clear by identifying Needs within domains of personality traits called the Components.

These Needs will provide a roadmap to the facts your clients consider essential and the meanings they attach to them even if they don't consciously know what they are.

In this way, you can help them assess if their perceptions are illusory, irrational, or unreal, and causing problems in their lives. And you can do this with a great deal of accuracy.

If their perceptions are relatively valid and grounded and they are still experiencing obstacles they want to address, by being a certified Birkman Method® consultant, you can coach them into the best life decisions guided by their comprehensive Birkman Feedback report showing Interests and Career Preferences.

To sum up this point, your new knowledge will empower you to question and calibrate your client's perceptions to achieve the kind of lives they want. In the following chapters, you will learn how we humans interpret facts and create, maintain, and reinforce perceptions, giving you the tools to assist in their deconstruction and reconstruction on a more valid and grounded basis.

The precise opportunity we have as coaches.

"Perception depends not only on the presented stimulus but also on internal hypotheses, expectations, and stored knowledge," which we can see clearly with Birkman feedback reports. "Thus, perception can be regarded as an inferential process that is much influenced by conceptually driven or top-down processes. It follows then that perception is relatively prone to errors since the inferences made from our sensory input may be mistaken."i In fact, most of what we experience is shaped by what we've already experienced.

In his book, The 5th Discipline, Peter Senge uses the term, mental models, as "the images, assumptions, and stories that we carry in our minds of ourselves, other people, institutions, and every aspect of the world."ii Without mental models and their subsequent cognitive maps, we couldn't navigate our complex environment. If our models are not representative of shared reality, we're likely to wind up in the wrong places.

This clarity is the primary value of the Birkman Method ® to the coach. It shows us the details of our unique cognitive models by revealing our Needs. Our Needs are based on childhood expectations. And as we will see, childhood expectations formed many of our beliefs about ourselves and the world within which we live. Now, as adults, we need the world to meet those expectations.

And they were built on the innocent perceptions of children not fully capable of understanding their external worlds.

No ideal style.

We will encounter many clients with so many ways of interpreting and experiencing their lives that we need to understand there is no model or perfect style for which to strive. There is no ideal personality aside from its efficacy in relation to the external systems, i.e., social norms of the society in which we each live.

In more recent times we see ourselves differently thanks to discoveries in theoretical physics, evolutionary genetics, and the cognitive sciences. As noted earlier, we now see that much of what we ascribed to nurture is nature; that we are not blank slates iii when we are born. We come with genetically conserved core-learning intuitions iv that facilitate experiencing the world, and each of us comes with more or less innate capacity when compared to others.

We now suspect that the mind is more than an epiphenomenon[1] of the brain. We also know that we are shaped by the circumstances into which we are "thrown"v at birth. Regardless of our innate capacities, we will be influenced by the social experiences that make us who we are.

In precise terms, the tension between our individuality and our need for social contact shapes our public identities as we interact with the external world. Our unique neural maps are in constant tension with social

---

[1] An epiphenomenon (plural: epiphenomena) is a secondary phenomenon that occurs alongside or in parallel to a primary phenomenon.

structures, accepting or rejecting experiences and revising the structures of our internal experience.

Here's the coaching opportunity: We don't always have a realistic grasp of our shared reality because we live in a kind of subjective blindness. Therefore, we could all benefit from having a good coach.

Why is language the basis of an effective coaching methodology?

Because language is a key tool in the creation of complete human consciousness, which gives us the ability to: (1) create, maintain, and interpret our identities (2) establish, manage, and understand the social reality within which we live.

Why is culture a foundation for effective coaching practices?

Culture determines meaning. Without culture we have no context. Without context, we have no way of correctly understanding our language and its use. The meaning of words is based on how they are used in a specific context. Culture determines their use in that context.

"Skillful" language is the basis of this coaching methodology.

It's evident that skillful language is a vital tool in coaching methodology. It may not be apparent what is meant by "skillful."

Let's start with the recognition that our self and social perceptions are created and sustained in language.

This means that who we think we are and how we think the world is, are accessed by language. Then realize that our direct experience is mediated by language. For instance, we sense and perceive physically, and interpret linguistically. We just cannot experience the raw nature of reality as it is. We experience it as we interpret it linguistically. This means we:

1) interpret and create our personal identities through language.
2) interpret and create the social reality within which we live through language.
3) shift and change the above based on our interpretations and re-interpretations of the ever-changing context.

This linguistic creation and interpretation of our identities, our world, and each specific context forms the self and social perceptions that govern our actions in life. Given how we interpret our self, the world, and the background, we apply "rules" of engaging others. These rules determine how well we function in the world. We will see later that they are not like rules in a rulebook, but more like hypothetical guidelines that we can change from context to context. In fact, a coaching relationship is often the space to examine the rules we use to be sure they're appropriate within the context they're used.

Sometimes even skillful language is not enough.

Here's the problem most of us face when working with our clients: These rules are not consciously accessible to us in normal circumstances. We can't just ask the client what they are and expect a clear and concise answer. We usually become aware of them when they are being violated or don't work for us anymore.

And discovering rules is not something we can automatically expect in a coaching situation. Unless we have an instrument that can assist in making them available, we can't know what they are and examine their efficacy. The right professional psychometric test can make the client's subconscious rules available to work with descriptively and prescriptively. As a certified Birkman Method® practitioner you know the assessment is that tool.

The golden moment of coaching.

Most all my experience has revealed a standard theme: We make a robust effort to maintain our points of view even in the face of undeniable facts and irresistible forces to the contrary. So even when life is screaming at us to change our perspective we have a difficult time choosing to see ourselves or our worlds as though with new eyes. This is compounded by the fact that we aren't always aware of precisely what personal rules are being challenged when we resist the new information that might just be what we need.

This is the precise opportunity—the golden moment—that presents itself to a professional coach (or anyone who works with other people.) This is also the challenge we all have when we are faced with learning a problematic lesson of our own.

Human personalities are created in language and maintained in neuro-cognitive structures. And the skillful use of words is the best tool the coach has to assist in the deconstruction of the ineffective and the reconstruction of more effective ways of being. To begin, we need to know what to deconstruct. Be clear here. Deconstruction is a threatening process, and your client will need to trust you. The Birkman feedback will build that trust most efficiently.

Table of Contents

Chapter 1 – The coach

If you bring forth what is within you, what you bring forth will save you. If you do not bring forth what is within you, what you do not bring forth will destroy you.

***Jesus**[vi]*

This chapter consists of three segments: 1. My personal observations on coaching. 2. Important features of a linguistic approach. 3. The coach as observer.

My personal observations.

My career consisted of forty-plus years of experience in many different organizations and industries with individuals from different sectors of society. I found that I needed to *change my view of change* to be a more effective coach. Having this new view allowed me to understand others with a full appreciation for and acceptance of their unique attributes. Consequently, it has allowed me to interact with people more productively. But first I had to face a challenge. I had to let go of my death grip on my self and social perceptions.

In subtle ways, this new perspective has become apparent to me as I have examined my experience more critically. My consulting and coaching methodologies had been formed and shaped in the social sciences, from which evolved the Standard Social Sciences Model. The problem seemed to be that these theories didn't work in practice. Somehow, someway, the people I worked with didn't quite fit the model, and when I did see change, it didn't seem to last very long.

I began to see that a good deal of what we call personal and organizational change happened at the level of *social behavior*[2] but was not truly incorporated by the individual or the organization. When I took away the stimulus, most behaviors returned to previous states.

Social behavior is shaped by the ethics of our times or circumstances. It is how we behave to conform to our current conditions, but it doesn't change who we are at a more authentic level. In fact, we can become lost in social behavior. One merely needs to review all the programs, initiatives, and new management methods that come into and go out of favor in corporate America to see the result of this phenomenon.[3]

It was becoming more evident that I was working with *social* and not *authentic* behavior. For the most part, people are blind to the fact that we create and live in *socially constructed realities.*[4] So it's easy to lose ourselves and become numbed to knowing who we are.

My clients were not purposely trying to fool me. They were as confused as I was about the issues. They were simply conforming to the situational standards that prevailed at the time.

I think that I might still be analyzing this dilemma were it not for the ten years that I spent in the career services

---

[2] This is what The Birkman Method® refers to as usual behavior.

[3] A Wall Street Journal article in December of 1994 pointed out that only about 10% of corporate change programs have lasting effects. Not a very good report card for change agents.

[4] For an excellent discussion on social constructions, I recommend the book, Reality Isn't what it Used to Be, by Walter Truett Anderson, Harper Collins: 1990.

industry. It became apparent to me while coaching people in career or job transition that I was dealing with a lot less resistance. The ethics of the situation allowed, if not rewarded, less *socialized* and more *authentic* behavior. And more importantly, these people wanted to know themselves better so that their next career move might be more successful than their previous one.

The social sciences model pretty much fell apart in this environment. There was just no way that individual natures were merely the indeterminate material that the social factor molds and transforms. Each person was unique not only because of their personal histories but also because of their individual biological differences.

Connecting.

I experienced another personal awakening while working with people in career transition. It was evident that with fewer demands for socialized behaviors to get in the way we were both more open to *real human connection.* And authentic human connection is a powerful force in any methodology intended to help people.

As we are all experiencing the complexities of managing the changes in our culture, there exists tremendous pressure to cover up our authentic humanness with inauthentic social practices, so we can be seen as being tuned into what's going on. But we are increasingly disconnecting from the details of our own lives, and that diminishes our human connections. We are surrounding ourselves with gadgets and material comfort; we are cutting ourselves off from what matters most: our fellow human beings."[vii] It's almost as though we can tolerate the demands to conform to public standards for most of our day, but eventually, we need relief. And we find it in disconnecting for a while and being more authentically who we are in our private lives.

Psychometric tools.

In the areas of practice called *coaching and consulting*, there exists a recurrent argument: use or don't use assessments? Unfortunately, those who make the decision are not always qualified to make this determination. I have heard the case, "people are just people...they're all the same, so an assessment is not necessary." But the fact is that people are not all the same and not all people can change to fit the demands of just any job requirement. So, in many instances that I have observed, executives and managers have confused their structural authority for professional competence and in the process have caused a good deal of suffering for the people below them and a good deal of organizational ineffectiveness for themselves.

This lack of knowledge on the part of the many managers and executives notwithstanding, we change agents must produce the results that we have been hired to provide. Consequently, it is our professional responsibility to find and use the tools that get the job done.

Well-designed assessments can and do offer a significant advantage to the change agent who is appropriately trained and able to apply them professionally. The Birkman Method® is that tool.

I have used The Birkman Method® to assist my clients and to understand myself better, and as a result, I am now very familiar with my self and social perceptions as well as those of my clients. I need to know who I am and how I see the world before I can assist others. Otherwise, I run the risk of contaminating interpretations and feedback with my own biases.

I also need to share authentic information with others to point out how their concerns can be more broadly understood when comparing them openly with those of another person. This way, in assisting others, I never leave a client engagement without having an enhanced understanding of my own point of view which allows me to be even more effective in my next engagement.

As you read this book you will learn:

- About our difficulties in managing and incorporating the changes that come with finding our authentic selves.
- That these very difficulties come from our healthy cognitive processes at work doing what they should as they interact with the internal and external structures.
- How the biology of our subjective experience and our unique neurolinguistic physiology work to create, sustain and change our points of view.
- The power of language.
- How to assist by creating an awareness of new possibilities that clients may not see from their present perspectives.
- How to be a more authentically connected human being.

The superiority of language to change our experience.

Why do I propose that a linguistic method is so superior to other methods? Because, as some philosophers in the early twentieth century discovered, they could not even pose a philosophical question *out* of language let alone answer it. Because the linguistic structure of the question influences how it can be answered. A client question that has been illogically formed will not respond to a logical approach. Being that language is shaped by a client's system of logic, we are sometimes faced with coaching issues that are illogically formed. So, then how can we have a productive coaching relationship? We must first linguistically *re-form* the problem so that it is logical. Until we have well-formed language coming from a logical foundation, we must focus there. This is the essence of effective conscious human interaction. This is the essence of working with other human beings from teaching and counseling to world politics.

Language and The Birkman Method®.

Why is this linguistic method so superior to other methods when using The Birkman Method®? Because the forces that shape observable behavior are related to the Needs of the individual and Needs are usually not apparent. The Birkman report makes them apparent.

When those Needs are satisfied, our clients can be at their best. When they're not, our clients default to stress behaviors that consume far more energy for very little return. And all of this is determined by the client's self and social perceptions. These perceptions are based on linguistic interpretations. Their skill or lack of same shows up in the client's way of linguistically interpreting his or her experience.

All this said, the real challenge for the coach is to understand that interpreting is a hermeneutical phenomenon.[5] We interpret our experience by relating it to relevant features of context.[6]

The critical point here is that accurate interpretation is always determined by the correct assessment of the context. Key to the early development of what became The Birkman Method®, young Roger Birkman observed this when he was a bomber pilot in WWII. How other pilots interpreted their circumstances (the context) determined how well they functioned. Objectively, the context was the same, i.e.; all these young men flew missions with no guarantees of returning. How each interpreted their experiences affected how well they coped with the conditions. Some did well. Some didn't.

Language and consciousness.

Language is necessary for that irresistible introspection that there is an "I" inside our heads.[viii] The conscious creation, sustenance, interpretation of and reflection on experiences of the "I" in our head are linguistic processes. This does not mean that we cannot have experience without language. We can reflexively withdraw our hand from a hot fire without consciously thinking about it until after we have performed the action. But to interpret it, reflect on it and plan not to do it again requires conscious thought. And that requires language.

Ferdinand de Saussure proposed that language precedes thought. Others have suggested that language facilitates thought. And still, others consider language as

---

[5] Hermeneutics is the study of interpretation in context.

[6] In this vein, Heidegger and his followers spoke of hermeneutics, the art of interpretation in context, especially social and linguistic context.

expression of thought. I think of language as the conscious interpretation of our experience. And as Dr. Birkman proposed, that interpretation is often "illusory, irrational, or unreal."

Language + melodies = consciousness.

FMRI[7] research has shown that two sections of the brain are activated when people are engaged in experiments designed to discover how the process of consciousness works. The two sections that are activated are 1) Broca's area, the area that participates in articulating words, and 2) the auditory portions of the left temporal lobe, the area that activates when listening to a familiar melody without lyrics. Thus, both linguistic and non-linguistic materials are processed in the consciousness-related regions of the brain. But consider if you will, what happens when you hear a familiar melody. You soon begin to experience feelings and thematic thoughts[8] or start to reflect on the melody, both linguistic processes that make the experience of listening to the melody a conscious experience. [More to come on this topic in chapter 16.]

(A side note here is that the Birkman Interest category titled Musical is often found to be high in people who say they are not necessarily musical in any traditional way. It may be reporting the client's auditory preference for receiving and managing information.)

So, it seems our brain's innate neurolinguistic structure provides pre-conscious abilities (the ten learning

---

[7] Functional magnetic resonance imaging

[8] According to Antonio Damasio emotions are different from feelings. Emotions happen in the body and feelings happen in the mind. Feelings require language.

intuitions detailed in chapter two) biologically available, so we can learn to think consciously. In other words, all *neurologically normal* [9] humans come equipped with them when we arrive.

Fully conscious human beings.

One of those learning intuitions is a generative grammatical structure in place when we are born[ix]. All we must do is be exposed to a native language and then fill in the cultural schema. For instance, a baby would have an impossible job trying to learn everything it needed to be able to speak if it didn't have some basic faculty, to begin with. Observations of young children during periods of language acquisition have shown that they could not have learned everything they needed from the outside but are in fact demonstrating an innate ability that has been provided with their neurophysiology when they were born.

As a personal example, many years ago, I was on my way to see my granddaughter in Arizona. There was a toddler playing under the watchful eye of her mother in the airport waiting area. She was smaller and younger than my granddaughter but seemed to have a command of several dozen words, which she could use in short but complete sentences. I asked her mother how old she was, and she said fifteen months. My granddaughter was then eighteen months and used several single words and was beginning to use two-word phrases. More complex sentence construction seemed

---

[9] The term "neurologically normal" in this case includes people who cannot hear. In fact, signing is an earlier language skill and is observable in hearing-children as they learn to speak. One of the earliest ways a hearing child speaks is called a holophrase, which includes gestures and context as well as verbal utterances.

beyond her reach at that time, which I discovered later, was pretty much on target developmentally. I was impressed with this little child in the airport.

My visit with my granddaughter was wonderful, and I returned home with the anticipation of being able to communicate with her more completely someday. It was about three months later that I saw her again. And in that short time, she had developed the ability to speak in more complex sentences, and the apparent desire to tell me everything that came into her little mind.

In that period of two or three months, she acquired a language ability sufficient to carry on a cogent conversation with the adults in her life, even though her parents, like most parents, have never conducted formal instructional sessions in grammar or vocabulary. And if they did, could she have acquired all that she needed in that short time? This is an example of one of the innate cognitive abilities with which we are born.

Summary.

With language, we have the tool to create and sustain our human experience, and with culture we have the background to create the meaning of that experience. Take either away, and I question whether we are fully conscious human beings. Take them away during nature's developmental time slot and I doubt that we will ever become fully conscious, fully functioning human beings. I can think of no stronger argument for using a linguistic methodology in coaching. I believe it is what makes us fully functioning human beings.

If you are a professional and experienced change agent [a supervisor, manager, executive, consultant, teacher, counselor, or coach] who wants to develop a solid footing for your professional and personal life, you have the right book in your hands. If you are a Birkman Certified consultant, it will be even more valuable. Most importantly, although this book offers my understanding of how we humans function, I also respect the fact that you will modify these principles to fit your experience and point of view. Hopefully, then this book will add a tiny little bit more to the continuing discourse on understanding human behavior.

Language Reveals and Obscures Reality.

> "The limits of my language mean the limits of my world."
> **Ludwig Wittgenstein**[10]

A coach using a linguistic approach needs to understand certain characteristics before using it with clients. First and most important, "the life of the mind cannot proceed without presuppositions,[11]" and those presuppositions are held in language, *limited* human language.

The Futility of "Presuppositionless-ness" – Linguistic Turn.

Philosophers began the period called the Linguistic Turn in the early 20th century. During this period, they recognized the limitations of language in philosophical

---

[10] Ludwig Josef Johann Wittgenstein was an Austrian-British philosopher who worked primarily in logic, the philosophy of mathematics, the philosophy of mind, and the philosophy of language

[11] Dr. Bart Ehrman, New Testament scholar.

inquiry. A valued convention in philosophical inquiry is to be "presuppositionless." Hopefully by doing so, one can contribute innovative ideas that would move the discussion further into new territory.

They found that to be an impossibility. They had to acknowledge the limitations of language, which are all based on presuppositions. And presuppositions lock our thinking into a kind of circularity that defines the limits of any body of human knowledge, whether it be philosophy, religion, or science. (Rorty, 1992) They found that a great deal of what we think of as *reality* is really a convention of naming and characterizing; the convention which itself is called *language.*

As German philosopher, Martin Heidegger said, "language is a house of being."

Another way of understanding Wittgenstein's quote is to say that language both reveals and obscures our experience of reality and assists in the generation of our subjective experience. We live in this house called language, thinking that it contains all there is, blind to what we cannot distinguish.

And yes, you and your client both live in a house of being called language, but your presuppositions most probably differ in seemingly infinite ways. Suffice to say that this simple idea serves as a point of departure for a deeper discussion on the limitations of language and what lies ahead as you apply your coaching skills.

Here is our dilemma: Language is self-referential, circular. Think of it this way. Each room in the house of language has at least two doorways, an exit, and an entry. One can wander this house forever but never find a doorway that leads to anywhere but another room within the house.

We are born, live, and die in this house. The key point here is that no matter how clever one's argument is, for or against a point of view, everything we might say is limited within the House of Being we call language. So, when a client's point of view differs dramatically from yours, you are both limited by language. Language limits all our arguments, beliefs, rationalizations, theories and counter-theories.

Linguistic distinctions precede learning.

As an example, do we have brains as distinct from the rest of our body? No. We have brains only because we make the distinction that this "three or four-pound" "segment or area" in our "heads," (all linguistic distinctions), is our brain. Just as we have objectively defined all the sub-components of our biology, none of them exist as independent segments of our bodies. They are all of one undifferentiated unit of reality until we describe them.

Imagine that you are peering into the opened torso of a human body for the first time and have never studied physiology. What do you see? You see an undifferentiated mass of reds, purples, and pinks, until someone begins to point to specific areas and label them. But even then, you may only distinguish the heart, liver, lungs because they have been pointed out. But what of all the other parts that make up the mass? Unless you are taught the distinctions, you won't "see" vascular tissue, lymph glands, arteries, and veins, etc. They are linguistic distinctions that allow us to understand our biology with the aid of labels. Where it not for those distinctions we are simply whole, undifferentiated, conscious living beings (also a linguistic distinction).

If you're still having trouble accepting this to be true, think about how the 2500-year-old Chinese, Japanese and Korean systems called Acupuncture[12] provide a completely different set of distinctions used to identify the various subsystems in the same human body described by Western medicine. You won't find bodily meridians in Western physiology, yet the East has been using them to treat illnesses for 25 centuries.

In this context, it would be difficult to find any serious scholar who would argue for something we call *objective reality*. Yes, of course there is some "thing" that we all share. We call it our world. But it is as subjective in nature as our unique personal points of view. Reality is linguistically differentiated because we distinguish it as such. And each of us distinguishes it in our own way. As Dr. Birkman told us, sometimes, in ways that limit our effectiveness. This is one of the most important challenges for the coach: to help raise a client's awarenesses when their way of distinguishing "objective reality" is harming them.

So, as we progress in this book, keep in mind that we're all using linguistic distinctions that help us create our self and social perceptions. Odds are good that these distinctions differ in too many ways to be identified. In this way, we can see that while language assists us by discerning the factors that limit our clients, it doesn't give coaches a "God's eye view." But by just knowing these distinctions, we have the tool we need to understand how we function, and how we can resist influencing them with our personal preferences.

---

[12] Acupuncture is a component of the health care system of China that can be traced back at least 2,500 years. The general theory of acupuncture is based on the premise that there are patterns of energy flow (Qi) through the body that are essential for health. Disruptions of this flow are believed to be responsible for disease

In effect, trapped in Heidegger's *linguistic house of being* provides us enough linguistic capacity to describe that which we are evolutionarily fit to experience but leaves a great deal out that we experience on a subjective level; those first-person constructs of consciousness that are the focus of the philosophical area called phenomenology, or the study of subjective experience. As coaches using The Birkman Method® we have a tool that allows us to go deeper into subjective experience than just talking and listening alone.

In summary, the many differences in theories about our reality that seem to conflict with all the other theories about reality are what Nietzsche referred to when he wrote "reality is made up of competing stories about reality."

So, we all have our stories about who we are and how the world works. All these stories are interpreted with language, structured into our bodies, and imprinted upon our central nervous system. (CNS)

Unfortunately, most of us are not aware that our interpretations are not the world. Fortunately, we have coaching processes that can wake us to the possibilities.

The coach as observer.

"The real voyage of discovery consists not in seeking new landscapes, but in having new eyes."

—Marcel Proust
French novelist, critic, essayist

What does it mean to be observers? The classical definition is *somebody, who observes some object or event that is happening.* Implicit in this definition is the premise that observers are separate and apart from what they see and are seeing things as *they* are. So, what is missing in this definition?

As observers, our observations are influenced first by our evolutionarily adapted neurophysiology and then by what we already believe, how we know it, and how we validate and invalidate new information. In other words, our personal cognitive maps of the territory (external reality) determine what we believe and see.

Kathleen Taylor in her book, Brainwashing: The Science of Thought Control, calls them "cogwebs." It's her generic term for mental objects, incorporating cognitive networks and schemas, thoughts, concepts, beliefs, hopes, desires, action plans and so on."

Our natural tendency is to think the world is fully explained by our incomplete cogwebs as though they are whole and complete. These cogwebs come to life in the ongoing narrative in our minds. That's the internal voice that shapes our conscious thoughts and never stops. In our present world, these simple cognitive devices interpret our current experiences with our presuppositions. We may not be able to expand them to see all reality, but a skillful coach can help us expand them to see more of what we need to be more effective.

As cognitive scientists are now proving, our maps not being the territory, form our limitations to seeing more territory. Keep in mind the content of our cogwebs is interpreted by language, and we have already seen the limitations we experience because we live in our linguistic houses of being. When we accept these facts, it can be the beginning of our voyage of discovery. In other words, this can be the beginning stage of becoming a new observer. Of course, it will take an effort just to overcome our natural tendency to believe what we already think without questioning.

So, exactly what is a new observer? Well, it is not another person. As Proust points out, it is the same person with the ability to see the same reality as though with new eyes.

An Example of a New Observer.

A simple example of the new observer would be the pre-historic individual who saw that a form of transportation could come from a continually rotating object. Voila, the wheel! Rocks, logs, etc., rotating objects had been around for a long time, but this primitive human saw them as though with new eyes. In fact, this is true of all basic tools, e.g., rocks to smash nuts, sticks to reach fruit in the upper portions of trees, large leaves to use as shelter or to carry objects.

A later example is when Copernicus observed that the sun and universe did not revolve around Earth and gave us what is known as the heliocentric scientific explanation that opened a whole new level of understanding of our cosmos to be studied. In effect, these are the events when someone sees the same *reality* everyone else sees but sees it differently. When they do, a new paradigm[13] is born and that allows new choices to emerge to create a whole new range of evolving possibilities.

With each new observation comes the tug and pull of resistance from other people. There are those who take advantage of the opportunities emerging from new insights, and there are those, who are certain only ruin can come in their wake. Unfortunately, the new eyes Proust refers to almost always come with a need for protective glasses.

---

[13] a pattern of something; a model.

From the beginning of written history to our post-modern conflicts between conservatives and progressives, the struggle between opposing and transformative forces defines our species, both internally and externally. We seem always to be in a state of asymmetry, somewhat like a giant tug-of-war. Each side pulls the other toward the center until critical mass is reached and we move on – most of us do—some will die instead of changing their minds. Fortunately, for our species, these new observers eventually prevail, and we make progress, or we might still think Earth is the center of the universe.

"The plain fact is different observers, operating with different sets of distinctions, see different realities. Notice that we aren't saying (as our rationalistic scientific common sense wants us to) that one reality is true and the other false. In each case, each observer sees what he/she sees, and this is what is real for him/her. One observer may have more refined or sophisticated distinctions than the other according to certain standards, but this doesn't make him/her right and the other person wrong.

"We can recognize this very clearly if we think about an astrologer looking at the identical night sky as the astronomer. The astrologer will see a completely different set of groupings, noting perhaps that a certain planet is in a certain astrological house, and so forth. Neither is right or wrong. They are simply motivated by different purposes, operating with different sets of distinctions based on different systems of thought, and, as a result, seeing different worlds.

"The observer is generative: that is, we actually create the reality we cognize, and thus determine what constitutes knowledge for us. In other words, what we know depends on what distinctions we already have, which is to say, on the kind of observer we are." (Olalla 2004)

Herein is one of the greatest obstacles to understanding our clients without the aid of a psychometric instrument like The Birkman Method®. We may not have the new distinctions to cognize or represent our client's reality when examining it. We are using existing distinctions that don't always apply to the human personality. Even Brian Greene, a contemporary theoretical physicist, and author says it best: "Surely, reality is what we think it is; reality is revealed to us by our experiences. To one extent or another, this view of reality is one that many of us hold, if only implicitly. I certainly find myself thinking this way in my day to day life; it's easy to be seduced by the face nature reveals directly to us […] "I've learned that modern science tells us a very different story. The overarching lesson that has emerged from scientific inquiry over the last century is that human experience is often a misleading guide to the true nature of reality. […] By deepening our understanding of the true nature of our physical reality, we profoundly reconfigure our sense of ourselves and our experience of the universe. (Greene 2004)

If someone as materialistically grounded as a theoretical physicist tells us "we may be seduced by the face nature reveals directly to us," how far off might we be with the human personality? The point I'm making is many of our observations and perceptions, even our consciousness, is derived from what we already know. And what we already know is a very small, incomplete portion of reality.

How much do we know (for sure) ?

Dr. Donald Hoffman has shown we have evolved to be evolutionary fit but not have the actual ability to perceive the true nature of our universe. Now Dr. Marcus E. Raichle, a neurologist at Washington University, makes our experience of reality a bit more tenuous as he explains the limits of our perceptive capacity: "Such a thin stream of data could not produce perception if that were all the brain took into account; the intrinsic activity must play a role."[14]

In broad strokes, he is helping paint a picture that says we just don't have much of a grasp of the reality that we fight so hard to defend. Our experience depends a great deal on intrinsic activity. The substance of this intrinsic activity is our previous experience formed into those cogwebs mentioned earlier. We only perceive a tiny portion of the world around us. This tiny portion of our perceived world is screened and interpreted with what we already know and believe. What we already know and believe is the result of our previous highly-filtered sensing, perceiving and interpreting abilities and is contained in our internal narratives. New information is always modified and fit to our internal cognitive ecology—that is, our maps.

Then the intrinsic activity is coded into linguistic distinctions we call words.[15] These linguistic distinctions are one of the building blocks of our cognitive models[16] expressed in our internal narratives. In the simplest terms, we can understand linguistic distinctions this way: The dictionary is a book of linguistic distinctions, which, when each is understood, defines a tiny granular piece of our shared reality. If you do not know what a word means, you

---

[14] Scientific American: The Brain's Dark Energy by Marcus E. Raichle, M.D. February 17, 2010

[15] Linguistic distinctions are the way we artificially parse reality into manageable chunks of information with the use of words. They allow us to experience reality as though it were discontinuous and distinct. When, in fact, it is continuous and connected.

[16] Our cognitive models also contain other components of our sensory systems.

do not possess this distinction and, therefore, do not fully understand this little piece of our shared reality. The process of learning linguistic distinctions is a step in our cognitive development. Think of how a child develops a functioning vocabulary to be able to communicate and interact with others.

As is all of life, more distinctions give you the ability to be more effective. In other words, the more open your system of knowledge, the more effective you will be. (Simply taking the time to read a few words in the dictionary every day can open whole new panoramas of awareness.)

We live in closed systems of knowledge because they, like a dictionary, are usually circular, self-referential systems. Closed systems do not distinguish, let alone, ask the questions we may need to have answered to be more effective in our lives. This is the role of the coach; to ask those questions that our clients' closed system of knowledge don't allow them to ask.

How could a breakdown be a great opportunity?

The end of the effectiveness of a cognitive map is what Martin Heidegger[17], a twentieth-century German philosopher, referred to as a type of breakdown in the transparency of living. Paradoxically, this transparency creates a kind of fog of unawareness. Breakdowns of this nature happen when we become aware of some subconscious aspect of our life because it is not working as it usually does. It is an interruption in our way of being.

---

[17]Martin Heidegger (September 1889 – 26 May 1976) was a seminal thinker in the Continental tradition and philosophical hermeneutics, with a growing influence on Analytic philosophy.

Breakdowns in transparency are golden learning opportunities to become new observers. If we examine them thoroughly, they can show us the failure of our beliefs, theories, premises, and ultimately, our logic. By seeing and questioning them, we can become different observers. If we do, we create new possibilities we could not see before. In this way, we can see that possibility has been there, but the observers we are, could not see them without another's observer.

In summary, we live our lives without conscious awareness of all its details. We have evolutionarily adapted perception that makes us fit for survival, but it does not reveal the full and complete nature of reality. We have a filtering ability allowing us to sift out millions of bits of input data and focus on the task at hand. This gift is also a limitation because it causes us to miss so much going on around us. In other words, our normal state is one of being conscious of a minuscule area; what we call awareness. The rest is transparent.

When transparency breaks down, we might become aware of whatever is causing the breakdown (e.g., a belief). If the issue is urgent, sometimes the events change our point-of-view, and we begin to see as though with new eyes, becoming new observers. If we're not curious or insist that our view is complete and certain, life returns to transparency, and we remain the same observer we have always been. However, the cost of this reluctance is often dearer than the effort to change. It is up to us.

Often, when there are serious breakdowns in the transparency of our lives, we cling to what we have always believed until we just cannot hang on to it any longer. We take seemingly new actions, but they come from our existing point-of-view. They do not work; we try again. They continue not to work; we keep trying.

The key to new learning is the ability to question the observers that we are? In other words, questioning the way we see the situation causing the problem. A breakdown in transparency is a choice point—an opportunity to grow. When we use these opportunities, we can continue to expand our options. Instead of trying new actions repeatedly, trying to see the situation with new eyes may make all the difference we need to be more effective personally and as a species. The coach seizes client breakdowns as the opportunities they are. In some instances, as we will see later in this book, the coach uses breakdowns in a generative way.

Chapter 2 – An Ontological History of Reality

As their world changes, people feel disoriented and lost . . . they cannot see the direction that society is taking but experience its slow transformation in coherent ways. As the old mythology that gave structure and significance to their lives crumbles under the impact of change, they can experience a numbing loss of identity and a paralyzing despair . . . The most common emotions . . . are a helplessness and a fear of annihilation . . .[x]

Karen Armstrong

"Ontology is the philosophical study of the nature of being, becoming, existence, or reality. In this context, a very simple definition of ontology answers the question, "what's the basic nature of reality?"

Usually, the formal study of reality itself is the province of the physical sciences, and the study of personal "reality" belongs to psychology. But for our purposes in this book, we will conflate the two for brevity.

As Dr. Birkman explained in his research, it's not so much the facts we find but how we interpret those facts that shape our personality. Our interpretation is highly dependent on our ontological beliefs. Very few clients consciously know the ontology on which they base their opinions, so being able to listen for them in their languaging is a vital coaching skill.

Why do we need this information?

"There still exist fragmentary connections to our traditions,"[xi] even in these changing times. And most of us operate on unexamined historical presuppositions that come from those fragmentary connections all our lives. These are presuppositions that were formed in various ontological views by others and swallowed whole by us when we were children. The bedrock of human experience is based on presuppositions made by others, the origins of which usually cannot be explained by the person who holds them. Therefore, in our preparations to be a coach, we should review their roots and the historical evolution of ontological explanations.

We start by understanding an abridged version of the history of Western philosophical traditions. We will do this by reviewing the thoughts and works of those who offered opinions that have a direct bearing on the topics of this book. By doing this, we shed light on the history of our presuppositions and the origins of our client's ontology.

The work of a few selected philosophers that follows highlights the evolution of the principles of this book.[18] Their trajectory leads to the current discoveries in the

---

[18] I have chosen not to specify the empiricist and rationalist schools, although they do offer valuable insights to the reader, for no other reason than to limit the scope and length of this text. Empiricism is any view, which bases our knowledge, or the materials from which it is constructed, on experience through the traditional five senses. Rationalism is any of a variety of views emphasizing the role or importance of reason, usually including intuition, in contrast to sensory experience (including introspection), the feelings, or authority. Just as an extreme empiricist tries to base all our knowledge on experience, so an extreme rationalist tries to base it on reason.

cognitive sciences. We are indeed beginning to understand ourselves and our present world in ways that offer us better possibilities for the future.

Finally, although I offer no new philosophical revelations, I do propose a methodology based on a belief that the basis of being human, as distinct from other primates, is how we use our language. We use our words to negotiate the interactions we have between our internal neurophysiological structures and the external structures of the society within which we live.

A brief history of philosophical inquiry affecting our thinking today.

What follows is an overview of ideas that still influence us today. There are two essential points to keep in mind here: 1) This is Western tradition and doesn't include all the other philosophical explanations of reality. 2) French deconstructionist philosopher, Jacques Derrida[19] proposed, "There is nothing outside the text." Derrida meant all our signifiers (words) depend on other words. And if we deconstruct all the meanings of these words, nothing is being signified but other words. So, all text, (text being all human knowledge,) references itself with no universally agreed grounding. This means merely that old ideas will be covered over with new ideas and the process might have nothing to do with objective reality.

---

[19]Jacques Derrida was a French philosopher best known for developing a form of semiotic analysis known as deconstruction, which he discussed in numerous texts, and developed in the context of phenomenology. He is one of the major figures associated with post-structuralism and postmodern philosophy.

So, it seems essential to understand where our ideas come from, how they've evolved, and how flimsy are the attachments of meanings to reality. (There is an *evolutionary point* after each philosopher to show our intellectual progress.)

The Milesians (500-400 BC), who were materialists, concentrated on the study of the fundamental makeup of nature or *physis*, (Greek for nature) looking for the one essential component that made up the cosmos. We can call them the first physicists (from *physis*).

Evolutionary Point: Humankind tried to explain fundamental reality with a single idea. (Monism)

Socrates (469-399 BCE) and his student, Plato being meta-physicists, pursued their questions by proposing form and content and introducing the concept of *essence*. In their way of thinking "things" had an essence, which meant that something existed outside of physical reality.

Evolutionary point: *We tried to explain fundamental reality with two ideas. (Dualism)*

Aristotle (384-322 BCE) had a different view on the questions and gave us the basis of Western logical thought. He looked to what was "sensible[20]" for the answers. He proposed that the *essence* of man was rationality and examined the material world for his clues. He gave birth to scientific inquiry and held sway over philosophical thinking well into the 13th century.

Evolutionary point: We can believe what we physically sense. (Scientific method)

---

[20] Sensible in this context means available to our five senses.

Copernicus (1473-1543 CE) and Galileo (1564-1642 CE) were the first real *"scientific"* thinkers. They disputed Aristotle's view, but the Church had reconciled and incorporated Aristotelian logic into its theology. The dispute existed unresolved for years. Galileo was only recently readmitted to the Church after his excommunication and house arrest over 400 years ago.

Evolutionary point: There is more to reality than what we can physically sense. Mathematical calculations are to be trusted more than physical senses.

To Rene Descartes, (1596-1650 CE) being human consisted of being both, body and mind, or substance and essence. He thought that the mind was separate from the body. He is best known for his statement, "Cogito ergo sum." (I think therefore I am). His radical skepticism resulted in proof of "his existence." In other words, if he could ask the question, he existed because he could. But what forms questions if it is not language?

Evolutionary point: The mind and body belong in different domains of reality. (Created an unnecessary detour in the scientific study of consciousness)

Kant (1724-1804 CE) gave us a view of morality on a personal level and expanded the concept of *a priori* moral structures. To him, we were born with a moral structure in place. We could no longer simply accept dogma. He suggested that we take responsibility for our morality. He dared us to use our reason. Humankind was now responsible for ethical decisions guided by the world around us. He advanced the concept of moral imperatives to conduct our lives. His thinking sparked the idea of the individual's *rules of engagement* for dealing with their world. But he didn't abandon the concept of *categorical imperatives* that existed external to us as individuals.[xii]

Evolutionary point: We can find our truth and don't need to depend on revealed or institutional truths. (Self-sufficiency)

Austin (1911-1960 CE) proposed that words are not only descriptive but also generative. So, when we use them, we are creating something not just describing it[xiii]. This theory applies to *concept* and *idea*-based words. Thus, when we are speaking, we are creating what we speak. When we say "congratulations," we are not describing a thing or concept. We are in fact creating the congratulations that we state. Austin gave us a new respect for the power of our language to create reality from nothing but our words. He helped us see that language *is* action.

Evolutionary point: Language creates, reveals, and conceals reality.

Wittgenstein (1889-1951 CE) proposed that philosophical questions suffer from a lack of proper formation in language. Our language could be flawed or tangled in the asking of philosophical questions, and therefore we cannot answer them. So, these questions become impossible to answer. On the other hand, he said that if we untangle what he called our "language games" the philosophical questions disappear, and we have reality as it is…and no need to ask that philosophical question[xiv].

Evolutionary point: Language and logic do not reliably mirror the world. Much of what we speak is tangled and not grounded.

Heidegger (1889-1976 CE) was anti-Cartesian. He reunified the body and mind into a single being called

Dasein. Dasein, roughly defined, is each of us as we are in the world. But he went further and speculated the concept of the authentic (or private) self and the inauthentic (or social) self. His formula for personal peace was to be our authentic self, inserted and living in the "facticity" of our life. When he talked about the nature of existence, he proposed that in our natural condition of living we exist in unity with the world around us, so the world's objects are transparent to us.

Evolutionary point: Our personalities are made up of an authentic private self and a public social self.

Searle (1932-) goes on to describe and categorize our language process into Speech Acts. No matter what language one is speaking, their use of language can be categorized into one or more essential categories[xv]. When we speak we create action in the form of social commitments; that our statement connects and commits us to others in a way that did not exist before we speak. Our speech acts fall into basic categories. These acts are necessary for producing any coordinated action with other human beings. Used effectively, they produce effective action, the intended action. Used otherwise, they can produce entanglements, confusion, and chaos.

Evolutionary point: We can live more fully by the skillful use of the basic speech acts.

Structuralism.

Karl Marx (1818-1883 CE) and Sigmund Freud (1856-1939 CE) played critical roles in the evolution of the philosophical thinking called "Structuralism." Ferdinand de Saussure (1857-1913 CE) is given credit for evolving their proto-structural views into a philosophical model that might even be called scientific. In the process, he disagrees with the conceptual bases of ontology and epistemology claiming that they are superfluous in understanding the makeup of our reality. Of course, structuralism became the new ontological and epistemological explanations. (These three men shaped the methods of explanation used in this book.)

To understand de Saussure's structuralism better we need to know that Marx denounced the metaphysical basis of "being," i.e., the ontology. He introduced the concept of deeply embedded social structures shaping our individual states of being and with the evolution of the perfect system our lives would be much better.

External structures.

These are the external structures that shape our lives. Of course, Marx's perfect system was idealized socialism within which everyone would reach their highest level of functioning for the good of the group.[21] So the individual was shaped by these preconscious and pervasive materialistic structures that existed outside of the individual.

Internal structures.

And Freud, on the other hand, attacked the idea that subjectivity and logic was the essence of being human. He said it was the unconscious structures of the mind, specifically the primal and aggressive "Id" and the controlling and conscientious "Super Ego" that shaped who

---

[21] Although modern Communism is an attempt to apply Marx's philosophical theories, it fails because of its inability to overcome its authoritarian structures and the consequent creation of privileged classes, which are suspiciously like the social structures of Capitalism.

we are, i.e., the internal structures. The poor Ego is no match for these deeper structures. So, the individual was formed by these deeply embedded preconscious structures of the mind and not by thinking that comes from a unique personal ontology or from learned knowledge that had an epistemological basis[xvi]. Both men brought us back to the pure materialism of the early philosophers.

Structuralism as a tool for understanding personalities.

De Saussure developed these views into what we call Structuralism today. According to him we don't see or feel structures, but they shape us in everything we think and do. They have us we don't have them.

The Birkman Method® feedback reports make accessible what is not typically available to us as coaches—the **structures** that affect our client's personalities.

Structures are not originated from "things" that have meaning in themselves but rather on relations between things or their differences. For example, we now understand DNA and its power in making us who we are. One hundred years ago who couldn't have imagined that every instruction for making a living, breathing human being was organized into strands of code? Code made up of four nucleotides that we refer to as T, A, C & G.[22]? Alone these units don't mean much but strung together in a structure they provide the instructions for making a living organism.

---

[22] Five nucleobases—adenine (A), cytosine (C), guanine (G), thymine (T), and uracil (U)—are called primary or canonical. They function as the fundamental units of the genetic code, with the bases A, G, C, and T being found in DNA while A, G, C, and U are found in RNA. Thymine and uracil are identical excepting that T includes a methyl group that U lacks.

This is also true of the human personality. Alone, our self and social perceptions don't mean much. But when they interact with each other and the outside world, our personality shows up in our public behaviors. These personality structures are complete, logical, and all-encompassing. As psychologist, Dr. Don Doty, says, "psyches only come in one size, whole."

Even though every personality trait can be plotted on a chart as if they are static, they are in constant transformation and recreation. And this is what the Birkman Method® does. It gives us a picture of the structure of a unique human identity as a roadmap to guide the process of coaching.

This is the coaching thrill:

To be present at the formation and re-creation of interpretations that offer our clients unique new options and opportunities for fuller lives.

The gift of age.

With our focus and attention being pulled in every direction assessing what's real and what's not, we can become distracted from awareness, let alone grasp, of our fundamental human concerns. It all seems so confusing in these complicated times. But then we reach a certain age. That age often brings with it some degree of economic security or the courage we need to express our authentic selves.

We feel an irresistible urge to express in relationships, family, work, or other vital areas of our lives before we die. This urge often happens in our midlife and is the cause of a good deal of anxiety for those who are covered up in obligations that won't allow them to change.

Many clients arrived at my office after being outplaced from twenty-year careers with and without transitional financial packages. Invariably the questions came up "what have I been doing with my life," and more importantly, "what do I want to do now?"

I used The Birkman Method® to examine social behaviors and most importantly, give access to the more profound, more authentic needs, which make up our ideal self. i.e., who we truly want to be to enjoy maximum satisfaction.

Dr. Birkman and I met at this philosophical juncture. We had no interest in "changing others" but rather helping them find their innate natural aptitudes. In this context, change is more like becoming who we are. This is the only change that has a reasonable chance of permanence.

But it is not easy. We have identified ourselves by our social behavior for so long that in many instances we have lost contact with our authentic self. We might even surprise others when we attempt to fill our *real needs* by being more publicly authentic. We can begin to say and do things that others do not expect of us. We can seem very different in our attempt to be the same as who we are. The actions of gay people coming out of the social closet provide an excellent example of this process.

It is difficult to assess the personal cost, let alone the cost to society of people not realizing their full potential. Douglas LaBier, in his book, *Modern Madness*, refers to us as the working wounded. He says we are "healthy people adjusted at great emotional cost due to conditions that are good for the advancement of career but not of spirit."[xvii] To what other forces do we adjust ourselves at great emotional cost?

Our current cultural trajectory.

In my career of forty-five plus years of working with people, I found that lasting, substantive change—whether personal or organizational—is a rare event and is becoming more difficult for reasons which seem to have to do with our current cultural trajectory into *postmodernity.*[23] What I am now seeing is people making new choices that offer them greater satisfaction in their professional and personal lives. It looks like change, but in fact, it is a step in the process of self-discovery.

But finding the *self* is becoming more difficult. From the description notes of the lecture series, *The Self Under Siege: Philosophy of the Twentieth Century,*[24] by Professor Rick Roderick, Ph.D., Professor of Philosophy, National University:

The self has come under siege from the start of modernity to the beginnings of the postmodern age in the

---

[23] There is considerable discussion and disagreement about the exact meaning of the term "post modernity." In addition, many people disagree with the hypothesis that claims that we are currently in a period of post modernity. I use this term to clearly distinguish the qualities that seem to be related to modernity from those that are being ascribed to post modernity. This way, I am less concerned about the exact era we are in and more concerned with the changes that seem to be happening to our culture or our way of being in the twenty-first century.

[24] Rick Roderick, Ph.D., National University, Lecture Series, The Teaching Company.

late twentieth century. We come to see how in the nineteenth century traditional concepts of the self come under suspicion. As we move into the twentieth century, we encounter the <u>self</u> buried under oceans of complex technology and information, leading us to question whether it is at all possible to construct some small space within which an authentic self might dwell. [25]

And from Douglas Kellner, editor of *Baudrillard: A Critical Reader,*

In addition, the postmodern universe is one of hyperreality in which entertainment, information and communications technologies provide experiences more intense and involving than the scenes of banal everyday life, whereby the models, images and codes of the hyper-real come to control thought and behavior, where it is impossible to chart causal mechanisms and logic in a situation in which individuals are confronted with an overwhelming flux of images, codes and models, any of which may shape an individual's thought or behavior.[xviii]

The revolution of postmodernity was thus a revolution of meaning grounded in the secure moorings of the dialectics of history, the economy of desire. Baudrillard scorns this universe and claims to be a part of a second revolution, that of the twentieth century, of postmodernity, which is the immense process of the destruction of meaning . . . Meaning requires depth, a hidden dimension, an unseen yet stable and fixed substratum or foundation; in the postmodern world, however, everything is visible, explicit and transparent, but highly unstable."[xix]

---

[25] Ibid.

So, the challenge is explicit. If substantive change is indeed the discovery of our authentic self and the self is constituted in meaning, and if meaning is so ephemeral in our times, how do we find our foundations? How can we construct some small space within which an authentic self might dwell?

Most importantly, the process of self-discovery is not a methodical process given to models and techniques. There is no one-minute approach to this very intimate personal work. We need a good grasp of not only our human abilities, which both assist and inhibit us but also of how we are shaped by the times within which we live. And our personal histories are equally important. Our personal identities are reflections of our historical circumstances as well.

Teacher, manager, executive, coach, consultant, or friend, if any of us are to be successful in our roles, we must understand the dynamics of human behavior and how it is shaped and sometimes distorted by postmodern times.

The bad news for anyone paying attention is that to effectively manage complexity today is a very difficult task because of its sheer volume. The good news is that we all have the innate capacity to do it. We have survived for over 100,000 years. We are here, and our primitive cousins have long since disappeared.

Syncretism.

Syncretism is the conflation of different religions, cultures, or schools of thought and we are awash in it. The social history of the U.S. has evolved over about 400 to 500 years, and we can still find people who behave in ways shaped by many earlier traditions. Just one example is people who attempt to find and adhere to a single absolute ethics as a guide for all decisions in any situation. And people who believe that every case requires a relative determination of right or wrong. So, who is right?

Fortunately, I am not proposing to answer this question in this book. To some extent, I can find elements of truth in both above views. But upon more profound reflection, I see that many of these elements of truth conflict with each other. I think that this is true for most of us today. This conflict is the result of the syncretism that permeates our society. If you've ever concluded, "our society is schizophrenic," this is the reason.

With our external world being in such a state of confusion, we need to look to our personal resources for the certitude and assurances that we seem to need so much. Most people who have demonstrated an ability to confront their interpretations in the light of new experiences have been subsequently able to absorb most any impact, reassess and sustain themselves no matter what the circumstances.

In his book, *Man's Search for Meaning*, Viktor Frankl eliminates any doubt about this essential human ability.

"We who lived in concentration camps can remember the men who walked through the huts comforting others, giving away their last piece of bread. They may have been few in number, but they offer sufficient proof that everything can be taken from a man but one thing: the last of the human freedoms—to choose one's attitude in any given set of circumstances, to choose one's own way."[xx]

Although we consciously experience a reality shaped by a long tradition of intellectual inquiry, most of us probably don't know that tradition well enough to question the present-day assumptions that derive from it. In fact, we may not even know that they *are* assumptions.

I have come to believe the *software* of human consciousness gets filled with the raw material of assumptions we have incorporated with and without awareness. As I review my own life experiences, I find that my assumptions have changed many times. I have discovered that much of the time I have operated on unexamined historical assumptions. These are assumptions and social constructions that I swallowed *hook, line, and sinker*. Most of us do.

Finally, I offer no new philosophical revelations. I do suggest a methodology based on a belief that the basis of being human, as distinct from other primates, is how we use our language. We linguistically negotiate the interactions we have between and among our internal neurophysiological structures and the external structures of the world within which we live.

Chapter 3 - Knowledge from the Cognitive Sciences

Be not angry that you cannot make others as you wish them to be since you cannot make yourself as you wish to be.

Thomas a Kempis

"The map is not the territory.[26]" Our cognitive maps are representations of the world that we use to experience and function in it. More recent research has given us insights into how our maps are formed and maintained neurologically. One of the more potentially productive aspects of this view is also the most difficult to accept, i.e., we do not perceive the world the way it is. Instead, it is filtered by our unique physiology and moderated by linguistic interpretations. Our ability to perceive external events is a function of our biology, and biological structures differ from person to person.

This is not new news. The newer story is that we come with perceptual preferences that have been conserved genetically. These preferences can be thought of as propensities to perceive some experiences and not others. And these perceptual tendencies are the ones that gave us adaptive advantages eons ago in the jungle.

A skillful coach knows that the client's perceptions of his world are not the coach's perceptions and vice versa. In fact, neither the client's nor the coach 's perceptions are wholly matched with anyone's. Of course, there is overlap as we will see in the following text, or we couldn't

---

[26] The semanticist, Alfred Korzybski

communicate at all. "All cognitive experience involves the knower in a personal way, rooted in his biological structure. There, his experience of certainty is an individual phenomenon blind to the cognitive acts of others, in a solitude which, we shall see is transcended only in a world created with those others." [xxi]

"Early perceptual competence is matched by cognitive incompetence. Much of the reorganization of perceptual representation is dependent on the development and construction of cognitive structures that give access to a world of objects, people, language, and events."[xxii]

This process begins with our earliest experiences as infants and is shaped by those who raise us into adulthood. The weakness of early perceptual competence is cognitive incompetence. And the baseline of our expectations, and eventually our needs, start with interpretations based on this immature cognitive incompetence. Much of the reorganization of perceptual representation is dependent on the development and construction of cognitive structures that give access to a world of objects, people, language, and events.[xxiii]

So even though we come with the raw materials for building cognitive structures, they are developed by the experiences that come from our native cultures when we are little children.

By now we should have a sense of the circularity of our developmental process. We now know we are born with these cognitive structures in place, and they shape and limit what we can experience. The concept of the *blank slate* is old news. We do not come into the world as empty vessels waiting to be filled with knowledge. "What makes our reasoning faculties different [...] is that they are not just broad areas of knowledge, analyzed with whatever tools work best. Each faculty is based on a core intuition that was suitable for analyzing the world in which we evolved.

Though cognitive scientists have not agreed on a *Gray's Anatomy* of the mind, here is a tentative but defensible list of cognitive faculties and the core intuitions on which they are based:[xxiv] "

- **Physics** - orientation to objects, space, movement, force, time in three-dimensional space.
- **Biology or natural history** - living things house a hidden essence that gives them form and powers and drives their growth and bodily functions.
- **Engineering** - make and understand tools and other artifacts designed to achieve a goal.
- **Psychology** - Other people are not objects or machines but are animated by an invisible entity we call the mind or soul. (beliefs, desires cause behavior)
- **Spatial** - used to navigate the world with our human bodies.
- **Numbers** - ability to register exact quantities and small amounts of objects and to make estimates of larger quantities.
- **Probabilities** - the reason for the likelihood of uncertain events based on past experiences.
- **Economics** - an awareness of the concept of reciprocal exchange.
- **Database and logic** - represent and store ideas and infer new ideas from old ones.
- **Language** - share ideas from our logic based on a mental dictionary.

And Innate Human Emotions: [27]

- **Anger**
- **Fear**
- **Disgust**
- **A moral sense of right and wrong**.

Our earliest perceptions don't mean much to us until we develop the cognitive competence to interpret them. But that doesn't stop us from ungrounded assessments that lead to declarations about the world, all linguistic processes. Add this to the fact that we come with these ten genetically conserved faculties in place and we can see how our early beliefs about the world can limit our possibilities as adults.

This says we depend on these cognitive structures to make sense of our perceptions and these structures bring biases with them that have evolved from our species' need to survive in the distant past. As Steven Pinker points out, our subjective experience is organized by these structures and based in our nervous system. To understand personal experience, we need to recognize that the human neurophysiological structure represents conserved evolutionary biases for surviving in the jungle.

Our linguistic faculty.

As noted before, Noam Chomsky is known for his theory that we come into the world with a deep generative language structure that allows us to learn language when we are children. [xxv] We can think of this deep structure as a pre-linguistic universal human grammar. It is like a bio-program that allows us to take on the difficult task of learning our

---

[27] This is a list of inborn emotions.

native language. As noted earlier, it's like a species "non-linguistic language" that facilitates learning a functional language. Steven Pinker calls it "mentalese."[xxvi]

Mentalese is not a public language per se. It is another kind of language that might be thought of as belonging to the pre-conscious mind where raw human meaning emerges. It is why we can communicate and connect with other human beings across cultural and linguistic differences and why understanding other animal species intelligence is so difficult.

This is just one of our natural learning intuitions that allow us to make sense of our experience of the objective world. We come genetically prepared to live and learn in the physical world, but it seems to be the world to which our ancestors were adapted at the time of the emergence of what we refer to as the first *modern* human beings, Homo Sapiens, between 100,000 and 200,000 years ago.

Metaphors of internal structures.

The use of the metaphors—schema, schemata, scripts, and rules give us an organizing structure to study the application of our language. As noted, the premise is every human being comes with the raw linguistic ability called "mentalese," but each of us learns a native language unique to our culture. It is with our native languages that we begin the process of cognitive development as we evolve from infants to adults.

By using these specific internal structures, 1) schema, 2) schemata, 3) scripts, and 4) rules, we can examine how we relate to our surroundings by creating our self and social perceptions.

It is important to note that these definitions are meant to be used as tools for analysis and preparation; not for immediate recall in every coaching moment. To be precise, they can be instrumental in preparation and analysis using the Birkman Method® feedback because it lays out the details in clear and concise terms.

Important clarification.

In his article, The Empty Brain, Robert Epstein[28] disputes the common, but erroneous, metaphor for how our brains work. We are not computers! We are living organisms.

"Because neither 'memory banks' nor 'representations' of stimuli exist in the brain, and because all that is required for us to function in the world is for the brain to change in an orderly way as a result of our experiences, *there is no reason to believe that any two of us are changed the same way by the same experience* [...] Those changes, whatever they are, are built on the unique neural structure that already exists, each structure having developed over a lifetime of unique experiences.

"For any given experience, orderly change could involve a thousand neurons, a million neurons or even the entire brain, with the pattern of change different in every brain.

---

[28] Robert Epstein is a senior research psychologist at the American Institute for Behavioral Research and Technology in California. He is the author of 15 books, and the former editor-in-chief of Psychology Today.

"What's more, as the neurobiologist Steven Rose pointed out in *The Future of the Brain* (2005), a snapshot of the brain's current state might also be meaningless unless we knew the *entire life history* of that brain's owner – perhaps even about the *social context* in which he or she was raised.

"To understand even the basics of how the brain maintains the human intellect, we might need to know not just the current state of all 86 billion neurons and their 100 trillion interconnections, not just the varying strengths with which they are connected, and not just the states of more than 1,000 proteins that exist at each connection point, but how the moment-to-moment *activity* of the brain contributes to the integrity of the system.

"Add to this the uniqueness of each brain, brought about in part because of the uniqueness of each person's life history, and Kandel's prediction starts to sound overly optimistic. (In a recent op-ed in *The New York Times*, the neuroscientist Kenneth Miller suggested it will take 'centuries' just to figure out basic neuronal connectivity.)"[xxvii]

As Birkman philosophy holds, there is no idea style, and everyone has a unique view of our shared reality.

Loosening our grip.

Most of us will fight like crazy to defend our point of view. Given what the preceding information, how accurate is our perception of reality? There is a clue in this excerpt from an article by Amanda Gefter in Quanta Magazine, in September of 2016. She writes, "As we go about our daily lives, we tend to assume that our perceptions — sights, sounds, textures, tastes — are an accurate portrayal of the real world. Sure, when we stop and think about it — or when we find ourselves fooled by a perceptual illusion — we realize with a jolt that what we perceive is never the world directly, but rather our brain's best guess at what that world is like, a kind of internal simulation of an external reality. Still, we bank on the fact that our simulation is a reasonably decent one. If it wasn't, wouldn't evolution have eliminated us by now? The actual reality might be forever beyond our reach, but surely our senses give us at least an inkling of what it's really like."

Not so, says Donald D. Hoffman, a professor of cognitive science at the University of California, Irvine. Dr. Hoffman goes on to explain that "getting at questions about the nature of reality, and disentangling the observer from the observed, is an endeavor that straddles the boundaries of neuroscience and fundamental physics."

It's individual perceptions all the way down.[29]

In fact, the world we experience is a collection of the perceptions and interpretations of many individual conscious agents including every sentient life form, not only human beings. A kind of matrix of consciousness creating what appears as our objective reality that doesn't exist as we think it does. It's difficult to understand, I know. An example might help.

This again from the same article by Amanda Gefter, Dr. Hoffman explains, "There's a metaphor that's only been

---

[29] "Turtles all the way down" is an expression of the problem of infinite regress. The saying alludes to the mythological idea of a World Turtle that supports the earth on its back. It suggests that this turtle rests on the back of an even larger turtle, which itself is part of a column of increasingly large turtles that continues indefinitely (i.e., that it is "turtles all the way down").

available to us in the past 30 or 40 years, and that's the desktop interface. Suppose there's a blue rectangular icon on the lower right corner of your computer's desktop—does that mean the file itself is blue and rectangular and lives in the lower right corner of your computer? Of course, not. But those are the only things that can be asserted about anything on the desktop—it has color, position, and shape. Those are the only categories available to you, and yet none of them are true about the file itself or anything in the computer. They couldn't possibly be true. That's an interesting thing. You could not form a true description of the innards of the computer if your entire view of reality was confined to the desktop. And yet the desktop is useful. That blue rectangular icon guides my behavior, and it hides a complex reality that I don't need to know. That's the key idea. Evolution has shaped us with perceptions that allow us to survive. They guide adaptive behaviors. But part of that involves hiding from us the stuff we don't need to know. And that's pretty much all of reality, whatever reality might be".

So, as we cannot envision the actual "innards" or the insides of our computers by seeing the user interface, we cannot envision the actual "innards" of the reality we're so fond of arguing about.

Taking this metaphor a bit further, each of us is the computer operator. Our sensory systems are the graphic user interface, the system that interacts with the internal and external data. They are our computer screens. By our subconscious directions, our sensory systems call up the arrangements of particles that make up what we observe in our subjective experience. (on the computer screens of our lives)

Think of it this way; the underlying reality is like the contents of a computer file on our screen. It appears there in a form that we can comprehend. It doesn't remotely resemble what it looks like in the memory of our computers. Our request to observe it makes it a recognizable computer file. We do not see the actual nature of the electrons that make it up any more than we see the actual reality of our universe.

And the key point is?

As coaches, we need common denominators for assessing all the possible variations in the perceptions and interpretations of our clients. As you already know, The Birkman Method® provides the first level, the personality traits, and neuro-cognitive science offers the next level down.

These structural terms, schema, scripts, rules, etc., are metaphors. They are organizing principles that allow us to examine the construction of a client's personality and guide our efforts to assist. They do not represent real physical structures any more than the term, "the four corners of the earth" represents real geographical features. Remember, as de Saussure, pointed out, structures are arrangements of what is real.

Schema:

Think of a schema as the internal framework that exists within our pre-existing cognitive faculties (those ten listed above by Pinker). They are learning intuitions that seem to be ready fit with open slots that are designed to accept and make sense of the stimulus that comes from the external world in each of these categories. For example, take our innate neuro-cognitive faculty of physics: when we interact with an object such as a table we can fill an open physical object slot with our unique experience. It's a table, a physical thing. We don't confuse it with a rabbit, a living thing.

Schemas seem to have default settings. These are the human universals that allow people from all cultures to form the basis for what we call the human experience. For instance, the slots for mother, father, son, and daughter are probably species schemata[30]. In other words, everyone in our species has these schemata regardless of what culture they come from.

When coaching people from other cultures, the objective here is to keep in mind that their default settings might be filled with different content information. For instance, the default settings for *respect* in the Far East are filled with entirely different practices from the West.

Schema comes with *tags*. Tags are like flags that come up when a new experience comes along that will not fit within an existing schema. When this happens, the tag relates this experience to a similar schema and in that way the individual can make sense of his new experiences. Of course, this is a very fertile place for misunderstandings and disconnections.

How many times have you or your client reacted to a present situation with an older response that seems to come from nowhere? Phobias are a good example. Our extreme fear of something in the present is probably a response to a past frightening experience being called up by a tag— something that reminds us of the past.

Occasionally there are experiences that are so foreign to us we have no tags to older ones. This little story makes an interesting point about them.

---

[30] Schemata is plural form

Curious, I took a pencil from my pocket and touched a strand of the (spider) web. Immediately there was a response. The web, plucked by its menacing occupant, began to vibrate until it was a blur. Anything that had brushed claw or wing against that amazing snare would be thoroughly entrapped. As the vibrations slowed, I could see the owner fingering her guidelines for signs of struggle. A pencil point was an intrusion into this universe for which no precedent existed. Spider was circumscribed by spider ideas; its universe was a spider universe. All outside was irrational, extraneous, at best raw material for spider. As I proceeded on my way along the gully, like a vast impossible shadow, I realized that in the world of spider I did not exist.[xxviii]

In this case, the spider seemed to have no previous cognitive schema or tags for this experience. People from very different cultural backgrounds have similar gaps in experiences. It's also possible that people from very different regions of the same country might not share schema. As a coach, it's important to know and be aware of this possibility. You cannot assume your client has the same cultural schemata as your own.

Schemata:

Schemata consist of structured groups of concepts, which constitute the generic knowledge about events, scenarios, actions, or objects that have been acquired from experience.[xxix] Although schemata are the plural form of schema, it can also be used to denote a set of *related* schemas.

For instance, we could say that our schema for table fits within the schemata for furniture. Once again, a very fertile place for disconnection's in relationships with people who are very different from us. For instance, if we think of schemata as cultural, we can see how difficult it can be to communicate clearly across their boundaries.

Scripts:

Schank and Abelson[xxx] extended the idea of schemata to explain how knowledge of complex event sequences is represented. These knowledge structures called scripts represent the elements common to repeated experiences of events. A script consists of a sequence of goal-directed actions, which are causally and temporally ordered and includes the actors, objects, and locations that are typically involved. In Birkman terms, we would call this a script that leads to Usual Behavior when Needs are satisfied and to Stress Behavior when not.

Script elements function as default values and allow us to supply missing elements and to infer what is not explicitly stated.[xxxi] In Birkman terms, this might also lead to Stress Behaviors if the default values are not fit for the situation.

The Birkman qualified coach has the perfect tool to guide the examination of what script elements, acting as default values, may be misleading a client. The answer to this question is found in a review of the client's Stress Behaviors. Using inappropriate script elements is an ineffective practice and produces Stress Behaviors. To use a theatrical metaphor, is the actor using the correct script for the play or should the actor find another play where his script fits? Keep in mind, changing the actor is not an effective strategy. There are leading men and ladies and there are character actors. Generally, they're not interchangeable, i.e., the "round peg in a square hole," situation.

The anatomy of an erroneous judgment.

These structures are accessed by the cortex assisted by the hippocampus. If the hippocampus is working well, it identifies them based on the themes that guide each interaction. This means we will find the closest previous experience to fit the interaction[31] An exception might be when a stimulus is directed around the cortex and directly to the amygdala producing a more primitive response such as a reaction to a threatening event. In this case, our response might be to trigger the "fight or flight" response, which does not require a linguistic interpretation.

Other than that exception, if we were having a conversation about a specific event, the script that contains actors, objects, and locations that are typically involved in similar circumstances will guide our interaction. Our scripts then interact with the structures of our previous knowledge with the help of our hippocampus and can reconfigure the information needed to fill an empty slot.

It should be obvious how this process can get us into all kinds of misunderstandings by merely using inappropriate past experiences. And remember, syncretism permeates our society and our society influences our thinking. So it's no wonder that we can seem very confused at times.

Our internal neural structures constitute our potential. They allow us to experience the external world

---

[31] Most recently I read an article about the discovery that in London, England the brains of taxi drivers have been found to have enlarged hippocampus seemingly due the fact that in order to gain a taxi license it is necessary for a driver to memorize the entire city of London. This means that the average taxi driver in London can find and retrieve details of every street in that enormous and complex city.

through the stimulus we receive from interactions with that world. But as we can see, we also make inferential leaps by substituting old information if the new information is similar to what we already know.

We don't have a single neuron dedicated to each unique bit of information. Consequently, we need to use seemingly infinite combinations of existing neurons to manage new experiences. (See Dr. Epstein's article above) This is a function of our central nervous system and serves the purpose of conservation and retention, but we need to be aware that this process can be the cause of how we can misunderstand and misuse new information. Even our client's most strongly-held beliefs can be based on these ill-formed cognitive structures. Ours can be too!

If we are to be competent coaches, it is essential that we become discerning in our interactions to improve the quality of our own connections with the outside world. Or we might just be responding to new stimuli with previously held information from the neural networks that form our subjective experience.

In other words, we can say that the quality of our connections to the outside world determines the efficacy of our subjective experience. This leaves us with the challenge of continuously improving our connections. Given this description of our cognitive structures, how do we then take actions?

Production systems.

In this case, our production system is that system that generates the decisions that produce action in our lives. Although one could identify several production system models from the research of information-processing psychologists, we will use a generic form to demonstrate the relationship of cognitive processing as it shapes behavior.

In Birkman terms, this is the entire process of decision making described by the interactions of the Usual Behaviors, Needs, and Stress Behaviors. As an example, "When I have time to make decisions, I am deliberate and cooperative. If my need for sufficient time to make decisions is not met, I can become resistant and non-compliant."

We perceive a sensation and interpret it as like or the same as a previously experienced event. In one instance, a Need is being filled, we have access to our strengths, and we have Usual Behavior. In other words, our desired conditions are met, our rule fires and related action is called for. In some instances, more than one rule is called on. This is called *chaining* and it happens subconsciously.

This process continues until the rules don't work or the situation ends, and then another script is called for. Sometimes, a Need is not being filled, and we have Stress Behavior at the cost of efficacy.

All this experience is then reinforced by restructuring our brains providing access to our long-term memories. In this way, our cognitive functions can and will be influenced over time gradually shaping our scripts new information to make them more effective in situations where they apply and less effective in situations where they don't. Rules are considerably more challenging to change as we will see.

The fallibility of human decision-making.

We live in an incomprehensibly rich world. We also enjoy a neural system adapted and evolved to negotiate that world. At its best, we can only sense, perceive, and interpret a tiny fraction of the whole. That is further influenced by what we already know and can detect with our ten evolutionarily developed learning intuitions. There is probably no better reason for staying connected to others lest we believe our own limited experience alone. And this is certainly the best reason to have a coach.

We make our decisions heuristically.[32]

Under conditions of uncertainty, we depend a great deal on our history to make sense of our present experience. Therefore, we humans make many mistakes.

Heuristic decisions allow for much more variability than an algorithmic[33] decision would. They are made with incomplete information, where an algorithmic decision is formulaic and would use the same sequence of steps repeatedly like a computer.

Our challenge is to overcome our own cognitive devices that are designed to keep everything consistent with our existing point of view. This is the process of consciousness working for and against us.

Enhancing connections.

To restate my premise here, to promote personal growth more effectively we must enhance and maintain our connections to the external world through interactions with others.

---

[32] Heuristic is any approach to problem solving, learning, or discovery that employs a practical method not guaranteed to be optimal or perfect, but sufficient for the immediate goals.
[33] A finite set of unambiguous instructions that, given some set of initial conditions, can be performed in a prescribed sequence to achieve a certain goal

An excellent example of this is the coal miner who knows that his working life is over because the mines have shut down. Until he can experience himself as able to learn new skills, he will live in a state of despair. Some miners may be able to overcome their own subjective experiences based in the past, but most will need the help of other people. This is the yoke of a single individual view of life without the aid of people on the outside of their personal experience.

The more willing a person is to question self and social perceptions, the quicker he or she will reach their objectives. Conversely, if they are not able to change interpretations, they are doomed to very long and frustrating efforts with uncertain outcomes.

Case in point.

A case in point was a 50-year-old woman who assessed that no one wanted to help her so she wouldn't make any requests. She was unemployed for two years when I lost contact with her. There seemed to be no way I could convince her that others were ready and able to assist her in her job search. She refused to make the connections she needed. She may be still unemployed.

On the other hand, a man I worked with had been outplaced at the age of 61, and he assessed that this was the opportunity that he had been waiting for to move to a warmer climate and be closer to water and his boat. Within six months he was re-employed in Florida. He had openly accepted his need to make connections with others.

Both people had marketable skills, so it wasn't the external factors that limited them, but their respective perceptions and resultant declarations had either opened or closed possibilities.

After coaching people in transition, I am convinced that those who refuse to recreate their world with new declarations never get around to making the requests needed to get through change in a healthy way. They stay stuck in their own blind subjective experience and blame it on the world around them. But they don't seem to know that this world of limitations comes about through their creation.

Know thyself.

An unavoidable truth is you need a practical understanding of how human neurophysiology and social assumptions shape who you and others are before you can reach your optimum capacity to assist your clients. Because as coaches we are tasked to work with the unique human neurophysiological structure of each of our clients as they interact with their world of social structures. What's not so obvious is that we are also affected by our personal neurophysiological structures and history of experiences.

This can be a major challenge but can also be the basis for enormous breakthroughs in our work. Because all cognitive experience involves people in a personal way, rooted in their biological structures. There, experience of certainty is an individual phenomenon blind to the cognitive acts of others, in a solitude, which we shall see, is transcended only in a world created with those others. [xxxii] In other words, we all live in a state of subjective blindness, and the only way to bridge over to a better understanding of our world is to have authentic contact with other people.

So, if our hippocampus is working well, it calls up our scripts based on the themes that guide each interaction. We will find the script to fit the interaction. As noted above an exception might be a stimulus going around the cortex and directly to the amygdala producing a more primitive response. In this case, our reaction might be to trigger the *fight or flight* response, which does not require a linguistic interpretation.

This is good because we do not need to learn new information each time we have an interaction. But it's problematic in managing change because we also erroneously use previously stored information to fill in a slot that is close but not exactly accurate in the current interaction. And as we store more information in each new interaction, it becomes more generalized to fit the existing information. In this way, we mediate the incoming information, so it conforms to our existing point of view. The practice called *racial profiling* is a good example of this process in action. A reminder here: This is all happening in our subconscious.

Remember, our internal neural structures constitute our potential. They allow us to experience the external world through the stimulus we receive from interactions with that world. But as we can see, we also make inferential leaps by substituting old information if the new data is similar to what we already know. And more importantly, we are now scientifically proving that idiosyncrasies in our neural structures will affect the actual perceptions of our external world.

So, it is very important that we become discerning in our interactions to improve the quality of our connections with the outside world, or we might simply be responding to new stimuli with information that is called up in our neural networks.

In other words, we might say that the quality of our connections to the outside world determines the quality of our subjective experience. This leaves us with the challenge of continuously improving our relationships. Generally speaking, this process continues until the rules don't work or the situation ends and then another script is called for. All this experience restructures our brain's neural networks which we think of as long-term memories. In this way, our cognitive structures can and will be influenced over time, gradually shaping our scripts with new information to make them more effective. This restructuring gives us the ability to decide and act quickly, but it comes with the potential for errors.

By now, you can see the difficulties in store for the person undergoing significant change. Every natural cognitive mechanism is working to preserve the integrity of past experiences and the compensating strategies that evolve from them. But somehow, we need to negotiate that *gap* between our personal experience and that of the world around us if we are to develop the new strategies necessary to manage new situations. I call this gap the nexus.[34]

---

[34] I use the term "nexus" not because I believe that we all have an actual space called a nexus but to communicate conceptually with fewer words by applying a linguistic distinction

Chapter 4 – The Nexus

"Each individual in society is a nexus where innumerable relationships of this character intersect."

Carroll Quigley

The nexus is the boundary space of connections; the continuous instances of interactions between and among the cognitive structures of our subjective experience and the external world. These interactions are instantaneous and unremitting. Once had, they cannot be recalled. Once done, they cannot be undone. All our experiences, up until the instant of each interaction, come into play in that instant. They are, in fact, automatic even though we think that we are using choice. Research has shown that our automatic responses begin nanoseconds before we become consciously aware of them. Then we add the explanations for the action we have just taken. We tell the tale that fits our story.

Does this mean that we are machines? No, because although we are fixed in a specific action, we are flexible for all subsequent actions because we can learn new responses and add new options to our automatically triggered repertoire of behaviors.

The Nexus is where the *social self* publicly expresses. Our social self is our public identity. Our public identity consists of a rough historic record of our repeated public actions and their linguistic interpretations by others. For example, if others interpret my actions as consistent with a person who keeps his word over and over again, my public identity will be that of an honest man.

Our *authentic self* is often kept hidden within our web of beliefs, which remain private for fear of the judgments of other people. And these judgments are grounded in the categorical imperatives of our native culture.

But even with the complications that seem to abound at this boundary between our internal and external worlds, we can and do connect. Helen Keller found a way to connect to the outer world even though she was blind and deaf. She went on to become an inspiration to us all. Steven Hawking lived entombed in his own body but produced theories of cosmology that enhanced Einstein's theories of the universe. How did these two extraordinary people manage to connect with their external world when they were so well insulated within their own subjective experience? In fact, they are like every other human being that now or has ever lived. Except that they used extraordinary means to penetrate the *boundary.*

Does negotiating the nexus or boundary of our personal experience require conscious effort? Maturana and Varela propose that living systems are *structurally coupled.* In other words, when there is a history of recurrent interactions leading to structural congruence between two or more systems, there is structural coupling.[xxxiii] So even if I choose to stay in my private subjective world, I am affected by the world around me. I can be influenced in ways that are not even conscious to me.

The nexus is the boundary point of these repeated interactions.

When humans structurally couple with other humans, language is usually initially involved in some form or another. Once in place, structural coupling does not require language. A good example is a pet that can anticipate your next move.

In Helen Keller's case, once her guide had connected the concept of a word to her physical experience of water flowing over her hand, progress began. And in Steven Hawking's case, electronic representations of words were the carriers of his sealed subjective knowledge such that he shared the immense power of his intellect.

To some extent, we are all like Keller and Hawking. But most of us have easier access to the tools of language in a given social context and community of common linguistic distinctions. We can talk and understand each other rather simply if we so choose. But nothing changes the fact that our subjective experience is one of solitude, unknowable by others as theirs is by us. The nexus is that familiar boundary space where the repeated connections must occur for us to transcend our solitude and create the external world within which we live with others.

A simple metaphor is that of a common spark plug in an automobile. It is designed to have a gap between two points on its body. If the gap is properly set, the electronic charge *sparks* across the gap and ignites the gasoline/oxygen mixture, and the internal combustion produces the power that we all take for granted as our car accelerates away from the curb. The gap is a space that allows something important to happen. It is not a thing. Without it, the two *physical points* on the plug won't function correctly.

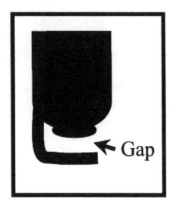

But there is more to the picture when we view it from a broader perspective. The gap exists on a single unit. It is of the same piece. So, the spark plug is interacting with itself to form the gap or space within which action will occur.

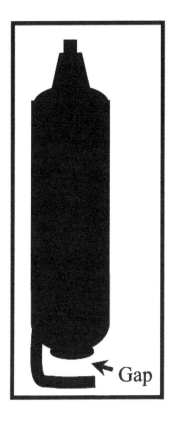

The plug connects and reconnects with its environment in the gap. This is what I refer to as the nexus or the point of repeating connections. In the case of the spark plug, it is creating a space of interaction that allows it to function. We, humans, generate this kind of space or nexus between our perceptions and external reality that allow us to function in the world with others as we reveal our public self. It is an illusion that we are interacting with the real world. In fact, we are interacting with our central nervous system's responses to perturbations from outside itself. We are structurally coupled systems interacting deterministically with each other and are limited to our own subjective experiences.[xxxiv] If each of us live in the solitude of our subjective experience, how do we create the outside world of interaction with others?

Enhancing connections

To restate my premise here, we must maintain and enhance our connections to the external world through interactions with others to deal with change more effectively. If we are to assist others, and ourselves, as change happens all around us, we have two primary linguistic tools to use. One, our *declarative* language acts must be grounded in shared reality. Two, our *performative* language acts must be synchronous with that reality and synonymous with our intentions. The first one means untangling and properly grounding our assertions, assessments, and declarations. The second means that we make requests, offers, and promises that are possible and are synonymous with our real intentions. [More to come later on these language acts.]

As I coached people in transition, I learned that those who refuse to [declare] recreate their world with new assessments, assertions and declarations never get around to [perform] making the requests, offers and promises needed to get through change in a healthy way. They stay stuck in their own subjective experience and blame it on the world around them. But they don't seem to know that this world of limitations comes about through their creation.

Chapter 5 -- The Power of Language

The quality of our thoughts is bordered on all sides by our facility with language.

J. Michael Straczynski

Why is language the most potent coaching tool? The obvious answer is we use it to communicate with other people. While this is true, there is so much more to understand. A coach needs to recognize and make use of the full power of language, not only to communicate, but also to create ourselves and our reality. When we understand this power, we begin to get a full grasp of its capacity to assist in coaching. We are continually using language to interpret the perceptions that create our inside world of experience and our interactions with others in our community.

Our neurolinguistic central nervous system.

As previously noted, our cognitive development is a neuro-linguistic process. Consequently, the most productive method for intentionally stimulating our CNS resulting in an experience is language. This doesn't say language is the only way, but a primary device for affecting us.[35] As Chomsky said, we are born *wired* for it with a kind of universal grammatical bio-program. Speaking and listening, whether to ourselves or others, are the essence of consciousness.

This is not to say we don't experience life without language, but to be whole, we need to have a language of some sort or another. The fully conscious interpretation of

---

[35] The others are emotions and body (physiology).

our every experience requires language. Language creates the syntax or structure of our lives. Our highest ability that of reflection is language in its purest form. So, in addition to being biologically primates, humans are linguistic beings. We are forever changed by each language act in which we participate.

The neurologist Oliver Sacks description of an eleven-year-old deaf boy, reared without any language for his first ten years, shows what life is like without language and subsequently without syntax:

Joseph saw, distinguished, categorized, used; he had no problems with perceptual categorization or generalization, but he could not, it seemed, go much beyond this, hold abstract ideas in mind, reflect, play, plan. He seemed completely literal-unable to enter an imaginative or figurative realm...He seemed, like an animal, or an infant, to be stuck in the present, to be confined to literal and immediate perception, though made aware of this by a consciousness that no infant could have.[xxxv]

Joseph had not been taught any language and therefore could not experience structure or syntax. He had no sense of the future. His consciousness was not fully formed. To some extent, he was like some lower primates who can experience events in the present but are unable to learn from the past and advance their knowledge and abilities into the future.

Language can also keep us *stuck* in our limited subjective experience.

The natural reflexive act of cognition is to apply *idiosyncratic certitude*[36] to life as it comes at us. We think we *know what's right* from the past and unconsciously apply it to our actions in the present. But this act commits us to the continuing solitude of our subjective experience.

When we realize that our subjective *certitude* and that of the client is based on presuppositions, and those are based in language, we have a robust coaching tool. And when our coaching engagement is successful, we are facilitating theirs and our transcendence from the solitude of subjective experience to being in the world with others. In simple terms, we are connecting.

The resistance.

It would seem anyone would want to add new information to their point of view if it meant getting relief from not knowing what to do in a strange situation. But my experience doesn't support this premise. In fact, the opposite seems to be true. Most of us will try to find others who agree with us rather than change our point of view. For instance, today we all seem to live in media bubbles or echo chambers, which continuously reinforce our existing point of view.

Having our point of view confirmed is comforting; limiting but comforting nonetheless.

---

[36] A uniquely personal feeling of certainty

Case in point.

As an example, I worked as a change consultant contracted to AT&T before and during the divestiture in the early 80's. At the time it was the most extensive change effort in the history of modern business. Over a million people in a company with a 100 plus year history and a highly influential organizational culture were to make a change from doing things the "structured, Ma Bell monopolistic way" to becoming a fierce competitor in the deregulated telecommunications market.

My first assignment was to help the field service people in a single Midwest division to become more flexible and nimble in the conduct of their daily activities. Supervisors who had never managed more than eight people were now going to lead 20 "*craftsmen*[37]." This span of control is not unusual in a manufacturing company where people stand in one spot all day. It was extraordinary in a field service organization where the manager was responsible for people distributed over a large geographic area.

Here is the remarkable part. The craftsmen who were going to get much more freedom from supervision, which they had requested in the past, were the most reluctant to accept the new reality. They couldn't or wouldn't believe it. They were not equipped to interpret these new circumstances correctly and depended on each other to reinforce their skepticism. They were applying their certitude, or what *they* thought was true, to an entirely unknowable future.

---

[37] This term was used to denote people who worked "with the tools" in their vernacular.

Why is the power of our subjective experience so strong?

Why does it hold us so tightly? The answer might be found in understanding that we are structurally determined beings[38]. As much as we would like to think we make decisions based on the needs of the immediate situation, our first responses are subconscious and automatic. And even if we pause and consider our present need, allowing new information is a difficult process.

How do we learn something new if we think we already know it all? This is one of the adult enemies to learning. At its most basic level, the first step is learning new language. We may need to manage our emotional resistance to new information, but language is the human representational form (metaphors) of the physical and the conceptual worlds. When we attempt to make sense of new information, we sometimes don't have the linguistic distinctions (words) to make use of it. Without these distinctions, we are lost. When we learn them, we open the door to new competence.

New linguistic distinctions (words) can lead to new competence.

The first step of learning new competencies is becoming aware there are new competencies to learn. How do we do that? We learn the linguistic distinctions (words) that define the concepts and or objects involved in the area we want to learn about.

---

[38] Our central nervous system determines our behavior and certain experiences become patterned into it such that we can function pre- or subconsciously without thinking about the actions we take.

Case in point.

For instance, I invite you to join me for a day of sailing. You have never been aboard a sailboat. You arrive and come aboard, and we leave the harbor and head out on the water. We clear the channel marker buoys, and I ask you to help me hoist the sails. You are very willing and ready to assist. So, I say, "grab that main halyard and unfurl the mainsail while I steer the boat into the wind" as I point to what looks to you like several neatly arranged loops of ropes. You turn to me with a quizzical look on your face. But then I begin to name each of the *ropes* and explain their purpose. At the end of our little discussion, you can discern each category of *rope* and their purposes. You now have linguistic distinctions and can begin to learn actions that you could not perform before. For what had previously looked like just a *bunch of ropes* are now halyards, mainsheets, jib sheets, or dock lines, and you know what they do.

You will never be as helpless again when and if you are onboard a sailboat. Has anything in the boat changed? Of course not, but you can now linguistically distinguish all the different *ropes* because someone taught you to see and name each of them and their function, and you are now able to take actions that you couldn't take before. You have learned something new, and you started by learning linguistic distinctions.

For the most part, I know of no one whose point of view is threatened by learning new information about a sailboat. (Except maybe a few power boaters I've met) But when it comes to so many other essential issues in life, I know of many people who don't want to see another point of view because it threatens their own even if they can learn how to do something they couldn't do before. Are these people somehow strange or faulty in some way? No, they are you and me.

You don't think so because you are more flexible, open-minded, you say. Okay, let's try a word experiment. Determine the truth of each of these statements on a scale of one to 10. One being absolutely not true and 10 being absolutely true. (Keep in mind, this is an experiment and I am not arguing for or against these positions.)

- Abortion is the right of every woman to determine what she does with her body.
- The Israeli's have a right to take Jerusalem as their capitol.
- Terrorists are doing what they should to protect their religious beliefs and are justified in their actions.
- People with darker skin color are intellectually inferior to those with lighter skin.

You already know, there are as many people who disagree with you as agree. And people have died for their point of view in situations related to each instance above.

Is this process a result of our upbringing?

Could our parents have done a better job with us, so we could have a more open mind? Maybe the answer is yes. The more critical issue is that our point of view is biologically conserved in our central nervous system. First, it's in the form of genetically conserved cognitive structures that are biased toward the behaviors that provided an adaptive advantage in the past. Secondly, those biases can be further enhanced by the external systems with which we interact throughout our lives. Things just feel right when they match our point of view.

Think of our central nervous system as the *structure* that holds our experiences in the form of our linguistic distinctions and past responses. We respond to language as a child responds to a pinprick. It is automatic and out of our conscious control. But we do have the choice of enriching that system with new information such that when the next stimulus comes in, we have more possible responses.

Word association.

To demonstrate this point, our automatic response mechanism is the basis for the *word association* test used by psychologists. In this test, you are given the word (a stimulus), and you are to respond with the *first word* that comes to your mind (automatic linguistic response). This is the word that comes to you before you add additional considerations as to its political correctness or the validity of your response. So, this test intends to gain access to your automatic linguistic responses to gain insight into your psychology. If you ever take the test you might be surprised at your answers.

Most importantly, external stimulus is neutral.[39] We add our interpretation linguistically. We have the power to re-interpret any external stimulus. But first we need to add new experiences, so we have new choices. It is only through this process that we grow and develop. If we stick to our point of view, we are doomed to miss a changing world as we attempt to view it through old lenses. This may be scary,

---

[39] This statement is not meant to include situations intended to harm us.

but it is the only way we can make progress in dealing with an ever-changing world.

Allowing new information to transform us is the difference between having many years of experience or having one year of experience many times.

The influence of external systems.

We don't live in a vacuum. We live in a world with others. We also have external pressures on us to maintain or change our point of view. Remember that we share relationships with others by being structurally connected to them. This not only facilitates our interactions with others but it also places demands on us to respond in previous ways. It's called habitual patterns.

In some instances, people continue to respond to patterned interactions that are not happening. In other words, our expectations are so structurally installed that we will react to familiar stimuli according to habit.

As an example, I have friends and business associates in England who I visit from time to time. As you know the English drive on the opposite side of the road. When I'm a passenger in an English car, I am on the U.S. driver's side. My foot presses a phantom brake pedal every time I perceive a traffic threat.

Another example is married people who don't listen to each other anymore. One talks and the other hears but the interpretations are somewhat out of sync with the speaker's intentions. You've probably seen the classic comedic skit that demonstrates this phenomenon.

The couple is sitting at the breakfast table chatting. The wife notices that the husband is not paying attention to what she says. She says that "her head fell off and she re-attached it with dental floss," and he continues to respond as though she was making sense. In this instance, it's good for a laugh. But what about the times when real communications fail because a usual auto-response misses a crucial message.

Case in point.

In a previous career, I was sent to a manufacturing plant in a rural setting to help with a problematic labor relations situation. Every word that came from my mouth was interpreted from a history of management abuses. This was a most unpleasant situation that took much longer to resolve than it should have. The workforce was structurally coupled with previous management representatives. I was too like those management representatives to stimulate a new or different response. My words were pre-interpreted. The system was closed. Ultimately, I did have success in building trust sufficient to improve overall relations. It was a long upward climb that took most of three years.

This process is somewhat explained through the study of *pragmatics* (more later in this book). Pragmatics is the study of the relationship of the signs (words in this case) to the interpreters. The interpretations are unique to the people sending and receiving the messages.

In summary, even when examining the power of language, we cannot ignore how it will be maximized or minimized by how it affects the people around us. Throughout the entire discussion about our linguistic capabilities keep in mind the origin of language was our need to coordinate actions with other people.[40] This is still its most important use.

---

[40] Some theorists propose that it was to win arguments and have our personal point of view prevail. It seems like both reasons are so interconnected it doesn't make any difference.

The most useful cognitive faculty for negotiating and enhancing connections at the nexus is language because it is what we use to interpret our inside world of experience and our outside world of interactions. It is with language that we create our personal identities and live in community with others.

As we have seen, language is required for complete human consciousness. And we've seen that language is necessary to interpret our perceptions and make sense of our interpretations. In other words, language is the most effective method for stimulating our central nervous system resulting in meaningful subjective experience. We are born *wired* for it with a universal grammatical bio-program. In the next chapter, we will examine the language acts that come with our grammatical bio-programming.

Chapter 6 – Basic Language Acts

"Say what you mean and mean what you say."

Anonymous

There about 6000 different languages spoken on the planet. It's doubtful anyone knows how many dialects there are. So, to get a practical handle on the use of language seems like an impossible task until we realize that there is a straightforward template we can use. Speech Act Theory is such a template but would take us far afield from a coaching application. Instead, this chapter offers a variation or derivative as a practical tool.

Understanding intention is the key to the effective use of language in coaching engagements. As simple as this is to understand on the surface, it is not always as easy to spot in a coaching session. Even outside the coaching relationship, we are confronted with language being *intentionally* and *unintentionally* misused every day. Sometimes, it achieves underlying and hidden agendas but sounds like it is doing something else entirely. (Politics is a good place to listen for intentional misuse.) Sometimes, its intention is not consciously known to the person doing the talking.

Six useful language distinctions.

1. Assessments, 2. Assertions, 3. Declarations, 4. Requests, 5. Offers, and 6. Promises. These six language acts can help us understand the construction of our self and social perceptions. They create our world and how we function in that world. At various times, they are used consciously,

unconsciously, attentively, and inattentively. They produce Usual <u>and</u> Stress behaviors. Sometimes they produce what we want and sometimes not. Nevertheless, they will always produce something.

In the following chapters, we will see how they can be used to deconstruct the Birkman component feedback and examine the structure of the conversations (personal and public) that hold them together.

The categories.

To begin, we classify the six essential acts, three language acts each, into two categories, Declarative and Performative. These are the most useful for understanding our topic because the first group creates our subjective experience of the world through conscious and unconscious declarations. The second group defines the strategy we use to act (perform) in that world we create through our declarations.

We'll call these the Basic Language Acts[xxxvi] for our convenience.[41] When you get to know these acts, you can classify most individual statements into one or more of them. It is by using these linguistic acts that we create ourselves, our worlds and effective action or stress in our everyday lives. And we don't need to utter them out loud. Our thinking affects our lives just as dramatically.

Wittgenstein proposed the logic of language often doesn't match the logic of our shared reality, tangling what he call the language game. The Birkman coach can examine a client's component score feedback narratives (the client's

---

[41] These are not the original linguistic acts found in formal Speech Act Theory.

language game strategy) for the illusory, irrational, or unreal interpretations that Dr. Birkman pointed to in his research.

Another set of definitions:

Throughout this text I have referred variously to the human communications process as language, speaking, talking, speech acts, linguistic acts or moves. These terms are considered *basic language acts*, which is the general phrase for describing what we do in language.

Why not just call it talking and hearing?

Speaking or talking are physical moves that create vibrations in the air that can be sensed by another. Language is the composite of the words and meanings we use. But the language acts include not only the utterances that come out of our mouths but also the physical gestures we make that can evoke responses in others. We also distinguish listening as different from hearing.

Hearing is a biological process. Listening is a linguistic process. Listening happens internally to the person receiving the sound waves. You will recognize the difference immediately if you have children, particularly teenagers, who have heard you but apparently aren't listening.

By its title, it is easy to understand what a speech act is. It is the act of speaking. But what is a language act? It is a speech act or a physical gesture to which the listener ascribes meaning. For instance, I can perform a *speech act* by asking "What time it is?" or I can perform a *language act* by getting someone's attention and pointing to my wrist with a questioning look on my face. In the proper context, the "listener" will interpret my gestures as a request for the right time. Of course, if the context is ambiguous who knows what the listener might think.

We can understand a great deal of the meaning of a conversation by watching body movements. Here's a simple exercise anyone can do. Go to lunch alone and find a seat where you can observe other people in the restaurant. Then watch the conversations happening all around you. You will notice that speaking is just a portion of the communications process.

It's also interesting to note when people are in rapport,[42] their overall physiologies seem to mirror each other, and their hand and head movements seem coordinated. The opposite is true when people are not in rapport. This is an important clue to watch for in coaching sessions with your clients. When rapport is not established and maintained, the efficacy of the work is at risk.

Context.

The practical use of any language requires a commonly understood and agreed on social context to create and communicate intended meaning. Of course, this says that listening requires knowledge of and agreement to the context of the speaker if there are to be effective communications between the two.

Context determines the language game being played and tangling that game happens when that context is purposely or accidentally confused or distorted. As noted above, in this instance, we're pointing to your client's narrative on each of the nine Birkman components as their

---

[42] a close and harmonious relationship in which the people or groups concerned understand each other's feelings or ideas and communicate well.

strategies for individual language games. For instance, the meta-structure of the Birkman component language game is "if my Need is met, I will do *X* (where X denotes Usual Behavior*)*. If *my* Need is not met, I will do *y*. (where Y denotes Stress Behavior)"

Untangling language games requires that we know the intended context, usually the social or public form. As Birkman coaches, we have it clearly stated in the component narratives of the client's feedback report.

The importance of context cannot be overstated. The reason is that our client's understanding of the context determines their effectiveness. And their effectiveness depends on the use of their language acts. Remember again, Dr. Birkman made two critical observations central to his research:

- Behavior is not determined so much by objective facts as by the meanings the individual attaches to those facts.
- The perceptions of some individuals about "most people" and/or "self" may be illusory, irrational, or unreal. Nevertheless, these perceptions are real and reasonable to the individuals, and so, influential on their behaviors."

As a coach, you know clients function as both real and social selves, continually interchanging based on the specific circumstances. The social self is often inauthentic and can create inauthentic and misleading context. In other words, tangling the language game. And very often this happens unintentionally because much of the time clients don't know their authentic selves. Even so, as coaches, it's our responsibility to distinguish and assist our clients to identify and express their authentic selves fully.

Categories of the Language Structure:[43]

I've identified two additional distinctions, or categories, to facilitate coaching with the Birkman Method®. They are Declarative and Performative. They are intended to assist in the interpretation of the client's use of the language acts as they apply to the nine personality components.

Declarative category.

The first three language acts belong to the category called *declarative* because we use them to declare how our world is and how we are in it. Although we don't necessarily use the canonical form such as, "I declare," we make these proclamations by our assertions, assessments, and declarations in our everyday language. I find it useful to think of declarations coming from a background of our assertions and assessments.

So, when examining a declaration, look for the assertions and assessments that usually precede it. When a coach can successfully confront either, the declaration loses its power to affect the future.

---

[43] For a decade, from the early 80's to the early 90's, I studied with Fernando Flores, Raphael Ecceverria, and Julio Olalla. My understanding of their work in linguistic philosophy influences much of what follows in this chapter. Specifically, they taught me about the language acts. I added the classifications of declarative and performative as a way of helping me deconstruct further in order to see the impact of these language acts in concrete terms. I can no longer identify exactly where their work ends and mine begins but I want to acknowledge them for their contributions to this text.

Performative category.

The second three language acts belong to this category because it is with these acts we then perform actions in our world when we request, offer, and promise. There is a cause-effect relationship between these two categories.

To summarize, the declarative acts create and sustain our interpretations of our self and the world, and the performative acts produce our actions based on those interpretations. i.e., "this is the way the world is, and this is the way I'm going to act in it."

Chapter 7 -- Declarative language acts: Assertions, Assessments, and Declarations.

This category of language acts can be used to examine how assertions and assessments lead to declarations, and how those declarations affect the client's future possibilities. For instance, if a client is making a declaration about their "perceptions of some individuals or about "most people" in their lives, listen for the assertions and assessments that lead to their declaration. Are they accurate and grounded or is this an illusion that works against the client's effectiveness? In Dr. Birkman's terms, are they "illusory, irrational, or unreal?"

Assertions.

An assertion is a statement of certainty that requires evidence. Different from an assessment, when we make a legitimate assertion we commit to provide evidence to support it. That is if it is to be taken seriously. If not, we are either purposely tangling the game or being irresponsible in the use of our language.

We usually hear assertions made when we enter a courtroom, hopefully. A good lawyer is not going to make assertions without facts and is not going to allow his opponent to do that either. Opinions (assessments without evidence) are not going to hold up in a court of law. We use assertions when we want to win an argument or make a point. But sometimes our assertions can be proven wrong, and we must retract them. Why? Because we don't have the evidence, or we have distorted it to support our position.

Assertions made with no intention to provide evidence is one of the primary ways we destroy our credibility and entangle our lives.

The generative power of assertions.

Assertions can be the reality upon which we base our perceptions. I know that this sounds backward, but we very often find the data we need to support our opinions about ourselves or our world. And in our world of information blizzards without filters, it is not very difficult to find supportive data.

But the problem is we often confuse our assessments with assertions. That is, we think that we have the facts but don't. Then, it's a short step to building personal realities that are not consistent with shared reality. We can be out of touch and less effective in our lives. We should think of assertions in the framework of objective statements that can be verified with evidence regardless of how we feel about them.

In short, an assertion produces the evidential background for the performative act that produces the space of action. If an assertion is based on facts that can be confirmed, our statement is probably on solid footing. For instance, if I assert that I can drive a car, I can offer to prove it and do just that. But if I assert that I can leap from one tall building to another, my assertion, as well as any similar performative, is invalid. I can offer to prove it by jumping, but I'm sure to fail. For an assertion to be considered true, it must be backed with evidence in the external world.

Assertions commit us to providing the facts or evidence for our claim. If we can't, our assertion is probably just an opinion. But don't be fooled by this easy explanation. Once formed, opinions are remarkably perseverant. (A note about facts: Facts are those "things" that remain even after you stop believing them.)

Assertions gone bad.

Assertions go bad when we can't provide the evidence for our claim. But very often the listener may not be discerning enough to ask for proof. In this case, another person can be injured in the process. Think of the damage that has been done to people who were wrongly convicted with evidence that was not accurate, and later released when DNA tests (the real evidence) proved them innocent.

The major errors in assertions are twofold. The first is confusing an assessment with an assertion. This can happen when a person believes their claims wholeheartedly even in the face of evidence to the contrary. The other error is when a person gleans out the favorable evidence and ignores the rest thereby misinterpreting the facts in support of their claim. I can recall times when someone was so committed to their position that they presented the evidence incompletely or with a particular spin to make it fit their assertion. As most of us know, even statistics can be used to justify a point of view, if they're manipulated enough.

How to make corrections.

If you make an assertion that is actually an assessment nothing works better than admitting your error and making sure you don't do the same thing in the future. Being thorough in the collection and evaluation of your facts is a sure way to stay out of trouble while making assertions.

Making healthy assertions.

When making assertions be sure to:
1. Have the facts
2. Verify them with other observers
3. Leave some room by saying "based on these facts...."
4. Use them sparingly

Assessments.

Assessments are opinions and are fully linguistic. If they have a future related action, they can become declarations. (more on declarations follows below) Assessments can be grounded or ungrounded, valid, or invalid. Grounding is like getting validation from others who share your assessment.

There is one hitch. Grounding an assessment requires a community of common linguistic distinctions, what we refer to as a culture. In other words, people of the same culture usually speak a common language of shared meanings. This does not mean that people of the same culture always agree with each other on their respective assessments but at least the language used to make the assessment is common, and meanings are relatively consistent.

Case in point.

If I go to Saudi Arabia and offer my assessment that women are not treated with full equality, I might have a tough time finding agreement, even from some women. And of course, I must be speaking a language familiar to the listener to be understood. They probably will disagree with my assessments, but more importantly, they consider theirs to be facts.

In cross-cultural situations, it's not always as clear-cut to determine what constitutes valid assessments. If you live in a culture where status or authority is enough to make your opinion indisputable without facts, it can be very difficult. For instance, in some fundamentalist religions, the clerics' assessments are sometimes considered to be facts without evidence, unless you consider their interpretations of ancient texts to be reliable evidence.

History is full of examples. Remember the scientist-priest, Copernicus? He observed and calculated most of his life. His findings indicated that the earth was not the center of the universe. He had discovered the evidence to support his argument. Of course, the Church hierarchy had different ideas, and they even had evidence for their beliefs. Everyone could see the sun go "around" the earth every day. Their assessment was more potent than his assertion. Poor Copernicus. His discoveries didn't get much public attention until 80 or 90 years after his death.

How are assessments used?

We live our lives immersed in our assessments. They are a short-hand method for negotiating a complex world. They facilitate our heuristic decision-making. "That's a beautiful house." "She's gorgeous." "He's a hunk." "Fords are better than Chevy's." "Sony makes the best electronic equipment." These are all assessments.

We should be clear that our assessments are just that, our assessments. We have a right to them, but we don't have the right to impose them on others as the truth. If there is **a** truth, it is probably grounded in an external context and not in our subjective experience. But so far 2500 years into the process, the philosophers of our Western Intellectual tradition have not agreed to what it is.

Most importantly, assessments are the basis for our self and social perceptions. To each of us, our perceptions are how the world really is and how we are in it. They inform our decisions to act or not through our performative language acts. When we mix them up with assertions, we can create a world that is so inconsistent with shared reality we become disconnected and irrelevant.

Why do we need them?

As previously noted, we need assessments because we don't have time to gather all the evidence we need to make decisions. Remember, we're heuristic decision makers. Sometimes we rely on our assessments to let us move on to the next decision. It might be something as simple as the choice of a movie or as complex as who we marry.

Used with care and awareness they can assist us. We even use them for entertainment. How could we gamble if everyone agreed on the winning horse? Most betting is just the result of differing assessments. Who will win the World Series, the Super Bowl, etc.? There are thousands of people ready to give you their opinions and put money behind them.

Expert assessments are not assertions.

We often pay people for their professional assessments. We hire interior decorators. We hire image consultants to tell us what we should wear and how to apply makeup. We ask for recommendations from all types of experts whose opinions are validated by popular opinion in our cultures, but that still doesn't make them assertions. The obvious danger here is that even an expert 's assessments can be inaccurate, and they can build shaky grounding for the actions we take in the world.

The generative power of assessments.

Assessments have power. They provide the basis for declarations. They can change the future. In this way they are generative. They create realities.

For instance, there was a good example in a past instance of self-image research. Little girls were asked to assess dolls and decide which ones were the prettiest. The African American girls assessed that the light-colored blond dolls were the prettiest. These girls had grown up in a culture that assessed blond white children to be the prettiest.

In another instance, research psychologists selected children randomly and told the teachers that these were the children with the most potential. By the end of the semester these children had done better in their studies and in fact were the most popular with the other children. Random assessments had affected how these teachers interacted with this group so powerfully that even the other children were influenced.

How do assessments commit us?

There is probably no better place to explore erroneous assessments than the area of racial relations. How often have you been surprised by the reality of meeting a person from a different racial background who didn't conform to your assessments? How about the assessment that women couldn't possibly be good business executives? What about the assessment that all Americans are infidels? How about those Israeli's and Palestinian's assessments of each other?

One of the most disgraceful assessments is that "starvation on the planet is just an unpleasant fact and it cannot be resolved." We have the food. We have the distribution capability. We have the technology. We have the communication systems. But, unfortunately for the starving masses, we also have an assessment that there will always be starvation on the planet[44].

Grounded or not.

Not only do we often mix up assessments with assertions, but we also mix up "grounded" with "ungrounded." Grounded assessments are merely opinions that have some form of support or agreement from qualified experts who have been granted that qualification from a culture. For instance, a famous fashion designer, or drama critic.

What is grounding? It's the agreement of the expert whose opinion we accept. It can also be the shared opinions of other people. Can we make a grounded assessment without other people's agreement? Well yes, we could if we happen to have information that is not available to others. This is probably the most difficult assessment to sustain. For example, Homeland Security officials often assess high alert situations on information that's not available to the rest of us.

What about ungrounded assessments? They indeed are easier to make, and there seems to be more of them. They are often someone's offhand remark offered as an opinion with no consideration for proof of any kind. Of course, that implies that those who make them are more reckless with

---

[44] The Hunger Project is an effort to end starvation on the planet caused by this assessment.

their languaging. If one makes an ungrounded negative assessment as though it were fact without having any basis for it, there is a good possibility for damage to the speaker and the person being assessed.

The ungrounded assessment has the potential for creating a great deal of human suffering and ineffectiveness. It's not unusual for a person to make an ungrounded assessment and then spend a good deal of energy trying to defend it. It's not a comfortable place to be. It would indeed be better not to make the statement at all. But we all make them from time to time.

The best strategy is to admit an error, apologize, and retract it when we are called upon to defend it. We have all experienced the pain of defending or seeing someone defend an ungrounded assessment. And we've probably experienced the relief and reduction in tension when someone, or we, admit error and offer a retraction.

Untangling assessments.

When we make ungrounded assessments, we open ourselves and others to the impact of their possible lack of validity. In a reality created by our erroneous assessments, we can create circumstances that are inappropriate and impossible to realize. The Birkman Method® coach should listen for how an ungrounded assessment might be instrumental in the misapplication of a client's declarations about themselves or their world.

For instance, a client might say with confidence that his manager is unfair and consequently he needs to protect himself with so much documentation it makes him less efficient in his job. But upon further consideration sees that his assessment was not grounded in shared reality because none of his workmates agree with his assessment.

Case in point.

In my earlier career, I owned and operated a company that produced custom training programs for manufacturing clients. After several years of doing work on specification, I decided it would be a good idea to begin creating programs on topics of common interests that could be sold to larger audiences through distributors. This was a significant market, and many distributors were looking for program content. The only question was "what topic were we to focus on"?

At the time, the Hazardous Materials Communication act had been passed, and every company that used hazardous materials was required by law to train their people in proper handling methods. This seemed like a natural for my little company, I assessed. So, we went to work with writers and actors and location shoots to produce a full set of high-quality videos with instructional integrity for this market. About three months and a hundred thousand dollars later we went to market. The product failed to sell. I was confused and began talking to people in the manufacturing marketplace to find out why it was not selling. It seems that I had assessed incorrectly.

In my mind, I had assessed that manufacturers would want to conform to the spirit of this new law and would buy a product that fulfilled that requirement. The people I talked to had assessed that the legal obligation was not so explicit, and my product was overkill, and too expensive. They merely wanted to meet the minimum requirements to pass an unlikely OSHA[45] inspection. Our

---

[45]Occupational Safety and Health Administration is an agency of the United States Department of Labor.

product was designed to teach the skills people needed to know. The market was buying a product that barely skimmed by on conformance to the law. Of course, they were right because they didn't buy my product.

Finally, I saw that the market invalidated my assessment. (I could have saved lots of money and suffering if I had asked more and better questions grounding my assessment before I produced the product.) We went on to recreate the product to meet the market's assessment of the legal requirements and the need for a lower price. We began to sell the product, but it was too late for a complete recovery. It was an expensive lesson that I could have avoided if I had paid more attention to the difference between my ungrounded assessment and *the reality* of the marketplace.

Declarations.

Declarations are powerful tools for creating the future. Different from assertions, declarations transcend the need for evidence. They are statements made as claims about the future, and they are entirely linguistic. Most of us are familiar with the greatest of these speech acts, "the Declaration of Independence." There was no evidence for this declaration. No nation had ever existed as a proof of the concept. But our founders just *declared* that this country would be what it became. By the way, the English didn't agree with this declaration, and we paid for it, but we apparently prevailed. I mention this because for a declaration to be taken seriously it must be possible in the real world or you set up a tangled language game.

Declarations are a kind of assessment or opinion about the future. So, they create possibilities that weren't necessarily there before. As we've seen, sometimes we act as though our assessments are assertions and they are the "truth" which tangles the game. If a declaration is based on this, it tangles the future too. Many hare-brained declarations are made every day with no possibility of becoming a reality. Unfortunately, some are taken as real, and the tangling continues.

Whole racial groups have been declared inferior, and generations of people lived within this declaration. It's scary to think about how much of our self-image is based on other people's declarations, made with flimsy grounding if any. We live with them as though they are the facts about us. And it's not unusual to fight like hell to keep that part of us protected.

When we grow up, what do we do with the declarations like, "you're a clumsy little oaf", "you're a dumb little girl", "you are not very attractive", "you're lazy", "too short, too tall, too fat, too skinny, etc."? How will we reflect these declarations in our performative language acts and further tangle our languaging to keep them in place?

Case in point.

I returned to corporate life as a part of the sale of my business after being self-employed for several years, and it was an eye-opener. As an example, declarations were regularly made that produced stress and chaos in the daily lives of employees, and remember declarations require no evidence. A case in point was the annual declaration of how much revenue and profit would be realized in the coming year.

The declaration was made in the fall of the previous year and was supported with little substance but instead guided by a formula which presumed that "if this year was x good, next year could be $y\%$ better." Financial spreadsheets were formatted and sent to all the field executives, and it was their job to create scenarios that satisfied this formulaic declaration. Of course, people conformed and then were held to *their* commitments. One can say that this is a positive thing because bold declarations can open the possibilities to exceed that which is considered realistic. But these declarations were not based in the same reality that existed at the operations level.

Nonetheless, they were quickly formed into expectations and the operations executive, by agreeing to them, had created a *promise* that may or may not be fulfilled. So where is the problem?

The problem was in the *cognitive imperative*[46] that ensued. It was no longer possible to use facts in discussing day-to-day operations. Everything was interpreted in the context of a promise that the operations executive had supposedly made to *meet the numbers*. Real facts, if different from the declaration or perceived promise, were interpreted as excuses. If operations were, in fact, doing better than the plan it was attributed to the declaration because it was empowering. Therefore, the credit was taken from the people who were doing the work and kept by the corporate folks who declared it so.

Operations people were smart. They had learned that each year was to be a more aggressive year than the year before and began to "save" revenue for the next year. The system of logic at work in the organization was based on the myth that had been created by the formulaic year-to-year declarations. As you already know, this company is not unusual. Many corporations operate exactly like this.

---

[46] A generally agreed way of thinking that may not have been consistent with reality but pleasing to the organization's authorities.

Finally, declarations can also produce results that seem impossible at the time they are made. President John F. Kennedy declared we'd go to the moon and we did. It was within the space of that declaration that we created the technology to get there. Declarations are powerful; powerfully good or bad, but powerful nonetheless.

Chapter 8 -- Performative language acts

Requests, offers, and promises are the language acts that we use to produce action in our lives. They are formed in response to the conditions that we create in the declarative acts.

Requests.

Requests are language acts that constitute our asking for something we want. When we tangle them, we don't make explicit requests, and the listener is left to read our minds. Then when we don't get what we want, we're disappointed. Sometimes we blame the listener who didn't agree to fulfill our unspecified conditions and many times doesn't even know we made a request. Requests should be sincere. We should tell the other what our conditions of satisfaction are so people don't need to guess what we want.

So, what are we protecting when we tangle requests? Maybe we assess our self-image as one of an independent person who doesn't need any help from anyone. Or we think that admitting our real wants and needs is shameful or weak. Or we think we need to suffer rejection because it's consistent with our self-assessment. This is a way of fulfilling our self-perceptions. It keeps our stories intact and our fears in check. Remember, it feels right when our point of view is validated.

Why do we have problems with requests?

The reasoning goes something like this, "Well if I have to ask for something from a loved one, do they really love me? They should know what I want."

I'm going to go out on a limb here, but I think as many marriages are broken by this thinking as from broken promises. In either case, these are entanglements of language. Examine the issue of resentment in marriages, and you will probably find the problem of one or another's failed efforts to deliver to unclear or unstated requests.

The structure of a request.

A request is a linguistic move that asks for something from another. It is not always made in the canonical form like "I request...." In fact, it doesn't even need to be spoken. I can point to the salt on the dinner table and in the process, send a request to another guest. I can use terms like "Can I have..., or please, I need the..., or I want a...etc. Any form will work if I am specific about my conditions of satisfaction. That is, how will my request be fulfilled to my satisfaction. In the simplest examples, the conditions are easy to state, the salt, the pen, or directions to the park. But in the more complex forms, they can become very ambiguous. "Please make me happier in our marriage...try harder."

And in the most complex forms, they are impossible to fulfill. "I've lived with that woman for 23 years, and she still doesn't give a damn about my needs." "He doesn't know what he wants. I can't seem to satisfy him."

Why do we need requests?

The generative power of a request lies in its ability to produce the desired action to get what we want—fill our needs. Ask yourself how often you have not been satisfied in a relationship in your life. Now think about how you formed the requests you made of that person. Did you make clear and unambiguous requests for what you wanted? Were you afraid or ashamed to ask for what you wanted? Or did you merely assume that the other person could read your mind? Or worse yet, did you hold the other person responsible for filling your conditions of satisfaction not knowing what they were yourself?

A well-formed, fully intended request can produce satisfaction for both you and the other person. If your request is sincere (remember intentionality) and you know what you want, the other person is empowered to say yes, no, or counteroffer. If you are not satisfied, you can try another approach. In both instances, you have a better chance of filling your needs, and the listener has a better chance of responding because of knowing what you want.

A sincere request commits us to receive and acknowledge its fulfillment. If we make requests that are insincere, we will soon lose credibility with others. For instance, if a manager makes requests and then doesn't follow up on their completion, she sends the message to her subordinates that she's not sincere. Very soon her requests will be ignored. In this case, her actions will speak much louder than her words.

Making healthy requests:

Making healthy requests depends on the declarations about your world in your declarative acts. If the world is very different from how you perceive it to be your requests will reflect that misjudgment.

Take these elements into consideration when you make requests.
- Intention
- Clearly stated conditions of satisfaction

- Verbalizing or otherwise communicating the conditions clearly
- Limitations of the other to fulfill them
- The other's freedom to agree, decline, or counter-offer.

Requests, an example.

Slavery was an atrocity in the history of the United States of America. The unfortunate reality is that it still exists in certain parts of the world yet today. But one aspect of slavery and why it is the monstrous act that it is can be found in the examination of the structure of requests. A valid request must allow the other to agree, decline, or counteroffer, and slaves do not have that option. Every disguised *request* becomes a demand.

Is this true just in the institution of slavery? No, it is not. In fact, there are many places today when requests are improperly formed such that the receiver cannot refuse to comply without suffering painful consequences.

Case in point.

Very early in my management career, I was the Comptroller of a manufacturing company. We were in the completion process of taking our annual inventory, which was being conducted by an outside auditing firm. The standard procedure was when the final reports were submitted it was my responsibility to sign them signifying my agreement with the findings of the independent firm.

For several months before this event, I was bothered by the methods we had been using to value our inventory. It was my opinion that these methods did not fairly represent the real value and were at their least, misleading, and at their worst, criminal. The decisive moment was coming for me.

Upon review of the auditor's report, I found that they were, in fact, reporting a value that did not correspond to the real value of our inventory resulting in not recognizing certain losses that had occurred during the previous year. This error resulted in an overstatement of profits for the year. I refused to sign the required documents that I had been *requested* to sign. I soon found out that this was not a *request* that I was going to be allowed to refuse. The request soon became an order and then a threat. Either I would sign it, or my replacement would. I had three small children, and their support was my most important concern. I did not want to experience the pain of losing this job and my career with this company. I signed the documents. Some might judge me harshly for this. Others might know this experience in their careers. And still others might make the argument that there are many ways to evaluate inventory, so my position was perilous to begin with. Regardless of anyone's judgment, this incident reveals how, in many instances, demands are classified as requests when in fact they are not.

Offers.

Offers are linguistic moves that contain our intentions to do or give something to or for another. Sometimes we make offers to meet the approval of others in social situations. When we make insincere offers we tangle the game.

As an example, a colleague says, "If I can ever help you call." Then you lose your job and need some networking help, and that colleague doesn't return your calls. So why do we make offers that we don't intend to keep? As noted, one reason is to seem socially acceptable in the moment. We might think it looks admirable in the sight of others if we step up and make an offer to do something for someone else. We may assess that it's a part of the social discourse that fits the situation; the socially acceptable thing to do. We might forget them or simply decide it isn't necessary to deliver on our offers.

Much like a request, an offer is a way of producing effective action by volunteering to do something. It could be giving directions or advice. It might be financial assistance or help moving furniture across the room. In its simplest forms, an offer is easy to fulfill. In its more complex forms an offer can be damned inconvenient. But remember intention. Does the offeror mean to fulfill the offer or is it a socially accepted thing to say?

Has someone ever said, "Would you like to go to lunch?" (It's not the canonical form but an offer nonetheless). So, you say "yes, let's put a date on it," and then wait for a response. "I'll have to get back to you on that...er... I'll call you." Of course, this is not always the case. In many instances, offers are sincerely made and fulfilled. The sad commentary about our times is that we are becoming skeptical of offers. And why not? Our life is full of suspicious offers being made by auto manufacturers, cosmetics companies, diet food producers, etc. But insincere offers cause serious disconnections between and among us. In other terms, they tangle the language game.

Why do we need offers?

Like other language moves, the generative power of an offer can be understood by examining its impact on our lives. An offer to invest in a new business commits us to take a risk with our hard-earned money and possibly suffer a night or two of worry. An offer to marry means a commitment to a whole new life with another person. An offer to work for an employer brings with it a responsibility to perform to the best of your ability even when it's not convenient to do so. An offer is a kind of one-sided pledge that is made voluntarily without a request from another.

When one makes an offer, the other person becomes engaged in the process and is affected by it. For this reason, offers should be made with sincerity and clarity. Insincere offers can create a lot of distrust from others and loneliness for you.

Bad offers.

What happens when an offer goes bad? The most powerful negative effect on the person doing the offering seems to be the erosion of our self-respect. Who can make and break offers repeatedly without beginning to think of ourselves as untrustworthy. When our private guilt is joined by public assessment, we have rendered ourselves less effective as human beings.

Offer errors can be corrected. First, we must admit the mistake we've made. Remember that we all make this mistake. Then we need to make good or ask to be relieved of the offer. The other person should recognize your mistake as one they also make. The real damage is done when we act as though our offer still stands and we have no intention of delivering. When we do, we set up an "unreality" that both parties to the offer must deal with. Nothing is more chaotic than acting as though something is there when it is not. Remember the story about the Emperor's clothes.

Making healthy offers:

Take these elements into consideration when making offers:

- Sincerity of intention
- Ability to deliver
- Managing the offer
- The other person may have changed something in their life with the expectation that you will deliver
- Unsolicited offers not kept are an invasion into the life of another
- The ultimate damage for unfulfilled offers will be the erosion of your self-esteem and eventually your public image

Case in point.

I was working away from home and spending alternate weekends on location. A business associate who lived a few miles from my apartment offered to take me to dinner and said he would bring his wife. I had heard a lot about her and wanted to meet her. It was a Friday night, and some of my other associates asked me to join them for a drink and dinner. I declined and thanked them.

Six thirty, the agreed time came and went as I paced my tiny Extended Stay unit. Somewhere around 7:30 I phoned my associate to find out if something had happened and if he wanted to cancel. There was no answer. It was raining heavily so I thought that traffic might be a problem and I waited another hour or so.

I finally resolved that his offer was not going to be fulfilled and decided to eat in and watch a movie. Was there damage done? Well, not damage to any significant degree but I could have made other plans and avoided the irritation of waiting for over two hours.

Promises.

Promises are our commitments to perform an action or actions in the future. Sometimes we make a promise even though we have no intention of keeping it when we make it, resulting in tangling the game. "Yes honey, I'll get that washing machine fixed this week." ("Whew…maybe that will satisfy her, and I can get some peace around here tonight") It's short-lived but this kind of promise may help you get away from a situation you don't want to be in without facing the reasons why. But the aftermath might be pretty negative.

Promises are sometimes made as a way of fitting into our culture. We can promise to be faithful in marriage, fulfill our job duties, defend the constitution, keep a secret, with no intention to fulfill our promise. In all these and similar instances, we tangle the resultant language games.

The language act of promises:

Promises are agreements made between a speaker and a listener. One might consider that they are the merging of requests and offers. But sometimes promises are made without a request. They commit us to some future action by mutual consent. To have a promise we need a speaker and a listener, and of course some potential future action. In some instances, we are promising to ourselves. In this case, we are playing both roles.

Promises have taken on a moral tinge. Our culture has placed an assessment of "morally wrong" when we don't keep a promise. In this book, we are not dealing with these moral implications but rather with the impact of promises on the quality of human interactions. One might say that not much effective coordination of action would take place without fulfilled promises. When you think of a promise as being the union of a request and offer that statement is probably true.

A promise is a powerful generative language act. Our life is full of promises made by individuals, institutions, and agencies. A major promise, that of marriage, is very often, the basis for our own origin. It was probably a promise between your parents that created the relationship within which you were born. It was the promise between your teachers and the community that opened the space for your education. It was the promise between you and your employer that allows you to earn a living. Of course, all these promises are not as obvious as the marriage vow, but nonetheless, they are there. And certainly, they are as powerfully generative in their ability to create reality.

By the way, the employer is not always the culprit. At one time or another, we have all forgotten the promises we've made to an employer. I know that when I was focused on my employer's faults (and they all have them), I was usually letting myself off the hook for my end of the promise. In that way, I could justify actions that didn't meet my promise. Mea Culpa!

How is it used:

A promise is used to commit future action, so the future is key if the promise is authentic. One cannot promise something in the past. The past is over, and we did or didn't do what we said. In many instances, a promise is really a form of declaration. When we marry we promise and at the same time declare that we will be committed to the person we marry. This is a public promise, and we ask others to witness it. We often make private promises to ourselves, like to lose weight, or to stop smoking. Sometimes we deliver and sometimes we don't.

Once again what's important is that we shouldn't make promises without the intention to keep them. But if we fail, the best action is to straighten out the mess by admitting our error, taking responsibility for it, and learning from the experience. Hopefully, if we do this enough, we will become more aware of our broken promises and do better in the future.

The generative power of promises should not be underestimated. They have a binding effect on people who are party to the promise. We need to go no further than the marriage vow to examine the chaos created by breaking promises. When we promise to marry we are creating new realities and all the responsibilities that go with them, mortgages, children, loyalty, respect, and consideration.

But what about divorce? Without making this a moral judgment, a divorce is the retraction of a promise. In this way, our retraction is public. Like the marriage vow, other promises can be retracted. One is not bound for life by a promise.

Promises don't always commit to future action. They can commit us to future inaction. We can promise not to do something. Some people in Christian religions promise not to take certain actions during Lent as a way of preparing for the Easter season. Muslims promise not to eat between certain hours during Ramadan.

What action is produced?

Promises commit us to do or not do something in the future. To some extent, they make the future somewhat predictable. They establish expectations and then set up the circumstances for meeting them

Bad promises.

We have all broken a promise or two in our lives. Sometimes the intention was sincere when we made it, but something changed later. This is not a problem if we retract the promise properly. The problem comes in when we act as though the promise is still valid with no intention of fulfilling it. Once again, marriage is a good example. I know several people who remain in marriages of appearances only. The vow made so many years ago has long since been broken but hasn't been acknowledged publicly.

Although the facts may not be discussed, the reality is revealing. Both people in this kind of marriage are dissatisfied and disconnected. A broken promise creates one of those situations of unreality that I mentioned earlier. The parties know that something is wrong but don't talk about it. Sometimes, we are more concerned with appearances than with our silent suffering.

Errors.

Making a promise commits us to action in the future. If we have no intention to fulfill the promise, it is best not to make it. Or when we lose the intention later, we should retract the promise to stay clear of the insanity of "acting as though."

One of the most obvious places that promises are broken is in politics. We have all experienced the candidate making promises that the incumbent never fulfills. The result is subtle but important. We have a more difficult time trusting the candidates of the future, and trust in all authority figures can begin to erode.

I can recall hiring a residential inspector to check out a house that I wanted to buy. His promise was clear enough, I thought. I paid him a few hundred dollars, and he would find the problems before I bought the house. I trusted our arrangement. I later found out that the house had significant problems that he had not discovered. When I went to my copy of the contract, I found that the "fine print" had all but relieved him of his liabilities. In America, we have had so many promises broken that we don't even respond as we did in the past. In Tom Brokaw's book, *The Greatest Generation*, he said that these people were so committed to fulfilling their promises that they died in the process. We have lost something in the last 70 or so years.

Corrections.

Admit the error! Broken promises are like lies. When we try to cover them up, we make the problem worse. It's not always comfortable or convenient to admit we made a mistake but it's the right thing to do. When we do, we and everyone else feel better. I can forgive a broken promise, but I have a hard time with someone who lies about a broken promise I depended on.

Making healthy promises.

When you make a promise remember to:

1. Be sure that you intend to keep it
2. If you change your mind, formally retract it
3. Have the capacity to deliver what you promise
4. Realize that someone's life has been affected

5. Be responsible for it
6. Manage your promises once made.

Sometimes a promise is implied, as in the relationship with your employer. Simply stated, you promised to work, and they promised to pay you. In my time as a career consultant, I became aware of many victims of downsizing living in resentment for an employer who had "broken a promise" that wasn't explicitly made.

Case in point.

I recall a conversation with a man in his mid-fifties. He was having a difficult time accepting that he had been downsized out of a job and career of 30 plus years. As we talked, it became evident to me that he believed a promise had been broken. I asked him if his ex-employer had ever explicitly promised him lifetime employment. He said no. I asked what they had promised. He responded, "his pay and benefits in exchange for his performance." I asked if they had delivered on their end of the bargain. He said yes. And he began to see that the promise he had thought was there, was not, and that both he and his employer had delivered on all the conditions of the promise.

So very often we think that a promise has been made and it hasn't. This is the cause of a good deal of pain and chaos.

To summarize, the declarative acts create and sustain our world and inform our use of the performative acts that we use to produce action in that world. And if you haven't noticed both categories are within our control to use as we choose.

Your conceptual grasp of the preceding six language acts gives you an ability to distinguish how they are used by your clients. And by having this ability you are better able to diagnose when your client is misusing them and falling into the trap of "illusory, irrational, or unreal" interpretations of their circumstances.

Chapter 9 -- Listening

"I said what I said, and you heard what you heard."

Fernando Flores

The first lesson of listening is we are not listening to words; we are listening to people. Although we need to recognize the difference, it doesn't end there. We must distinguish the differences in meanings that might be happening between the speaker and the listener. Because m*eanings* are not in words, they're in people, both the speaker and the listener. Hearing is biological, and listening is linguistic.

Listening is the coach's most important skill.

It's also the most difficult because we think we're listening and we may well be, but to the wrong conversation. We might be listening to our private internal conversations and not the one we're having with our client. We might assume the words we use mean the same thing to the listener they mean to us. We might miss a contextual shift in the conversation, so we misinterpret another's intentions. We might start agreeing or disagreeing with our client and distort the conversation. We might become lazy, tired, or bored and make all these mistakes.

The Birkman Method® feedback report is a wonderful aid to a coach. It exposes the key coaching issues with a great deal of accuracy. But that's where the work of skillful listening starts. If we're going to unpack the conversations that create the client's coaching issues, it will take excellent listening competence. The main point here is the key to good coaching is our ability to get a complete grasp of our client's self and social perceptions, so we have no option but to become skillful listeners.

Attentive listening encourages our clients to reveal more. Distracted listening discourages them. Attentive listening happens at a deeper level than hearing. You will recognize the difference immediately if you have children—particularly teenagers, who have heard you but obviously aren't listening.

Is our challenge semantics?

The late S. I. Hayakawa, then a professor at San Francisco State University, helped to popularize semantics in our nation's narrative. During his time as an author and academic, he was one of the most publicly known semanticists. In his public life, he was able to create an awareness of the subject if not a comprehensive understanding. Unfortunately, there is a great deal of confusion about the exact meaning of semantics.

Semantics is the study of the relationship of signs to the objects to which the signs are applicable[xxxvii]. So, if we can all agree on exactly what words will be used in a shared context our communications problems would be over, right? Wrong!

To examine the way our language works effectively and how it fails, we need to understand the notion of *pragmatics.* An awareness of semantics is not enough. Pragmatics is the study of the relationship of signs to the interpreters.[xxxviii] So we are not only faced with the challenge of agreeing to the common definitions of words (semantics), but we also must consider what those words mean to the speaker and listener when they are spoken (pragmatics).

Case in point.

Here is a favorite example of mine from when I would speak to one of my sons in what I thought was unambiguous language.

- "Son, take the garbage out. It is piling up and stinking us out of the kitchen."
- "Ok, Dad."
- (One hour later)
- "Son, I thought you said you were going to take the garbage out."
- "I will, Dad."
- (One hour later)
- "Son, I'm tired of telling you to take the garbage out. Do it now."
- "OOOOOKKaaaaayyyyy, Dad."
- (One hour later)
- (Me) "I've had enough…I'll take it out."
- (Him) "Dad, what are you doing? I said I would take it out. It's my job."

Was he lying? No, he was not. We just had a mix-up that involved *semantics* and *pragmatics* as follows:

To me, "take the garbage out," meant "do it now." (semantics).
To him, it meant, "when he gets around to it." (pragmatics).

Most of us who have raised children recognize this story. But how often do we recognize it in our everyday dealings with adults? Listening is the fine art of distinguishing the differences between and among:

- Our culture's contextual semantics if we share a culture
- The different contextual semantics of our different cultures.
- The unique individual semantic choices of the speaker.
- The unique individual semantic choices of the listener.
- The unique individual pragmatic interpretations of the speaker.
- The unique individual pragmatic interpretations of the listener.

Is it any wonder why communications is often the primary reason for failures in human affairs?

The meanings are not in the words.

So much has been written about listening that is incorrect and persists that one is not sure what to believe. Let's begin with the most popular and erroneous model. That is the "words are boxcars that carry meanings in them" theory. In this theory, when people speak, they choose imaginary boxcars (words) that contain their intended meanings, line them up like a train (a sentence) and deliver them (utters them to the listener). In this theory, the meanings are in words.

Unfortunately, this is just not true. Words have no absolute meanings, people do. Many factors, like context, intention, need, etc., all affect the meanings we attach to the words we use. And to make matters worse, people have the compounding habit of making meanings for every word they hear, even if it is an unintended or erroneous meaning. So not only do we have the problem of choosing our words carefully, but we must now consider the fact that others will automatically put their meanings to our words. So, no matter what you intend with your words, the other person will make their own meaning of them, initially. This is automatically happening constantly. In fact, it would be better if we humans could not make meanings of words unless they were the intended meanings.

As an example, this is an old story, to which I cannot give proper attribution, but it serves our purpose very well. Two men are talking. One says, "I like fish." The other says, "I do too." But they imagine two different meanings as they speak and listen to each other. The first is thinking of his hobby, raising tropical fish. The other is thinking of his hobby, fine dining in restaurants. One sees a "beautiful multi-colored tropical specimen' in his mind's eye. The other sees, "a properly presented, freshly grilled trout on a platter."

How do we avoid communications breakdowns?

Getting a *receipt of comprehension* is a good idea when speaking and listening in important communications processes. That means taking the time to be sure that the other person properly comprehends your communications and that you properly comprehend theirs. So, communicating with language is not a 50-50 responsibility. Its 100-100 percent the responsibilities of both the speaker and the listener if we are to be sure that our communications are effective.

For instance, in my time in the U.S. Coast Guard Auxiliary, I was taught how to be sure that I was listening correctly. When I was asked to take over the helm of a boat underway and given the course, I was to repeat the course and speed as a confirmation that I had heard it properly.

- The previous helmsman, says, "holding a one eight five-degree course at seven knots."
- The new helmsman repeats, "holding a one eight five-degree course at seven knots."

If you have ever listened in on a conversation between a commercial pilot and the ground control center, it goes something like this.

- "United two three four heavy…climb and maintain…three thousand on a course of two nine zero degrees. Hold speed steady at three hundred knots."
- "Roger tower…climb and maintain…three thousand on course of two nine zero degrees…steady at three hundred knots…United two three four heavy."

When the results of misunderstood communications can be disastrous, we have mechanisms for validating that we understand the intended communications. As coaches, we need to do it as well.

To whom are we listening?

Of course, before a *receipt of comprehension* is even possible, we need to listen to the right conversation. It has been my experience that this is not the easiest thing to find in everyday life. In far too many conversations I've been a party to in business circumstances, people are listening to their own internal conversations and missing what the other person is saying. This is usually relatively easy to discern. These conversations sound disjointed and more like arguments than real dialogues.

We have all been present when no one was listening to anyone else in the room. Then, when a kind of quasi-agreement is reached, is it any wonder why nothing happens after the meeting. One of the gifts of human consciousness is that we have *steerable attention*. All we need is to practice the discipline to use it effectively. We also have the urgent need to modify what we hear to match our present point of view. Its natural but can be controlled with practice. As the clinical psychologist and Buddhist teacher, Tara Brach, once said in a lecture, "the world is divided into people who think they are right."

Our natural tendency is to spend a lot of time protecting our perspective as though if we acknowledge the validity of another, we will disintegrate. But in fact, we will only grow in the richness of our experience of the world around us. Linguists still don't agree on the reason for the origins of language. Was it to coordinate our actions with others or to win arguments?

Be quiet and listen.

A common flaw in the coaching style of many people I have trained has been their seeming inability to stop talking long enough to listen. I suspect this is about "managing anxiety" in many cases. Nonetheless, it gets in the way of productive coaching. It is better to find a way to manage the anxiety outside of the coaching situation so that we can listen to the client.

At the risk of inventing a technique, I suggest that the coach should probably speak no more than 10-15% of the time. It is very clear that we cannot speak and listen at the same time. It may seem that we can, but it is not possible to fully understand the other person when we are talking.

Case in point.

As an example, I was coaching a new coach who had been previously trained and certified in a specific coaching model when I noticed that she was ignoring her client's present state and attempting to fit him into her model.

In other words, the client was not following her script, and she was distracting herself with trying to get him into the *correct place* as defined by her model. (He should be at step 4 by now, and he keeps ruminating at step 2) Several problems were beginning to emerge, and they began to accelerate. She was losing the confidence of this client and very soon she would not have been able to recover. We took a break and went out to discuss the situation.

She was completely unaware of the client's state and argued for continuing her agenda. I introduced her to the idea of *utilization*. I urged her to utilize what was in front of her at that time. Her client was giving clear signals that he was not staying on her course and it was not productive.

Effective coaching requires recognition of the client's current state, which she could not see because she was distracting herself. She needed to fit him into her coaching model. His resistance to her model was the issue he was demonstrating, and she needed to utilize it as the focus of her coaching. This is not an indictment of any coaching model but rather an attempt to point out that models can take us away from the authentic issues that may be the keys to assisting another.

We returned and *utilized* the fact that the client seemed to be stuck at this exact point in the discussion. This turned out to be the coachable issue that she needed to address with him. When she began to let go of her coaching model and trust herself, she began to make progress, and the session ended successfully.

Practice.

Listening is like any other skill. It must be developed and practiced if we are to be professionals. So much has been written about listening that I will only offer those ideas that I think exemplify a skillful listener. They follow:

- Listen to the other person's concerns about the future, shaped by their past. Remember we need to experience people in their past, present, and potential future states.
- Listen to the *stories* people use to explain their actions and perspectives in the present. These are the stories that reveal their interpretations of the events in their lives.
- Listen *to learn* about how they experience their experiences. Ignore your urges to either agree or disagree with them; think of this as a learning opportunity.
- Do not pass judgments. You are interpreting from your own subjective experience. Your point of view is not a "God's eye" view of the world. And you cannot stand apart from it.
- Stay aware of the context of the conversation so that you have a good chance at really understanding their implied meanings. A shift in context can happen at any time in a conversation, so pay attention.

- Stay aware of the power of pragmatics on your interpretations of what the other is saying. (pragmatics is how you interpret the words that they are using as possibly different from their intentions).

- Listen for the deeper mood, not just surface emotions and feelings by watching the other's physiology and "listening" to what that tells you. A good way to increase your skills at listening to another's physiology is to borrow that person's physical presentation, try to match is as close as possible, duplicate it in the privacy of your office later and listen to your internal dialogue with yourself. I promise you will be amazed at what you will learn.

- Listen for personal history and experiences, particularly the recent past and how it relates to your client's earlier history.

- Listen to your client's *listening* into which you are speaking. Try to ascertain how they are listening to you as you speak. This is a clue to get to his or her pragmatic interpretations of what you are saying.

- And when you finally open your mouth to speak, speak to the other's place of listening. Do not use *jargon, idioms, figures of speech* that may confuse the listener. If you are trying to impress your client, you need to close the coaching session and regale him with your wisdom. But when you are coaching, forget the "show" and pay attention to him or her.

- Be *willing* to hear whatever the other has to say, no matter how difficult it may be to hear. If you haven't read the classic Carl Rogers book <u>On Becoming a Person</u>[xxxix], get it and read it. Sometimes we need to do nothing more than to be a non-judgmental listener.

Finally, listening can't be faked. We all know if someone is listening or not when we speak. Most of the time we don't call them on it. We're too polite.

Chapter 10 -- Language Games

Everything is vague to a degree you do not realize till you have tried to make it precise.

Bertrand Russell

Like it or not, when we enter a coaching relationship, we enter a language game. It is a game because it has rules, actions, and an objective. The critical issue here is that sometimes you are playing one game and your client is playing another. This is most likely to happen when your client is being directed to "get a coach" or "being assigned to you for coaching" as often happens in business organizations. The obvious first step is to ascertain that you are in the same game and come to an agreement about the game and its rules early. If it can't be done, the coaching relationship will not be very productive.

Some might object to using the word "games" to classify the language acts. It is not used to make light of the power of language. But "games" as we saw in the previous chapter was Wittgenstein's reference for classifying groupings of related language interactions and how they function as a coherent and unitary process.

The term *language game* refers to a specific linguistic event that is *framed by meaning.* The event has a core purpose and could have a related set of definitions, and those related sets don't change the core meaning. For example, if I were talking to a friend about the opera that I enjoyed last night, that would frame the core purpose. When I describe the orchestra or the audience I am referencing related sets but am not changing the core purpose.

But when I begin talking about an experience I had on a fishing trip; I have shifted to another overarching theme of the conversation. A traditional game is much like this example. If I'm playing basketball and I execute a "lay up" shot, I'm still in the same game. But when I try to "tag another player out with the basketball," I'm in another game.

Language games are coherent sets of conversations and actions. They are more than linguistic frames. They can contain multiple linguistic frames, but those frames follow a cohesive theme. Traditional games, like language games, stay coherent when played by the rules. Otherwise, they create entanglements and confusion. One difference between regular games and language games is that the rules of ordinary games are usually understood and agreed when we play. Game rules are usually clearly stated, and we adhere to them if we want to play. Sometimes we even have an official, like an umpire, who enforces the rules.

In language games, we follow the rules too. But all too often the rules are not known, shared, or applicable to the circumstances. Sometimes the other person doesn't know or agree with the rules we are following. Occasionally, we are in entirely different games even though it seems we are together. And sometimes we seem to be in the same game, but one of the players is playing with hidden rules trying to achieve another agenda. Coaching other human beings requires we are playing by a mutually agreed set of rules and have a mutual objective in our interactions. And coaches don't have the advantage of a referee to help.

Case in point.

This challenge is particularly significant when an external coach attempts entry to an existing group. It is critical to any successful intervention.

In a case in point, I finally gained the confidence of a group of senior managers that had tolerated me for several weeks because their "boss had hired me." An outside coach or consultant can get paid this way (for a while) but is not very likely to produce any results.

This case took place in a large Midwestern telecommunications company. These were field service managers who felt disconnected from the formal corporate authorities to whom they reported. They liked to think of themselves as tech-savvy people who knew the only answers that were worth knowing. Although I hesitate to use the term because of its underworld reference, I will call these men "wise guys." They were sophisticated in a "street-smart" way and used that knowledge well, both to the advantage of the company, and themselves. They didn't trust the rest of the organization. To say the least, entry was not an easy task.

First obstacle: "the rules are not known, shared or applicable to the circumstances in which we are playing."

My formal introduction to this group came at a regular staff meeting conducted by the man I was hired to coach, my primary client, the senior manager of the district. Among other topics on the weekly agenda was—me. I was introduced as his personal consultant. The reason for my presence was, "corporate said he needed an outside consultant." He went on to say that, "he didn't know why." I knew that I had a lot of work to do to overcome that introduction.

Second obstacle: "The other person doesn't know or agree with the rules we are following."

It was several weeks before this manager and I were able to come to an agreed objective for our work together. Even though the corporate authorities knew the objective, were my sponsors in this work and he knew what they wanted him to achieve with my help, he continued to insist that he didn't know what we were supposed to do.

Finally, we agreed to an objective, but then we had to establish how we were going to get this work done. This took several more weeks. Of course, during these several weeks of various conversations, we made no authentic personal connection and subsequently, no progress toward anything of real value to the corporation. But I had been warned that this was going to be a long rough, road.

Third obstacle, "We are in totally different games even though it seems that we are together."

Even though we had seemingly established an objective and agreed to how we were going to achieve it, he was publicly saying one thing to me (and his boss) and privately telling his loyal subordinates to keep tolerating me because it kept the corporate people appeased, and out of his business. I had inadvertently become his pawn; a token concession to his superiors and a way of hiding his resistance to their plans for him.

My game had the corporate objective as its final goal. His game had the "continuation of business as usual" as its final goal. And although we were playing different games, on the surface he was able to satisfy the corporate requirement, "work with the outside consultant, me, to achieve the corporate objective."

Fourth obstacle," Sometimes we seem to be in the same game, but one of the players has a hidden agenda."

For some reason, unknown to me even to this day, I was finally able to connect with this group. I joined the group one night at an informal poker game while we were all at an off-site company conference. I wasn't aware of it that night, but the next morning I had an interesting conversation with one of the opinion leaders of the group. He said, "Well, last night you finally became a member of the group. You talked to us...connected with us."

Coaching the district manager's subordinates began to take on a different quality. From that time on it was more effective and rewarding for all of us, except for my primary client, the district manager.

Key point: Staying connected with other human beings requires that we are playing the same game with a mutually agreed set of rules and have a mutual objective in our interactions with others.

Several weeks later, as my manager was reviewing my work, it became apparent to me. Although my progress with his subordinates was good, I had still not connected with my primary client, the district manager. As difficult as it was going to be, I needed to have a conversation with him and withdraw my services. It seemed to be time for another coach to try it with him.

We sat at lunch, and for the first time he opened up and told the truth. He said he had never really bought into the work we were doing. He knew it was right for the others, so he allowed it. But he was going to leave the company and had used our time together as a way of buying time to decide on his future. He had finally concluded his decision and planning process. He thanked me for my work. That was the first time in our work together that I felt that we had connected.

The entire episode as described above was one big language game for each of us. The problem was that we each were playing different games.

The goal of language games.

All games have a purpose. To score the most goals in basketball; the fewest strokes in golf; to align the cards in Solitaire. In the example above, my client's objective was to buy time to make a personal decision.

In language games, we usually have the goal of producing or coordinating human action in one form or another. But, very often our most important goal becomes "to preserve our point of view." And as certified Birkman practitioners we know the power of "illusory, irrational, or unreal" interpretations to disrupt and disable our clients.

A cautionary note.

Theoretically, language games have at least two potential goals: 1) produce and coordinate action and 2) preserve our point of view. We have all known situations when we abandoned our original purpose in a conversation and gave in to our need to win the argument.

A classic example is a married couple who has given up on creating a happy and loving relationship and sunk into a continuing power struggle. Each person wants the final word on every issue regardless of its relative insignificance. The content of the argument is no longer the driving force.

"Putting the toilet seat down" or "hanging nylons in the bathroom" are not such significant events that justify being in constant tension with another human being. There must be another driver behind these common forms of language games.

To summarize, primal human motivation is like a coin that has "protecting one's point of view" on one side and a "desire for connection" on the other. These primal motivations are at the core of being human and consequently our language games? Even with this tension most of us want connection to others.

I have come to depend on the fact that the primary purpose of *language games* is the survival of our point of view and this belief has served me well when coaching others.

Given this belief, we can see why it is so difficult to give up our beliefs. Who's ready to just let go of their unique perspective even in the face of the difficulties that may come from holding to them. Many of us can make the same mistake repeatedly, and when pressed for change we will work diligently to find someone to validate our perspective rather than change it.

As an example, think of the people who go from company to company trying to find the situation that will conform to their view of how an employer should be rather than explore their own point of view and its mistaken notions about the employee – employer relationship.

Or spend a few hours in a public place, like a coffee shop and listen to the conversations between and among others. Invariably you will hear people reach consensus on common points of view in the face of all kinds of evidence to the contrary. In this case, connection, and confirmation of our point of view are more important than accuracy.

If we use Heidegger's distinction of the "authentic self[xl]" and apply this concept here, we might interpret his proposition to read "we live in fear of the demise of the real or authentic self." This means not just the physical self but also our real self-identity.

I have seen the existential pain of a fifty-year-old professional attempting to decide to explore the personally appropriate career direction while trying not to succumb to the external pressures of family obligations and expectations. It is often an urge that will not be denied. This intensity does not come from some external force. It emerges from the very core of the individual. It is a fear of the demise of that person's authentic self.

Think about our self-identity as a coherent set of compensatory interpretations and declarations from which we create imperatives[xli] or rules for engaging the world. In this way, we protect our identities, which include our "personality" (how we see ourselves) and our point of view of the world (how we think the world is). This process informs the creation of rules, but it does so within the limitations of the external structures that define *rules*[xlii] and the internal structures that define *us*[xliii].

Another way of saying this is "_when_ you are and _where_ you are shape _who_ you are."

Thus, my proposition here is that we are linguistic beings and our self and social perceptions are created and maintained in language. Therefore, a primary objective in untangling language games is to uncover the *rules of engagement* being used by examining our client's language acts. And in the process, clarify their self and social views of the world and maybe even get a glimpse of their structures. Then we are enabled to know what they are preserving and come to a better understanding of how they do this in language games.

Know the corporate game.

If you have spent as little as a month in a corporation, you know that games are central to their functioning. You may not be able to discern the theme, but you are, nonetheless, subject to the rules. In my experience, all corporate games have underlying dual purposes. The first rule is to maximize shareholder value. The second is to manage perceptions such that *everyone sees everything the same way.* If you don't understand the second rule, please refer to the first rule because most corporations believe their way is the way to maximize shareholder value.

As one enters corporate life, he or she must learn the game quickly. Those in the corporation are often not consciously aware of rules even though they guide them on a day-to-day basis. One way we learn corporate or cultural rules is to inadvertently break them. We will quickly find out what they are. In most instances, it is purely by chance that we trip over *the way things are done around here.* And if we aren't paying attention, we will quickly find that we don't have much of a future in that company.

The choice we have is to learn to see things the prescribed way and conform to that view of the world. This phenomenon in and of itself is not evil. Jack Welch, of GE fame, was considered one of the greats because he was able to influence the way everyone in that organization perceived reality. His will was irresistible. And that's a lot to say in an organization as large as GE. In Welch's case, one might assert that his point of view was a successful one. We merely need to check the results while GE was under his watch. But in so many corporations the leader's will is not going to lead to the kind of success that GE enjoyed.

Remember, "language matches our logic, and our logic sometimes doesn't reflect the facts" while we explore its application as corporate phenomena. It has been my experience in working with dozens of corporations that the clear majority of companies are more prone to maintain their point of view than they are to change because of new input; even if that input could improve performance. Although this seems very straightforward and easy to prove or disprove, it isn't.

Remember, in corporations we are dealing with socialized behavior. (I have seen very little evidence of the authentic self in management below the C Suite[47] in American corporations. I won't deny its existence, but I have personally not witnessed it very much in my forty years of experience.)

Case in point.

For example, one such situation was a food processing company to which I consulted. Their primary manufacturing plant in the Midwest was experiencing a drop in quality and productivity levels. The senior plant executive was new and open to help and welcomed another point of view of his plant's problems. In the process of our initial analysis, we discovered an attitude of frustration on the part of the local management team. The plant needed significant maintenance and repairs, and the workforce was non-responsive to participating in any improvement efforts.

This plant was the premier operation in a large corporation with headquarters several hundred miles away. So, although local management received some level of pressure from the top, it was very manageable, and

---

[47] C-Suite is a widely-used slang term used to collectively refer to a corporation's most important senior executives as in CEO, CFO, COO, etc.

enthusiasm for taking on the challenges of a significant improvement effort was non-existent. The locals liked it the way it was.

Our work concentrated on developing a system of related improvement projects for which group managers and their teams would take responsibility. They, in turn, were required to bring whatever production and maintenance employees they needed into the process. Within a few weeks we had worked out the bugs, and things were improving, including employee morale. Within two months the results were beginning to get the attention of the corporate people. And a corporate manufacturing engineer was dispatched to *check us out*.

His visit consisted of interviewing several people in management and auditing the reporting processes that had been put in place. He did not meet with us but was still able to write a report. His report was secreted to top management. Unfortunately, we didn't get even a glimpse of it.

Soon we had a visit from the Vice President of manufacturing who had been the local executive in charge of this plant previously in his career. It was his opinion that this plant could not be improving the way the reports indicated. His conclusion was based on the fact that when he had managed the plant, it could not have achieved this level of improvement so consequently these improvements were an anomaly that could not be explained or reproduced consistently. In his opinion, they were an example of the Hawthorne Effect[48].

---

[48] The performance improvement related to the simple act of paying attention to the people who are doing the producing. Named after the Hawthorne Works of Western Electric where the phenomena was first described and recorded.

Indeed, the work we were doing was not to be considered the cause of the improving performance—in his opinion. In summary, he believed whatever caused the improvements was not to be credited to anyone, especially a group of outsiders who didn't understand the plant as well as he and his corporate staff engineers did. So, no thanks, we don't want another point of view even if it improves our performance.

The plant's performance continued to improve for the entire year of our involvement. We were contracted for another year and eventually were asked to come to another manufacturing plant to install the same improvement system. But to my knowledge, we had never been acknowledged openly as the reason for the improvements by corporate HQ.

In fact, the plant executive who brought us to the second plant had heard of our success and wanted our help. He had to overcome the strenuous objections of the corporate staff and his boss, the VP, and in doing so alienated himself. We made significant improvements, but the mounting stresses of our outsider's opinions eventually could no longer be tolerated, and our contract was called, the second plant manager was fired, and the first one left the company.

One might think that this was an isolated instance where one person's personality was at cause but read on. I was involved in another situation that illustrates this phenomenon again.

Another company had received a "Request for Proposal" of services from a large telecommunications firm. The requirements for submitting a proposal were exact and voluminous. The process began with the assignment of 20 different people to prepare the information for specific sections of the RFP. Each had been assigned an area of responsibility to develop information to respond. A senior executive had been appointed the role of coordinating everyone's input. And the work began.

When I objected to a specific statement, it became apparent to me that the job of the other nineteen people was to "invent" information that matched the requirements of the RFP. The RFP required a precise answer to a question of, "how many people worked in a particular classification." The answer that was being given inflated the number fifteen-fold. There were, in fact, two of us. The answer given in the proposal was thirty. When I pointed out that there were actually "one fifteenth" of the number being reported, I was criticized, and my input was dismissed. In other words, our job was to *create the right answers* to the questions being asked by the telecommunications firm, and not report the facts.

So, to be *a player* in this situation meant that you needed to ignore the facts and conform to the system of logic that the coordinator had created. And that logic was "to answer the questions to get the contract and not to represent the facts." I was told, "when we win the purchase order, we will make the situation match the 'facts' as reported in our proposal."

It was apparent that this company's goal was to get the business no matter what they had to say. The facts were irrelevant. It became evident to me why the requesting company would create such a detailed RFP. They were attempting to protect themselves from the very process that was happening.

In the end, this company did not win the contract. But the more important point is the example that was set for the twenty people who worked on the proposal. Telling the truth—reporting the facts—was not an acceptable way of doing business in this company. This is not a moral judgment here. I am merely saying that if we don't know the facts how can we fix the problems?

What if your rules don't conform to the rules of play in your current organization?

My advice is to get out and find another game to play. Unless of course you are the leader and can change things to match your ethics. Good luck! One needs to remember that when we go to work for corporations, we rarely decide what game is going to be played. Mr. Welch was as much a leadership anomaly as effective change programs are in corporations.

Chapter 11 – Rules

"Rules and responsibilities: these are the ties that bind us. We do what we do, because of who we are. If we did otherwise, we would not be ourselves."

Neil Gaiman

We all develop and follow "a structured set of rules of engagement" for interacting with the world[xliv]. These rules seem to be organized into categories. This whole process is guided by our imperatives, both *categorical* and *hypothetical*.[xlv]

Roughly translated, categorical imperatives are those we are not supposed to question. There are no conditions that would allow us to deny them. We should follow them without question. Of course, this sounds like religion. But think of them as secular in nature and formed from the overall experiences of a community. They reflect "what works" for a society. These are the universal rules of our communities that guide our actions so that we live as accepted members. This is a good example of how an external structure affects our individual behavior. For instance, a categorical imperative in our culture is "do not steal another's property."

Hypothetical imperatives are those that we create individually. They always have a condition stated as an "if." An example here would be, "If I think I'll get caught, I will not steal another's property." We can see the relationship of the *categorical* to the *hypothetical* as a decision process that answers the question "how will I (as an individual) live independently and yet connected to and within my community (my world)?"

The Enlightenment brought with it a new appreciation of the value of the individual and the individual responsibility to live with our own as well as externally imposed morals. As we saw earlier, Kant[49] said that we all have an inherent moral structure that deserves our attention. Call it the natural basis of having a *free will* if you like, and he dared us to use this moral structure to reason for ourselves.

We determine our path in life with this process. So, it is essential to understand how we go about it. Consider two factors: The first is our self-perception. This is how we perceive our self as a unique individual living in our world. The second is our social perception; how we perceive our world. This can be thought of as what we expect and eventually need from others.

These two factors establish our fundamental decision matrix for the creation of our hypothetical imperatives. They are uniquely derived, given the facticity of our individual backgrounds in a specific community. As we call upon our scripts to inform our actions, we also access the underlying imperatives so that they shape our "rules of engagement."

As an example, if my self-perception is that I am a competent person capable of getting what I need from others and my social perception is that the world is full of

---

[49] Kant, Immanuel (1724–1804), German philosopher. In the Critique of Pure Reason (1781) he countered Hume's skeptical empiricism by arguing that any affirmation or denial regarding the ultimate nature of reality ("noumenon") makes no sense. His Critique of Practical Reason (1788) affirms the existence of an absolute moral law—the categorical imperative.

cooperative and giving people when I call upon related scripts I will develop rules of engaging others that reflect those beliefs. In the case that my perceptions are opposite of these, I will call upon a set of scripts and set up a very different set of rules for engagement. In the first case, I may accept my community imperatives much more readily. In the second case, I may need to consider my personal rules a bit more carefully. And I may put more "ifs" into my decisions and subsequent rules. I might not be as ready to conform to my community's imperatives.

The term *hypothetical* reflects Kant's proposition that these were imperatives that we *hypothesize* will work for us in our world. The categorical imperatives are grounded in the collective experience of a community. The *hypothetical* need to be tested on a case-by-case basis.

So where does the problem lie if the process is this formulaic?

It lies in the durability of our self and social perceptions, which is being reinforced by the external structures of our community's related scripts. We and these external structures have a great deal invested in maintaining each other, uninterrupted and unchanged.

This is never more obvious than when we keep making the same mistakes repeatedly. The outcome is always the same and, yet we don't change our approach to the problem. Why? Because it would threaten the very core of who we think we are in the world. For example, consider the battered wife who struggles to prove her worth to an obdurate husband and stays in a bad marriage. Her efforts are never appreciated. He will never get enough from her to satisfy him.

At the core of this might be a wife who sees herself as a flawed person who needs to tolerate abuse to satisfy her self-image and the world as a place where others' opinions are more important than hers. Her existing rules for engaging, in this case, are probably keeping her in the cycle she finds herself in. What could happen if she saw herself as a healthy and deserving person, not willing to stay in an abusive relationship? What could happen if she saw the world as full of opportunities just waiting for a capable person?

Our rules help us know how to behave to get our needs met – we think. The most fundamental need is that of the survival of our unique point of view. Our point of view is the sum of our self-perception (who we perceive our self to be) and our social perception (how we perceive the world to be). A simple example of this is, " If I see myself as an incompetent person in a competitive world." My rule might be "Why try? I won't accomplish anything anyway."

On the surface, it would seem anyone would want to change a rule that doesn't work. But it's not that easy. Our self and social perceptions are very near and dear to our hearts. They have been in place for a long time, and we have lived our lives by applying the scripts and according to the related rules that derive from them. They are transparent to us. And in some unusual cases, we will die for them. Think of the "religious martyrs" that abound in Western history. Think of the modern suicide terrorists who kill themselves so that their point of view lives on.

If life were static and unchanging, we would have little need for examination of our self, and social perceptions let alone our rules. But in this era of constant change, we need the additional tools to help us function, even if we want to ignore the reality around us. We need a new understanding of what our rules are, what are they made of, how they get there and how we can add new and more useful variations. This is the role of the coach. The coach can act as another observer, offering another unique point of view that enhances and enriches the client's possibilities.

Awakening to our personal rules.

"Script elements function as default values and allow us to supply missing elements and to infer what is not explicitly stated."[xlvi] A rule is a script element. A script is a pattern of language that is called on in situations that seem similar to past experiences. This means that we will fill in the empty slots and make inferences based on our past history. So, to depend on them can be a tautological[50] error when we attempt to understand what they are. In other words, we will be searching for our rules in a closed system that provides the only answers it can, and more importantly, keeps them intact.

The best clue to discovery is to become aware of when, in Heidegger's terms, we have a "breakdown in the transparency of living."[xlvii] Our rules are transparent. If they are working, we don't think about them. We just use them to guide our interactions. They exist in a somewhat permeable but powerfully self-reinforcing system. But we can all remember a time when we became aware that what we were doing didn't seem to be working. We may have re-examined our approach and chose a new one, or we may have blamed the situation and persisted in our efforts.

Either way, this is an example of a time when we can become aware of our rules. It is an abundant opportunity for self- discovery. But it can be a time of uncomfortable emotional responses causing us to deflect, deny, or move too

---

[50] Needless repetition.

quickly to escape. We may feel better for the moment, but in doing so, we keep ourselves from learning what we need to know at that time. Change requires courage.

There is no more probable time for *breakdowns*[51] than during imposed change. In these times our rules probably no longer apply, and we feel the effects.

Case in point.

I was coaching a mid-level manager in his late forties. His breakdown had to do with retaining the people in his department. He was a professional engineer and well respected for his technical competence. But people did not want to be assigned to his team. In discussions, we discovered that he had two primary rules causing his problems. One rule said, "I need all of the facts before I can make a decision." The second rule said, "I must make 100 percent accurate decisions all the time." These two rules working together kept him in suspension.

He didn't have time to gather all the facts, most of which were usually not available anyway. But his "100 percent accuracy rule" wouldn't let him make a risky decision, even if the risk would be minimal. Of course, this conflict showed up in how well his "managing people" rules worked. He had to approve every detail of every piece of his department's output. No one wanted to work under those conditions. This was his moment of opportunity to discover what was not working, or rather, breaking down. He could not have found the cause of his breakdown alone. He needed

---

[51] Breakdowns are not negative but refer to instances when what has been working so well, we weren't aware of it. Then for some reason it stops working and we become aware of it. For instance, we're not aware of the tires on our automobile until one goes flat.

assistance. His response to the situation was to ignore it and act as though he just didn't understand what was going on. This was apparently not working, and he was failing in the minds of his managers.

What are Our Scripts and Rules Made Of?

Although we come with the empty slots (natural learning intuitions) ready for the filling, in all cases our rules come from self and social perceptions; those that are developed for us by others and those that we develop. Then we reinforce them with our subjective experiences. This whole process is created in language, enhanced with emotions, and structured in our bodies. As already noted, language capacity is one of the natural structures in us when we're born and provides for our having our interpretations of our self and social perceptions as well as the rules that we use to engage the world.

As stated, categorical imperatives are given to us from a community's experience of what does and doesn't work. Hypothetical imperatives depend on declarations that we make about what will work for us as individuals. These declarations are made both consciously and unconsciously from our experiences and by the people who raise us. But who knows with certainty how the world really is? So, to reach the conclusion necessary to make a declaration, we must make personal assertions and/or assessments about our self and the world.

In the manager's case above, we found that upon examination, he could verbalize what had been transparent to him before. This sounds self-evident. But individual rules are intertwined to form coherent structures and are not easy to discern as distinct phenomena. They tend to blend into our identity undistinguished from the whole. To make them less accessible, they are reinforced with emotions and structured into our bodies. To understand their power in our lives, we will unpack them a little further.

Origins.

As noted, when we share a common culture, we are also shaped by its *categorical imperatives*.[xlviii] These imperatives are not to be ignored even if our *personal rules* don't agree. That is if we are to be community participants in good standing. We also have our own rules of engagement. These are *hypothetical imperatives* that organize our individual behaviors. These two sets of imperatives work together to create the normally functioning *private* and *public* person that we are. In Birkman terms, we can think of these as N*eeds and Usual Behavior* respectively.

But sometimes we find that unfilled needs or the forced continuation of a public self are the very basis of our pain. Another way of saying this is, a private part of our personality isn't satisfied, and our public lives won't allow them to be. A good example is a wife who grows emotionally or intellectually in a marriage with a man who doesn't. The marriage no longer satisfies her needs for an equal partner, yet she feels obligated to stay in the marriage for religious reasons. Or the manager who was promoted for his technical competence but has no real management aptitude. His family obligations keep him in his position for the money alone, so he suffers the stresses in silence.

It follows logically that we are effective or ineffective in direct proportion to how well our rules fit our various roles in society. And this fit is best utilized when our rules allow our public self to reflect our private self and fulfill our needs.

How Do Rules Get There?

In the example of the mid-level manager earlier, he created his two problematic rules early in his life. And when a current situation felt like a familiar event, he employed the same script, which called up his rules and he was ready to apply them. His father was a perfectionist and taskmaster. If he made a mistake, he paid for it dearly. His father also told him he was not that competent. In response, he created rules that would allow him to survive as a "less competent person" (this, was his father's declaration that formed his self-perception) in a world where "authority figures were perfectionists with the power to punish" (his assessment that formed a component of his social perception). Given these perceptions, the rules become predictable; and most of us would create very similar rules.

Like external structures, personal rules continue to transform after our childhood. But the core declarations and foundational assertions and assessments that formed the self and social perceptions remain pretty much the same for most people. Occasionally we experience a significant emotional event that causes us to re-evaluate our lives at a deeper level. These are events like, but not limited to, the loss of a loved one, major illness, or religious conversion. In business, the loss of a job can be the event that causes us to examine our core declarations.

The common theme in all life-changing events is that they cause us to re-examine our view of ourselves and the world we live in. We are forced to re-examine the declarations we've made about how life is and how we are in it. In these cases, we can create new and revised rules.

Breakdowns in society.

Think about this in the context of the sudden shift that happened in America on September 11, 2001, when we were attacked. What declarations about the strength and power of the mightiest nation on the planet were called into question? What assessments about security in our country and the shared value of the sanctity of life had to be re-assessed? Some say that the event resulted in the loss of our sense of security as a people. It certainly caused us to re-examine our common assertions, assessments, and declarations, because they were based on a particular kind of naïve realism[52] about the world we lived in at the time.

This is change in its rawest form. Those who ignore this reality and attempt to apply the old rules will feel the most stress. But those who can accept that we live in a new world can then create new more effective rules to guide their actions and live in relative peace.

Case in point.

As another personal example, I became acquainted with Tom, an African American man who taught me a lot about rules and didn't know it. I got to know him because he was a disruptive presence in the manufacturing company where we worked together. He was quick to settle differences physically and in the middle of the

---

[52] In social psychology, naïve realism is the human tendency to believe that we see the world around us objectively, and that people who disagree with us must be uninformed, irrational, or biased. Naïve realism provides a theoretical basis for several other cognitive biases, which are systematic errors in thinking and decision-making.

manufacturing area. Yet when engaged in a civil conversation, he was intelligent and considerate. He was an enigma.

One day, after I had earned his trust during many interesting conversations, I asked him a simple question, "Why didn't you finish High School?" His response was an awakening for me.

He said that he had grown up in the Alabama of the 1940's. In those days the adult Black men he saw were Porters and Janitors. He believed that the best he could aspire to was a janitorial position. He saw no need for education to do such a simple job. His family was poor and could use another income, so he quit school and went to work.

His rules were based on a self-perception of inferiority and a social perception of a world with no possibility for a Black man. This conversation took place in Chicago, Illinois in the early 60's.

Chicago was a place that many Black Southerners came to find more opportunities. He had run into the same wall of prejudice in Chicago that existed in Alabama. So, when he faced similar issues he applied the rule he followed when he experienced trouble in Alabama. "I can't win...so why try."

How Can We Develop More Effective Rules?

First, we must realize that they exist. And then the task becomes one of accepting that we live by them. Finally, we need to become open to the process of discovery. Once we become open to discovering them, we can begin the process of conscious examination. Only after we have a conscious awareness can we start to examine their situational effectiveness. A coach can be instrumental in this process.

This is a difficult task for most of us. We live in a way that we assume that our perceptions are the way the world really is. To attempt discovery means that we need to admit that we may be wrong about assumptions that we have made and lived with our entire life. Who is automatically open to the implication that we are not who we think we are and the world is not how we think it is?

Freud said, "the neurosis strives to perfect itself." If we see neurosis as consisting of a coherent weave of compensations built to defend our self and social perceptions founded on our declarations, we begin to get an appreciation for the difficulties of change. Especially when every attempt to change them feels like an attack on the integrity of our point of view because it is.

In the case of the previously mentioned technical manager, he can now apply his rules more effectively. But he could also choose to ignore the rule if it wasn't going to work for him. In the case of Tom, the Black man he was able to see how his rule got him into trouble and did change it. In the process, he became much more successful in his life. With the revised rules that allowed new possibilities he had not seen before, he went back to school and eventually became a senior manager in that manufacturing company.

The lesson here is to re-examine self and social perceptions to be sure that they are based on valid declarations made from assertions and assessments grounded in current reality. And when this is done, to call up an existing rule or create a new rule that fits new perceptions. This requires other people who we trust, like coaches, to offer their observations.

Because it is only with these other people that we can escape the blindness of our own subjective experience. Such trusted observers can offer their views as benchmarks. With these benchmarks, we have something to compare our perceptions, interpretations, and our rules. This is the power of connecting to others that is so necessary for managing the inevitable changes that we all face in life. This is the true role of a coach.

Chapter 12 – The Birkman Method as a coaching aid

There is more than a verbal tie between the words common, community, and communication.... Try the experiment of communicating, with fullness and accuracy, some experience to another, especially if it be somewhat complicated, and you will find your own attitude toward your experience changing.

John Dewey

Although The Birkman Method® preceded the FFM it is based in similar personality theory. "The Big Five personality traits, also known as the five-factor model or (FFM), is a model based on common language descriptors of personality. When factor analysis (a statistical technique) is applied to personality survey data, some words used to describe aspects of personality are often applied to the same person. For example, someone described as conscientious is more likely to be described as "always prepared" rather than "messy." This theory uses descriptors of common language and therefore suggests five broad dimensions commonly used to describe the human personality and psyche.

"The five factors have been defined as openness to experience, conscientiousness, extraversion, agreeableness, and neuroticism, often represented by the acronyms OCEAN or CANOE. Beneath each proposed global factor, there are a number of correlated and more specific primary factors. For example, extraversion is said to include such related qualities as gregariousness, assertiveness, excitement seeking, warmth, activity, and positive emotions."[53]

This theory is based on the association between words but not on neuro-psychological experiments. We know that certain attributes described by words are neuro-physiologically based. So, these personality "super factors" are commonly accepted the bases from which all other personality traits evolve. The Birkman Method components provide the insights on those traits that have the most impact on understanding an individual's construction and maintenance of the private and public selves.

An important global awareness.

Check the Birkman Map to see if your client is more or less extroverted? The answer should shape an overall expectation on your part about their willingness to respond to external versus internal stimulation. For instance, what resistance will you encounter in the coaching process? This is an important observation to make early on in the coaching engagement. It gives you clues to the level of openness from external stimulus as opposed to that which comes from their internal world. In other words, what inside and outside structures are having the most impact on their perceptions and actions.

As you will see, this awareness will provide useful distinctions for assessing the *internal-external* orientation of the individual's focus. With this information, one can begin to see that creation, sustenance, and expression of the private

---

[53] Matthews, Gerald; Deary, Ian J.; Whiteman, Martha C. (2003). Personality Traits (PDF) (2nd ed.). Cambridge University Press.

self [versus the public self] represent different challenges when working with clients who have different orientations.

The Birkman roadmap.

The Birkman Method's® unique benefit to a coach is a clear and concise roadmap to the client's authentic self. The best route starts at the *Coaching to Needs* report. The first step is to ask what Needs are not being satisfied in the client's current circumstances. Although the objective isn't to change these Needs, the coach can assist by:

- Offering a reality check to the client by sharing differing interpretations of his or her perceptions. Sometimes Needs only feel unmet because of a client's misinterpretations of their circumstances.
- Helping to find ways the client hasn't considered yet for filling unmet Needs.
- Developing coping strategies when it becomes clear the client's Needs won't be met in their current circumstances.
- Helping to plan changes in the client's circumstances, i.e., make a career change, leave a relationship, move to a new location, etc.

The complexity of heuristics.

As we all know, life can be difficult. We are faced with daily decisions without enough information to make good reasoned choices. To reduce cognitive load, we have evolved heuristic[54] cognitive tools to facilitate our decision-making. This was an adaptive mechanism that evolved while we were still in the jungles where we could be eaten if we missed an important clue from our environment. These heuristic tools base our judgments on our pre-existing cognitive maps and are therefore highly prone to bias. None the less, as Dr. Birkman explained, those judgments have a powerful direct impact on our behavior in the present.

Because our behavior is based on decisions deriving from our pre-existing cognitive maps we can think of these as the factors that make up a personality; personality being the product of a continuous negotiation between our authentic and public selves. So, to facilitate our coaching efforts, we need to establish a practical and manageable frame of reference for their delineation.

As we've seen the personality "super factors"[55] are commonly accepted as the bases from which all other personality factors evolve. The Birkman Method® uses nine personality components to give us more specificity. Being coaches, we need to be aware of the degree of rigidity of each client's personality, component by component. This rigidity will vary based on the individual's biological makeup.[56] This resistance to change is our inborn

---

[54] Heuristic is defined as a trial and error system of discovery or learning that allows for judgments and decisions under conditions of uncertainty.

[55] The Big Five personality traits, also known as the five-factor model (FFM), is a model based on common language descriptors of personality. The five factors have been defined as openness to experience, conscientiousness, extraversion, agreeableness, and neuroticism, often represented by the acronyms OCEAN

[56] Dr. Birkman and I agreed that what looks like behavioral change is most often a client feeling his or her own permission to act out who they really are.

temperament or aptitude. Although our personality may seem supple, our temperament is not. It is biologically anchored and isn't going to change.

Knowing this, we coach anyway, because personality is the outward demonstration of the interaction between the private and public selves, given the circumstances in our lives. It emerges from temperament but is relatively flexible given our assessments on a situation by situation basis. The key point here is we can try to fit in or please others only for a finite period, and then the stress overcomes us. Each person is different in their level of flexibility. (More to come on the topic of temperament)

The point here is that the stresses being felt by the client are coming from the unmet Needs of the authentic self. A skillful coach will focus on those gaps and work towards re-interpreting erroneous perceptions and or finding circumstances that are more appropriate for the client.

What is the biological resistance?

There are three general aspects to understanding what will affect any effort to facilitate change in the client: (keeping in mind that what looks like lasting change is the expression of the authentic self.)

1. The range of personality characteristics are (structurally) determined and contained in our language, our body, and emotions. Change one and the others will work to bring it back to the original position. The term homeostasis is usually used to describe a biological system's innate ability to

remain in balance. Our personalities work the same way. In other words, they are extremely resilient.

2. Tendencies toward certain behaviors derive from our genetic evolutionary history both as a species and our personal history as individuals (ontogeny and ontology.) For instance, the above example of our genetically conserved heuristic cognitive processes that save us from dangers.

3. We are highly complex biological systems. We are not computers, nor do we function as one regardless of the many theories of brain functions based on digital processing. We are biological organisms that produce seemingly infinite variations of behavioral responses to different situations.

Some Birkman Method features and benefits.

Dr. Birkman devoted his entire professional life to the creation, development, and improvement of this instrument. It was formerly called the *Test of Social Comprehension* and was originally developed after he returned from World War II. Over 60 million tests have been administered since that time.

The nine delineated behavioral constructs (Components) being measured in The Birkman Method® work well for coaches because they provide the information needed to perform a comparative analysis that explains the gap between the (public) social self and (private) authentic self. As you know, the greater the size of this gap, the higher the costs in stress on the client.

Both the physiological and the linguistic aspects of these constructs are discussed and examined in the following text. In addition, the interaction between the physiological and linguistic is explored to examine the degree of difficulty involved in modifying those perceptions that will be the most beneficial.

The Birkman Method® is very valuable for timely and accurate analysis of behavioral constructs that make up the personality. By doing so it gives insight into the construction of the client's world view and allows the coach to get a quick grasp of the organizing principles behind a client's patterns, and subsequently their rules for engaging their world.[57]

Building confidence.

The most relevant aspect of this method is its accuracy. Without gaining a client's confidence, it would be very difficult to convince people to leave what they know and move on to the unknown. The method is so accurate as to create the trust needed for the client to consider difficult life changes.

I have conducted Birkman Method® assessments with over 100 clients, and in all cases but two, the client has substantially agreed with the results. In these two cases, these clients were experiencing traumatic life-changing events during the assessment period that were revealed in the feedback sessions. I consider these two assessments to be unreliable because of these circumstances.

---

[57] It has also allowed me to assess behaviors based in constructs that won't change and those that might. In about 50 percent of the cases I have managed or coached, it became clear that these people were in careers that brought them little satisfaction at substantial personal costs. They had the choice of continuing to use their energy to manage the stress that their present situation created, or they could use it to re-launch new and more rewarding directions for their lives.

Using the primary nine constructs identified and assessed in the report, we will show how to understand them in linguistic terms. In this way, we will see how our interpretations inform our behavior. And remember, Dr. Birkman, based this research and resultant method on the theory that those interpretations shape our behavior whether they are grounded and valid or completely unrealistic—the exact reason a skillful coach plays such an important role.

Reviewing the metaphor of language games.

A game is a good example that illustrates the orientation of an interaction with others. How we interpret it, determines what rules and subsequent scripts to apply. We might think of behavioral constructs as our way of playing the game we think we're in. They are not the game but are our unique orientation to the game being played.

Using a sports example, a player might be aggressive and impulsive, and another might be patient and thoughtful. They could be playing any game, but the way they play it is their unique orientation, or in our terms, personality construct.

For instance, the personality trait titled, *Insistence,* measures our orientation toward structure. The *game* being played might be a formal discussion like that of a courtroom debate. There, stricter guidelines are followed, versus, free-wheeling gabfests where anyone can jump in and change the topic. In this *game*, a person with high Insistence scores would be much more comfortable than someone with low scores.

In simple terms, we bring our personality to everything we do.

Preview of scripts and rules.

We can think of personality traits (Components) as our unique personal orientations that shape and hold our scripts and rules. Each construct is like a super schema that informs our interactions, guides the choice of our scripts and rules, providing structure to how we behave. The efficacy of rules and scripts is determined by their applicability to the game. For example, it would be silly to say rules and scripts are right or wrong if we didn't know what game we were playing.

In the previous highly structured example, a person with high structure needs will call on personal rules that work best in highly structured situations and they will probably produce what the Birkman Method® calls, the Usual Behaviors. If that person finds himself in a less structured situation he'll still call on rules for high structure situations and they won't work. If this goes on long enough, he will call up rules designed to deal with stress and the outcomes will rarely be as successful. They will certainly use up far more energy.

Given the *game* or domain of action we are involved in, our behavioral constructs are what we bring to the field upon which we play. Another way of saying this is that if we are on a football field we will probably be best advised to use the scripts and rules for football, or we might seem out of touch with the current reality. This is the precise definition of what Dr. Birkman saw in those people whose perceptions seem "illusory, irrational, or unreal." So, it's not a stretch to see how these people *might* call up and misapply scripts and rules. If left to our subjective blindness, we *will* most assuredly misapply them and may not even know it. A coach can be the link we need to validate the applicability of our scripts and rules.

As we have seen, we are structurally determined organisms[xlix]. And yet our central nervous system (or CNS) is a very flexible system that allows for learning and growth most all our lives. Because our behavior is structurally determined by our CNS does not mean it is predictable. Our past experiences and our unique personal history provide a full range of possible behaviors with which to react. We call this free will.

Additionally, it is doubtful that we are limited from reaching our cognitive growth boundaries by our physiology. More probably we set self-imposed boundaries based on a unique way of seeing the world. In other words, our belief systems are the limiting variables in most cases. They establish our comfort zones and our natural tendency is toward safety and away from the danger of the annihilation of our point of view[l].

Temperament vs. Personality.

Like mental capacity, temperament is a function of neurological systems whereas personality is a product of socialization. Think of temperament as the stem and personality as the flower. No amount of coaching will produce a Rosebud from a Lily stem.

Another way of saying this is we are biological, structurally determined beings, and all our behavioral constructs are neurophysiologically based. But certain of these are more related to the endocrine and autonomic nervous system functions and general CNS sensitivity-reactivity factors. Therefore, at the deepest level, our temperament, the roots of personality constructs are out of the reach of behavioral interventions like coaching.

In simple terms, when temperament is at the basis of a person's ineffectiveness in their current life circumstances, it is best advised to coach them into more appropriate directions. For instance, sometimes advising a change to a career is better than attempting to assist a client to change themselves to fit the career.

Keeping in mind that the goal of coaching is the full realization of the authentic self and finding that *perfect* place to fulfill it, we now come to the issue of durability. Even though all personality factors evolve from inborn temperaments, some factors seem to be more durable than others. By durable, we mean their power to influence the meanings of their interpretation of objective facts and the level of illusory, irrational, or unreal perceptions that influence their behaviors. In simple terms, how durable are their cognitive maps that take them to the wrong places.

Both the physiological and the linguistic aspects of these behavioral constructs are discussed and examined in the following text. In addition, the interaction between the physiological and linguistic is explored to examine which of these outward personality constructs are (a) not changeable, (b) somewhat changeable and (c) more easily changed. (Keep in mind; this refers to the outward personality manifestations and not the root temperament of the client.)[58]

To fully understand how our rules of engagement influence our behavior, we will examine certain Components

---

[58] Copyright © 2018, Robert T. De Filippis. This work has been designed to apply coaching skills with the aid of the Birkman Method®, a previous work of Birkman International, Inc. and is used with their permission. This method takes information about an individual obtained through a questionnaire and interprets that information by comparing that individual with a database of information about many other people. The database includes data from several thousand companies, including Fortune 500 firms.

from The Birkman Method® and how they point to scripts. These constructs can also be understood in linguistic terms to help us explore how a client shapes the interpretations that inform their behaviors.

Although explaining the use of scripts and rules suggests a very structured way of understanding cognitive functioning, it doesn't mean to imply that we operate with this perfectly logical flow. Rather, the explanation is offered as a way of showing how to deconstruct scripts with the hope of reconstructing them to help a client enhance his or her personal effectiveness. Also, the example rules are not provided as illustrations of right and wrong but only to show the differences that a script can make in the process of choosing how we might interact with others in different situations.

Reviewing up to this point.

Remember, rules must be assessed in a specific context. This context is the game, and although the related script derives from our previous experiences [external], it is also shaped by our behavioral constructs [internal]. As we have seen, we are structurally determined organisms.[li] And yet our central nervous system [CNS] is a very flexible system that allows for learning and growth throughout our lives. Just because our CNS structurally determines our behavior does not mean it is predictable. Our past experiences and our unique personal history provide a full range of possible behaviors with which to react.

Being structurally determined beings, all our behavioral constructs are neurophysiologically based. But certain of these are more related to the endocrine and autonomic nervous system functions and general CNS sensitivity-reactivity factors. Therefore, temperament, or the deep levels, from which the constructs emerge are out of the reach of ordinary behavioral interventions. When temperament is at the basis of a person's worries or concerns about their life circumstances, it is best advised to coach them into more appropriate directions. For instance, in a career counseling situation, in some instances, advising a change to a career is better than attempting to assist a client to change himself [physiology] to fit the career.

The behavioral constructs in categories:

Regarding changeability, this categorization reflects only the outward personality demonstrated in the client's repertoire of public behaviors. The temperament from which the behavioral constructs come is not changeable.

- **Group 1 -- Physiological – Autonomous reactions - not likely to change**
- Emotional Energy-- this is the construct of allowing our feelings or expression of emotions in day-to-day life.
- Thought -- this is the construct of action or reflection indicating how a person makes decisions requiring either more or less time for consideration.
- Restlessness -- this is the construct of dealing with and managing the changes that affect our daily lives.
- Physical Energy -- this is the construct of the preferred pace of action either with enthusiasm or conservation.

- **Group 2 -- Belief and values – May be somewhat changeable**
- Assertiveness -- This is the construct of directing and controlling or how we deal with Assertiveness.
- Incentives -- This is the construct of incentives and competition or how we approach incentive.
- Insistence -- This is the construct of systems and procedures or our planning and organizing style.

- **Group 3 -- Learned behavior – Relatively changeable**
- Self-consciousness -- This is the construct of sensitivity in relating to others or how we deal with people one on one.
- Social Energy -- This is the construct of relating to people in groups or how we deal with people in general.

Important

Keep in mind here the term **changeable** refers to **behavior**. It's the degree of flexibility in the client's patterns of behavior as described in the Component.

Psyches come in one size – whole and complete.

Even though the previous section shows the relative changeability of behaviors described in the nine personality traits, it is good advice to think of them all as impractical to modify in a coaching situation. There are at least two reasons for this advice: 1. Coaching engagements are usually too short term for lasting behavioral change, even when the client is very willing. 2. We cannot consider any one of these constructs without considering them all. And they will all be affected when we try to change one. The personality *system* will strive to balance itself and maintain stasis.

There is "no one simple thing" that changes everything. Given the complexities of a human personality, we are better advised to respect the balance of all these traits as we help our clients seek out and realize their authentic selves.

Theoretical case.

For example, if a client has a low S*elf-Consciousness* score and prefers to be very direct and frank in her communications, we might see an opportunity to help her make some behavioral adjustments. But we might also consider her *Emotional Energy* score because she may not want to express feelings and may think that being too indirect is being too *touchy-feely*. And then there are her *Insistence* scores. She may insist on order and systems as a way of keeping things very straightforward and clean without a lot of *messy* human being stuff. So even though her *Self-Consciousness* related behaviors might allow some movement, her *Insistence*-related behaviors will require an order of magnitude more effort and her *Emotional Energy*-related behaviors just aren't going to change because of your efforts.

In summary, we have seen that we can identify our neurophysiological orientations by using tools such as The Birkman Method®. And we have also seen that some of these orientations are more open to modification than others. The ethical challenge for us as coaches is to use this information in ways to assist others without regard for our own preferences but rather with respect for the unique internal ecology of the other people we work with.

Chapter 13 -- Discovering and Questioning Scripts and Rules with The Birkman Method®

"What you focus upon will always tend to rule what is experienced."

Steven Redhead

Although the Usual Behavior scores can show the themes and patterns of the client's contextually appropriate, or socialized behavior, the clues to a client's scripts and rules are to be found in the *relationships* of the Needs and Stress Behaviors scores. You can infer from this relationship which scripts are not working and which embedded rules may be failing. With your client's agreement, you can then begin to work with the client to produce an awareness sufficient to begin linguistic deconstruction and reconstruction processes culminating in:

1) The ability to discern the script and *rule set* that may be troublesome
2) New choices that come with discernment and/or
3) The revision and/or enrichment of our scripts and rules
4) The creation of additional effective scripts and rules.

To explore how we select and apply rules, we will use the following behavioral trait from The Birkman Method® as an example.

Group 2 -- Belief and values -- Moderately changeable

- Assertiveness – Your tendency to speak up and express opinions openly and forcefully.

This matrix illustrates the internal scripts that contain the rules

Behavioral Construct	Linguistic Construct	Declarative Acts	Performative Acts
Physio-logical orientation in an interaction	My rule	The world is . . . I am . . . I will be . . .	If so, I will R, O, & P[59] in this way . . .

Person A –

Asser-tiveness	Expressing oneself is a human right	The world is a place where I can speak out and express my opinions openly. I am a confident and capable person in it. I will be forceful and confident.	My requests will be firm and forthright. My offers will be seriously delivered. My promises will be kept without fail.

---

[59] R, O, & P refer to requests, offers, and promises.

Person B –

Asser-tiveness	The right to speak out must be earned	The world is a place where speaking out is not allowed. I am a simple person who will never have much power. I will hide my real intentions so as not to bring attention to myself.	My requests will be cautious and uncertain. My offers will be simple and few. My promises will always have a hidden caveat.

Aligning the application of the rules.

It is impossible to read the previous matrix objectively. Your level of assertiveness will influence how you react to the different scripts and rules that person A and person B use in their lives.

As tempting as it is to moralize and promote personal values, the properly aligned application of scripts and rules is evaluated by how useful it is in the context within which it is being used. [This sounds like relativism, but it's more about utility than morality]. That is, a rule is useful if it works to produce the results we want in a particular context. This seemingly amoral view is based upon the improbability that one can create a formula that can encompass all possible cultures, norms, beliefs, and value systems.

Morality.

Although it is not the coach's role to judge the morality of our client's point of view, we must evaluate and validate their grounding. If a client's social perception is so ungrounded as to seem out of touch, we have an entirely new problem with which to deal, which may include referral to the proper mental health professional.

That said, I believe people and society function more effectively grounded on a coherent ethical foundation. The fundamental interpretation of effectiveness includes the values of the environment within which the rule is being applied. If that environment is inconsistent with your values, don't take the assignment.

Remember that the efficacy of one's hypothetical imperatives, although individualistic, is determined by the categorical imperatives of the dominant culture and the specific context of its application. Culture and context determine efficacy.

One might argue today; culture's categorical rules are a bit less applicable given the actions of some of our elected officials.

Cultures exist in families, communities, businesses, and organizational contexts. And as we apply rules to these various and distinct cultures, the same rule can be both effective and ineffective. For instance, if I follow the rule "I will hug and kiss those people who I care for" in a family setting, my actions may be appropriate or effective in demonstrating how I feel. If I attempt to follow the same rule in my social community, I might be welcomed by some and rejected by others. If I follow it in a business or other more formal organization, I would surely be ostracized and possibly find myself the defendant in a lawsuit. The rule and behavior are the same, but the cultures and contexts are different.

So, alignment of the application of rules is a function of the circumstances within which they are being applied. This is a simple statement that sums up a large range of ineffective behaviors that are at the cause of much human ineffectiveness, isolation, and confusion. It's the answer to so many questions. Why can't the exemplary engineer manage people? Why can't the senior scientist reduce turnover in her department? Why does the intelligent and well-educated minority employee stumble on seemingly simple tasks? Because they are unconsciously applying rules in specific contexts that worked before but don't now.

Case in point.

Earlier in my career, I was responsible for managing a manufacturing company in a small rural community. This community was one that had functioned well for several decades before our company came to town and opened our facility. People lived simple but sufficient lives by earning their living doing a multitude of different things. Some owned small farms that made a few dollars. Some went hunting and fishing to supplement their food supplies. Some even had small side businesses that they could operate in their spare time. These were hardy and industrious people who had survived quite well before our company arrived.

During conversations with our Human Resources manager, I was informed that absenteeism was at an all-time high and we were having trouble keeping the plant at full production. He had tried several programs to manage the problem and none had been very successful. After careful consideration of our options, we approached the union and explained our dilemma. The union agreed that we had a problem but that whatever we did, we should stay within the parameters of the contract in taking further actions. No surprise.

Our contract seemed to allow sufficient latitude if we would simply apply the rules we had. So, we launched a new program directed at reducing the absenteeism that was getting to a crisis point for our operations. The program included strict adherence to a set of guidelines or rules. The rules were progressive in nature. That means at six unexcused (by a physician's note) absences, an employee would be sent home without pay for one day. At seven it would be two days, at eight three days off and at nine the employee would lose their job.

Because we were guilty in the past of unequal application of the rules, we erased each employee's previous record with a great deal of fanfare and started from ground zero. We wanted employee buy-in, so we gave them all a clean slate.

Within a few months, we knew that our new plan was failing. In fact, absenteeism soared beyond its previous levels. It seemed that most people would get to seven or eight absences and become very conscientious about being on the job every day. My first clue came when I realized that this program was modeled after a similar absentee policy that had been employed effectively in our Chicago plant. This little town was not remotely similar to Chicago, and these people were as different as they could be.

Fortunately, we had a few employees who didn't mind telling us what their peers were thinking. What I discovered was enlightenment for me. I discovered that these employees loved the time off with or without pay. They had gardens to attend. They had hunting and fishing to do. Their little side businesses had needs that had to be filled. So, the loss of a few days earnings was a fair trade for the time off to take care of their other needs. We had applied a policy that was based on a set of rules that worked in a different community and didn't work here.

What had seemed like a punishment was in fact interpreted as a reward. I didn't know it at the time, but this was an excellent example of the same rule not working effectively in a different culture. Was the rule inherently right or wrong? I don't know. If I apply a categorical imperative that says one owes his or her loyalty to their employer, I could argue that the rule was right. But I had found that this was not the categorical imperative of this community. In fact, it was just the opposite. One was a *sell-out* if they showed too much concern for their employer's needs.

The cultural heroes in this plant were the ones who gave management the most trouble. Were the cultural imperatives wrong? I don't know that, either. I do know that the community had survived for a long time by following their own rules. I also know that other companies had exploited them in the past. There had been industrial sabotage in the community's history. Illegal strikes were a regular happening here. If a local person was promoted to a management position, his extended family and old friends began to regard him with suspicion. "He must have sold out to get the promotion." So, the community's common experience had taught them to trust themselves and no one else.

Using rules to guide actions appropriately.

As we saw in the matrix at the beginning of this chapter, rules are embedded in scripts. So, to use rules to guide appropriate actions, we need first to find out if we are using the correct script. Once determined, we have the basis for deciding if our rules are appropriate.

The first challenge here is to be discerning about our scripts. Once we have accepted that our perceptions and actions shape our scripts and vice versa, we can examine them more effectively. Remember that scripts have flags that are used to call them up to match a situation that may be familiar but not the same.

If the script doesn't work and the situation *feels* too much like one that we have experienced before, we are often stumped when it comes to acting appropriately. So, make no mistake; the process of discerning a script at work is not the end but the beginning of the challenge. From there, we must be able to receive new information as objectively as possible, so we can make new choices as to how we will act. Unless we can do this, we are doomed to our past experiences shaping our responses to new situations.

So how do we do this magic?

To answer this question, I will again borrow a piece from Peter Senge's book, *The Fifth Discipline*. *Reflection* and *Inquiry* are the answers. *Reflection* is the process of slowing down our thinking to become aware of how we form our mental models. *Inquiry* is holding conversations where we openly share views and develop knowledge about each other's assumptions,[lii] (Assertions and assessments) Both methods allow us to stop our leaps up, what Chris Argyris calls, *the ladder of inference.*[liii]

The Fifth Discipline goes on to say that our ability to achieve results is eroded by our feelings that:

1. Our beliefs are *the* truth
2. The truth is obvious
3. Our beliefs are based on real data
4. The data we select are the real data.

In other words, we need to stop the process of believing that our point of view is the one correct way to see the world. If there is a place in this universe where we can go from one point to another without passing through the space between, it seems to be between the receipt of a stimulus and the conclusions we draw from it.

Our internal responses happen so quickly that it feels as though our inferences are the only way to interpret the stimulus. Fortunately, with practice, discipline, and diligence, we can slow the process down for reflection and inquiry. Here's a graphical look at the process of self-reflection for clarity.

Assumptions	Reflection	Inquiry
Our beliefs are *the* truth	Are my assessments about the world, others, and myself valid and well-grounded?	How do others see the situations that I feel so strongly about? Do others believe as firmly as I

	On what basis do I know this view to be true?	do, something that may be very different from my belief?
The truth is obvious	Am I mistaking my interpretations for facts? Do others share my beliefs and interpretations Can I think of situations when my experiences were different from those of others whom I respect?	Given a set of circumstances, how do others' beliefs compare to mine? Does someone's interpretation of a similar experience differ dramatically from mine? Do others sometimes see things that I didn't see in a mutual experience?
Our beliefs are based on real data	Am I confusing an assertion with an assessment?	How do others respond to the evidence that I offer to

	Is the data I call "real" verifiable by others?	support my assertions? Do others have data that I might consider that I hadn't considered before?
The data we select are the real data.	Am I interpreting this stimulus correctly? Is the data that I'm receiving being unduly influenced by my previous experiences?	What data are others using to make their judgments?

In summary, as coaches, we have a responsibility to respect another person's views of the world, scripts, and rules and at the same time be available to assist in their reflection and inquiry. Some of us can do that relatively easily. Others might find the task onerous. But for sure, no one can do it without having a conscious awareness of their own private and public selves. (See your personal Birkman scores)

If we can accept that everything a person becomes is unique to that human being and evolves through their neurolinguistic structures and life's experiences, we can come to see that there is no basis for argument. No reason to invalidate. Confrontation is not going to convince a person of the superiority of another person's point of view. Yes, you might get a socialized response to seem agreeable, but the authentic self is going to need a lot more than tricks or techniques.

Self-aware, authentic connection is the most crucial coaching attribute.

Personal certitude limits progress.

Teaching someone the methods of reflection and inquiry is a good goal to have. But first, the other person must be able to admit that his self and social perceptions are not necessarily the way the world is and then become open to the process of questioning them. This will come with a price. The price is the loss of that person's certitude and the assurances that seem to come with it. And in too many cases in my experience, people are willing to pay a very high price to maintain their personal certitude, which is an illusion of certainty.

Today we are all too aware of the Mideastern religious fanatics who have acquired a level of certitude from their skewed interpretations of their holy texts. The price of that certitude is a willingness to die as a martyr. In our own twenty-first century western world, we also read about a "fundamentalist this" or an "over-zealous that" who are as committed to their certitude as the terrorists are to theirs. They are just as committed as any fanatic from another land.

What enormous drives fuel these beliefs and actions? It comes from deep within that human being. And in some form or fashion, you may touch that force as you attempt to convince another to question their subjective reality. Be aware. Be patient. Be respectful. And learn to offer your view of the world in a way that allows others to sustain the integrity of their own. Remember, "In the process of enlightenment, there are only participants."

The deconstruction process.

You need a trusting alliance to reduce the client's resistance to discovery and change before you begin the work of deconstruction. The validity and credibility of The Birkman Method® give you a first step in the process of developing that partnership. Deconstruction starts with a review of the Birkman *Coaching to Needs* Report.

- Focus on each need in sequence and ask your client if that need is being met.
- Listen for the declarations they make and ask about how they arrived at that belief about themselves or their situation.
- Listen for their assertions and ask for the evidence.
- Listen for their assessments and ask for the grounding.
- Offer your opinions on each assertion and assessment
- Ask them to reconsider their assertions and assessments in light of your point of view.

The reconstruction process.

Indirectly you are asking about the underlying rules that are not working. These unsatisfied Needs point to the scripts and rules because they are expectations that are not being fulfilled. Asking for their evidence and grounding puts their declarations about their world to the test. Your client should leave that session with an awareness that allows them to answer the questions:

- Are your beliefs *the* truth?
- Is the truth obvious?
- Are your beliefs based on real data?
- Is the data you select the only real data?

If your client is willing, you can assist in the reconstruction of more effective assertions, assessments, and declarations that will work better. To be clear here, do not attempt to install your assertions, assessments, and declarations. Assist your clients in determining their own. And do not be disappointed if the only gain is your client's awareness of their subconscious decision-making processes at work to create their self and social perceptions. This is major progress.

The above steps require that the relationship have enough credibility and trust to allow open discussion about the breakdowns that come from unmet Needs. The reasons for these breakdowns are brought to consciousness and can now be examined openly. The coach needs never mention the words *scripts* and *rules* to affect them and help the client become more effective. You're asking them to explain how and why they act in the situations that seem to cause them the most amount of conflict or ineffectiveness.

This process is much like the work of a detective. Criminals leave clues. The effective investigator will discover and review the clues, look for and find the patterns, hypothesize the motives, recreate the crime, speculate about, and interview the suspects, and finally arrest and bring charges. [Not necessarily in that order] I don't know of too many crimes where the criminal calls an investigator and gives him access to all the above elements out of the goodness of his heart. Like it or not, the investigator must work for his results. Coaches are to some extent like investigators. Except that in most instances, the person being coached is present and willing to take help but is usually not aware of the underlying facts that need to be discovered to help. And of course, that person has usually not committed a crime.

Here is an example coaching application:

1. The process begins with asking the client if a particular need is being filled.

[In this case, the client's need to have others show genuine respect and appreciation for his feelings is <u>not</u> being met, and consequently, he is under stress. But his usual behavior belies his deeper need for respectful interactions. He seems outwardly plainspoken, but inwardly, he needs more sensitive relationships.]

2. Then by discussing the respective *Needs* descriptions in the report, begin to hear the underlying rules that are not working.

[This stress can be caused by a primary hypothetical rule[60] that sounds something like "people should show genuine respect and appreciation for my feelings if they want it back from me." But in this case, his rule seems to work

---

[60] Hypothetical Rule or "H rule" is an individually determined rule that contains a conditional aspect, which allows the user to circumvent a Categorical or "C rule." C rules are consciously or unconsciously assumed by the individual from external influences like family, culture, religion, etc.

one way. He interprets direct people as insensitive and yet he is direct and straightforward with them.]

3. Then examine the rules for the underlying declarations that the client has made about who they are and how the world works. This is what shapes the *Needs* scores.

[This rule is grounded in the categorical rule and sounds like a declaration, e.g., "people should be direct and straightforward but must base relationships on common activities and interests rather than on feelings of general warmth." So, your examination should be directed at what assertions and assessments provide that "being direct and straightforward with others and needing them to be more sensitive and appreciative for his feelings" is consistent. He assesses that they know that he means no disrespect when he is direct. He also asserts that direct people are honest people and he needs honesty]

4. Then question and confront the assertions and assessments upon which the declarations and subsequent rules are based.

[These are the declarative language acts at work. If behavioral change is going to happen, it will happen here. So, ask, "How do you know that people are aware that you mean no disrespect when you are direct?" and, "What is the basis for your belief that direct people are honest people?" Continue these lines of discussion until you have established that these are his constructions and offer examples that contradict his assertion and assessment]

5. Finally, assist in the construction of more effective assertions, assessments, and declarations that will work better for the client.

[With time and patience, engage the client in a discussion that allows him to reconstruct the assertions, assessments, and declarations. E.g., You might say, "Given that you need to have direct and straightforward interactions with others, can you establish a way of being okay if others are not so? What would that be like? Let's discuss the circumstances within which you could do that. What can you do differently if they are not the way you want them to be? Can you see how you send the opposite signals from how you want to be treated?" etc.])

To recap, we have the following:

Personality trait: Self-consciousness - sensitivity in relating to others.

Linguistic construct: It is best, to be frank, and direct in dealing with others, and they should be the same with me.

C rule: [Usual Behavior] People should be honest yet respectful in dealings with each other.

Primary H rule: [Needs] If others are straightforward, frank, and forthright with me and respect my feelings, I will be the same with them.

Faulty declaration: [Stress Behavior] If they do not treat me this way [primary H rule], I will become self-conscious and defensive. <u>This declaration is always ineffective.</u>

Change is inevitable.

We all know the folksy advice, that "all we must do is pay taxes and die." For those more enlightened thinkers, it has become "all we have to do is make choices and die." But in postmodern times, we need to add "experience changes" to the mix. Change is one of the two most difficult and inevitable processes we humans face. Even if we lived in some imaginary, sheltered environment, somehow protected from massive changes in external variables, we would continue to age. And with age, we are faced with significant changes to manage in the best of cases. So, no one escapes it. What does elude us is the need to create new rules for dealing with new situations. But this is far more difficult than it seems on the surface. This linguistic approach provides a method to assist the other person in managing the process through *reflection* and *inquiry*.

The Birkman Method® provides a credible and reliable assessment process that allows for getting to the bedrock substance quickly, so reflection and inquiry can begin. Although rules can be uncovered with the use of other *talking* methods, this method has served as an excellent tool upon which to base an approach. One drawback to talking methods when used without an assessment tool like the Birkman is that we are constantly confronted with *socialized behavior*. If we are excellent observers and with sufficient time, we can begin to see the discrepancies between how the client is behaving and what they would like to be doing. But in economic terms, we may not be allowed the time.

Socialized behavior.

In his book, *True Colors*, Dr. Birkman points out, "We quickly learn that there is one set of behaviors that we can use in the comfort and privacy of our own homes [. . .] But the rules change when we get out into the world [. . .] From childhood we begin to absorb the nuances of "socially acceptable behavior." Sometimes we wrap so many layers of such behavior around the core of our personalities that we find it hard to distinguish who we really are."[liv]

The Birkman Method® addresses this point very clearly in its ability to reveal the *authentic* self beneath the *social* self. Using the feedback results as described above quickly allows a look at the authentic self and provides the basis for understanding the socialized aspects of another's behavior.

Keep in mind that socialized behavior is situational, i.e., it is guided by the client's interpretation of the circumstances. If a client is engaged with you in a situation that he perceives as threatening, a good deal of his energy will go toward managing his behaviors and not revealing the information that is most useful. And we already know the distortion of constrained communications and its negative impact on finding the best answers.

Case in point.

In this case, I was asked to coach a senior financial executive. He was doing an excellent job at certain procedural tasks in his position but failed at providing the financial leadership that the company required. The president of the company hired me to work with him. She (the president) was supportive and wanted him to succeed but had serious concerns about the possibilities. This was her final investment in his development.

During my introductory meeting, I predicted that he would flood me with socialized behavior. And he didn't disappoint me. Had I not used The Birkman Method®, I may have never arrived at the level of authentic discussion that we needed to be productive. He couldn't deny or deflect the information presented in the feedback report. And within two sessions we were beyond the veil of the feigned situational behavior and were discussing the real issues at the core of his failure to provide financial leadership.

Several weeks of meetings did not produce an improvement in his performance but rather an awareness on his part that he was in the wrong job and that he was feeling frightened about admitting this to the president. At this point, he balked at doing what he needed to do to get this situation resolved to everyone's satisfaction. He needed to have an honest conversation with the president. I saw no additional value that I could add, short of having *his* conversation for him. When I finished the assignment, he and the president were circling each other with the intention of discussing the real issues necessary to resolve the real problem.[61] Even when the facts were finally known, the job of dealing with them openly is still a difficult challenge.

In conclusion, the added value of tools such as The Birkman Method® is that they can provide insight into the reasons behind behaviors that even the client can't explain.

An admonition.

More is not better! I have been engaged in situations where several tools are being used simultaneously. This practice simply confuses and creates more anxiety. Choose a tool that can provide the information that you need at several

---

[61] I found out a year later that the president had replaced him with another person and kept him in a job where he was able to be of more value to the company.

levels. The Birkman Method® has done this very well for me. For instance, one can use it in career transition and planning, team development, 360-degree assessment, leadership coaching, organizational planning and development. It has also effectively assisted me in some instances of conflict resolution, assessing interpersonal skills problems and communications consulting.

A final note on certainty.

Coaches should understand the power of a client's drive to achieve and maintain certainty. And most importantly we should understand how that drive will cause the resistance that we sometimes face when working with them. Certainty is defined as freedom from doubt. *Certitude* is based more on personal belief than on objective facts. It is not the test of certainty.[62] Certitude gives us a feeling of confidence resulting in the assurances we need to live our lives, but there is no such thing as absolute certainty.

In seemingly all cases where people claim certainty they only have convictions that create the assurances that they need to live in a world created by their self and social perceptions. This quest for certainty is a baseline of human need.

For fear of not having certainty, we create it. We see ourselves in *certain* ways. We see the world in *certain* ways. We reinforce ourselves with *certain* beliefs that provide certainty–we think. So, when someone attempts to change our self and social perceptions they will encounter the full impact of our resistance. In other words, they touch that powerful force that says, "no, I won't let you disrupt a level of comfort and assurance that has taken a lifetime to build."

---

[62] Oliver Wendell Holmes, Jr.

The certainty of death.

As we all know, one certainty in life is death. We also know making choices is the other. When we combine these two certainties we find another opportunity to make a crucial decision. The finality of death refers not only to the end of our biological existence but also the end of our self and social perceptions. But even while we're alive, sometimes our self and social perceptions need to die for us to have new life choices. To put a finer point on it, sometimes we should choose to kill them when they are obsolete and limit our future possibilities.

How many of us can do this alone? Very few people can be so discerning in the vacuum of subjective blindness. We need the help of others for this task. This is another opportunity for the professional coach.

Case in point.

I was coaching a younger woman who was having a tough time of it as a newly appointed manager in a male dominated organizational culture. One might jump to the conclusion that being a young woman brought with it uncertainties and ambivalence with managing older men. It was just the opposite. Her employees were complaining that she was too aggressive on even the most insignificant issues. She was strident as well as uncompromising—more competitive and intense than any other person in the company. Recognizing that different standards exist for women and minorities in management positions I wanted to check out these reports.

During an initial interview, I was impressed with her. She was intelligent and friendly. She talked openly and with a great deal of candor. I saw my opening and asked about her reputation. She gladly confirmed it for me with a story. She was merging into traffic coming into the main expressway stream from an entry ramp. As she edged her way onto the highway, one driver would not yield to allow her to merge. She collided with the other car purposely. I said that I had felt the urge to do just that myself but at the last minute avoided contact. I asked her why she did it. She said her father had taught her never to let the other person win; always come out on top, no matter what the situation. She also said that she would do it again if the situation warranted it. She made no apologies. She was convinced that the consequences were worth bearing as long as she didn't let anyone "beat her." And she wasn't willing to discuss her *certitude* in this matter.

Does this level of certitude show up in our coaching situations? Of course, it does. Maybe not in such a physical way, but I have coached many people who cling to their personal views with the same intensity. Even if their lives are not working out as they would like, it is much easier to blame it on their circumstances than to let go of the sense of certitude that they have created with their self and social perceptions. They are the ones we can see constantly colliding with all the other people in their lives.

Chapter 14 – Culture: The Golden Key to understanding others

"Seeing is more than a physiological phenomenon... we see not only with our eyes but with all that we are, and all that culture is."

Dorothea Lange, Depression Era Photographer

Culture helps us understand people at a much deeper level. It shapes individual behavior and determines meaning. Coaches cannot do their best and productive work without being aware of how culture affects themselves and their clients. You see, we know that there are differences in how we perceive ourselves and the world around us based on our cultural mores or ethnic heritage. Also, our historical times, unique family experience, and religion, all add to the final shape of our cognitive maps.

It is important to be able to discuss these areas with another person without fear of feeling as though we are being politically incorrect, bigoted, or insensitive. We can use this information to help or harm others. It is not inherently harmful; our intentions can be.

In the previous chapters, we examined a model for understanding and assisting others and ourselves in change. And as we've seen, The Birkman Method® is an important tool in revealing another's social and self-perceptions. These perceptions are partially based on our culture's values and traditions, which shape our social practices. These social practices guide our actions. Generally, people don't think they're making bad decisions and taking bad actions when they do. In most instances, clients are surprised by the fact that their behaviors are not getting the results they want. But to them, their actions are justified by their unexamined presuppositions and consequent views of the world usually shaped by their cultures.

As noted throughout this book, The Birkman Method® provides the framework upon which much can be done to assist others. But the other person's *whole* story, including their cultural background, needs to be *apprehended*[63] to increase our likelihood of helping.

We are not the independent thinkers we think we are.

As previously noted, it is erroneous to think that each of us is a blank slate when we are born. As Steven Pinker pointed out, we come with several learning intuitions in place. Then, as Heidegger proposed, "We are *thrown* into our lives and begin to develop our stories within the historical, cultural, and familial narratives that pre-exist us."[lv] Our stories, shaped by our learning intuitions, are written from the background of the world within which we live. They evolve intertwined within these pre-existing narratives and are influenced by conversations and interpretations from as much as 200 years before we're born.

The family narrative going back two hundred years is a strong and silent shaper of values and perceptions. Our first learning of what's right or wrong in the world doesn't come to us by reading the great authors. We learn it from our families and our level of society. If we are to understand another person, we need to know not only their personal

---

[63] As opposed to comprehended. Another person's story is too complex to be truly comprehended. The best we can do is get a tinge or flavor for it.

story but also the narrative within which they and their ancestors lived.

I have used several methods for improving my apprehension of a client's Birkman feedback in this regard. One approach is the process of conducting a preliminary open-ended discussion asking the following questions:

1) What generation in this country are your father and mother?
2) What country did they come from?
3) If they are second generation what can you tell me about your grandparents?
4) Describe some of your family's most important traditions.
5) What did you like and dislike most about your father and mother?
6) What did you learn from your father and mother?
7) How did your father and mother disappoint you?
8) What do you wish they would have been or done differently?
9) How are you like them?
10) How are you unlike them?

Asking these questions and listening before I review the Birkman feedback has provided valuable insights into the client's profile. This process has allowed me to get a temporal sense for the data that I read on the feedback reports in addition to how the client's current rules interact with each other. It has added another dimension to understanding my client. As Heidegger said, we are best understood in the context of past, present, and future.[lvi] We cannot fully appreciate a person's past without knowing about their family of origin and cultural heritage.

Alasdair Macintyre, the Scottish philosopher, historian of ethics and critic of liberal modernity offers an elucidating perspective here. We can see the basis of our postmodern *aporia*[64] because disconnected from our traditions, the establishment of meaning becomes tenuous. Postmodernism's continued erosion of traditions has made it even more difficult to understand a client without some knowledge of his or her cultural background. This is even more complex in the United States because we are country of immigrants from everywhere. And the clear majority of us come from immigrants who arrived within the last 200 years. (An excellent book on this topic is The Nine Nations of North America by Joel Garreau[65]). If we are to fully comprehend our client's deeper needs, we have no alternative but to become familiar with their traditions; because traditions are an observable outward expression of culture, i.e., the behaviors that we see.

Case in point.

I read an article that spoke to this issue some years ago. The purpose of the article was to describe cultural differences. In this story, a young man [in his early 20s] in India was being urged to go to a therapist for help. It seems

---

[64] Greek for "wayless"; a term used by deconstructionists to refer to what happens when a critic tries to trace a given signifier back to a single, stable signified . . . leaving the critic in a state of suspension in which meaning is always already deferred.

[65] Garreau suggests that North America can be divided into nine nations, which have distinctive economic and cultural features. He also argues that conventional national and state borders are largely artificial and irrelevant, and that his "nations" provide a more accurate way of understanding the true nature of North American society. The work has been called "a classic text on the current regionalization of North America".

that his *problem* was that he was trying to be an individual, and in the process was forsaking his obligations to his family of origin. This was a severe enough aberration in the normal behavior of a young man in India to send him for therapy. Here's the interesting part. Many young men in America come to therapy for the opposite reason. Their goal is to individuate. So, in India, desire for individuation can be considered somewhat of an emotional problem. And in America, individuation can be an emotional growth goal. Who is right? Of course, both are right in their respective cultural context.

But isn't it reasonable to say that if I didn't have access to the cultural background of the Indian man, I might make assumptions about his interpretations? And wouldn't those assumptions be based on my cultural biases? Now, who's right? He is, and I'm wrong. Because when coaching, I need to consider that his point of view is correct for him and if I'm going to be effective, I need to know its cultural basis. And if his coaching objective was to become more effective in our culture, I need to have this information if I am to assist.

Case in point.

Another example of cultural differences is a bit closer to home to me. In this case, I thought I knew the culture in question. I was consulting to a man in his early forties. He was first generation western European.

During a preliminary discussion with him, I asked him, "What did you like and dislike most about your father?" He went into a detailed description of his father's attitude when dealing with others. He described his father as "high-handed" and prone to make unilateral decisions without regard for how they might affect others. He took what he wanted. I immediately thought of Jared Diamond's book, *Guns, Germs, and Steel, The Fates of Human Societies,* within which he describes what happened to so many societies after they were *"discovered"* and subjugated and in some instances all but annihilated by western Europeans.[lvii]

As I got to know this man, I could see that he had learned his father's way of being but was not able to see it in himself. He had been in a therapeutic relationship with a psychologist who knew of our conversation. She reported that his mode of being was one of getting what he wanted when he wanted it without regard for how that affected others. She confirmed he was matching his father's behavior and didn't seem to have any awareness of this fact.

"Caring" is the cultural bridge.

Heidegger proposed that the core of our being human is *care*. That means that to be human is to care or be concerned about something. The concept of caring is a species phenomenon. What we care or concern ourselves with reflects the culture from which we come. It follows that culture is what provides the background for our caring at a personal level—about what we will care or be concerned with in our individual lives. One can travel to other countries to see evidence of these cultural phenomena.

As an example, on a visit to Germany I observed that the vineyards in the Neckar Valley were scrupulously well organized and maintained. Every square inch of the hills was used to grow the vines that produce their wine grapes. The vines grew in meticulously maintained rows. The hills were crisscrossed with perfect geometric patterns. The people in the valley seemed well organized, properly maintained, and dour.

On a recent trip to Mexico, I observed that nothing seemed to be well organized or maintained in the town I visited. A good deal of space was wasted with unfinished construction projects and debris. But the people seemed open, friendly, and happy.

It seems to me that the differences in these two cultures are obvious. One has a high level of concern with precision, utilization, and appearance. The other has a high level of concern with family, friends, and social conventions. Of course, neither is a full description of what any individual from either culture cares about.

Very few visitors to both countries would assess that the German and Mexican people are similar in their general orientations. One only needs to pay attention to see the differences between the peoples of both cultures and to see the differences in their attitudes and views of life. The general themes of care and concern in these cultures are identifiable.

So, if we consider that a core human attribute is *care,* and if care is shaped in culture, how can we connect with people without considering its impact?

Disconnecting from culture.

Our challenge today in America is the progressive disappearance of the connections between our actions and their meaning. If we are to assist others in self-discovery and change, we need to be aware of our postmodern condition and its effects on individual behavior.

Hans-Georg Gadamer[66] proposed that postmodernity is based on the *prejudice against prejudice.*[67] The attempt to escape from all prejudgments and preconceptions and our starting anew, with a relation between self and the world unmediated by previous culture, education, and tradition[lviii] has put us on a trajectory which is resulting in a disconnection from our traditions and the very social practices that gave us direction and meaning in the past.

But where do we find meaning if not in our cultural traditions? The individual who has attempted to disconnect from all previous meanings also disconnects his or her actions from accepted social practices, and consequently is at risk when and if trying to develop a coherent sense of morality. This action is reflected in the development of hypothetical rules without consideration for the categorical cultural rules within which other people live. In simple terms, it initiates the question, "what's in it for me?" Therefore, answers to questions of *right and wrong* are self-referent. This means that it is difficult to find convincing reasons to justify moral rules and the obligation to follow them. This makes moral judgments irresolvable, a pervasive feature of modern and postmodern thought.[lix]

Deeply philosophical? Yes. But vitally important in understanding the effects of postmodernism on our clients. Postmodernism is defined by a disconnection from reality and a fascination for the simulations that supposedly represent reality. Check out the popular movies today. They

---

[66] Hans-Georg Gadamer was a German philosopher of the continental tradition, best known for his 1960 magnum opus Truth and Method on hermeneutics.

[67] This does not mean prejudice in its popular application to racial or sexual differences, but rather in its formal definition as a prejudgment.

are simulations as are all movies, but they are simulations of comic book heroes, which make them simulations of simulations. The question is how does this emphasis on the simulated affect submersion of the authentic self and the accentuation of the social self in the coaching engagement?

Truly knowing the client.

Considering this, coaches have no option but to know another's cultural orientation, even if we think that person shares our culture. It's also important to recognize that though we are in a period of change and transition, there still remain *incoherent fragments of coherent traditions*[lx] to discover and depend on for understanding others and ourselves. The more difficult challenge is to discern the client's level of disconnectedness from his or her originating traditions. To the extent that when this disconnectedness exists, we have this additional challenge in knowing the other person well enough to assist. It is not our place to resist or evaluate the other's ways but only to know them.

In my own practice, I have discovered that the easier clients to work with are the ones whose self and social perceptions and subsequent social practices remain coherent with an identifiable tradition. In other words, their worldview consists of whole rather than fragments of a traditional values system. In these cases, I am empowered to learn more about clients and how they see the world through the magnifying power of their cultural lenses. When these social and self-perceptions are more whole, my grasp of them is more complete.

The more difficult challenge is to understand the self and social perceptions of clients who is attempting to reject and disconnect from their historical past. We can quickly lose our reference points. We need to listen very carefully to the clients' worldview, or we miss some of the most important information about them.

My good fortune has been that most of the people I have worked with have been in their late-forties and early fifties. They have not been entirely *postmodernized*. My greater concern comes with clients from younger generations who have been thrust into the confusion of the disconnected meanings of postmodernity. A most difficult bridge to cross is that of being a *"modern"* listener to *"post modernized"* person." The subtleties are deafening. If you are older than thirty-five or so, you may not understand them very well because they are, by and large, based on values and perspectives that may not be immediately recognizable from within your subjective experience. Hopefully, this text has raised your sensitivity to the challenge.[68]

It is important to note that a casual observer may find individuals from any culture who do not fit a pattern. The point is not to prejudge others but to become more familiar with the possible pre-existing orientations that often show up in observable behaviors in very subtle ways. The objective here is not precision but sensitivity.

Important caution.

I want the reader to be sure that I'm not comparing countries and their cultures to determine which is best. None is better or worse in objective terms. The evolution of human cultural systems is shaped by the survival needs of a group of people within their physical circumstances. So, each culture and its values can only be judged in a historical

---

[68] For more on this topic I refer the reader to the book, Generations, The History of America's Future by Strauss and Howe, (Quill- New York: 1991)

context by asking the question "has this way of being been successful in helping these people to survive?" If the answer is yes, the culture has been effective. But that answer is not sufficient for assessing the culture's efficacy for the future. And we need to consider this reality when dealing with people from cultures that are different from our own if we are to be effective when coaching.

I am obviously biased, but I will make a judgment here. Cultures that allow people to starve to death, that offer no hope for the future and offer mysteries and superstition to answer critical questions of science and survival are obsolete. They are failing. And their need to repress individual freedoms is the evidence. The individuals who come from these kinds of cultures are no less inclined to be resistant than the culture itself. Excellent examples of this phenomenon are the many failed governments on the planet today that have caused one of the greatest migrations and displacements in the history of humankind.[69]

The German culture works for the people in Germany. They have survived for centuries. The Mexican culture works for the people in Mexico. They too have survived for centuries. Of course, this is an oversimplification of how cultures work. In its essence, this is not very different from the way a cultural anthropologist or ethnographer would assess any culture.

When we get past our value judgments, we find that all cultures are to be assessed on their own terms and their ability to assist their members in coping effectively with the world around them. They are what they are, and it is important for us to understand them if we are to indeed

---

[69] I am not making a political argument here. I simply want the reader to see that culture effects the actions of the individual in powerful ways.

apprehend the worldviews of the people who are influenced by them.

Once again, our present-day concern with the *Islamic extremists* and their penchant for terrorist activities is an appropriate example. If we attempt to measure and compare their cultural values, through our own lenses, to those of western civilization, we will quickly conclude that western values are superior. But we are using our own measurement criteria to make that determination. If we allow them to do the same, i.e., use their measurement criteria for judging our cultural values they can justify our annihilation. In fact, in many instances, one culture can justify the subjugation of other cultures when using its own criteria to judge.[70] This is the essence of *ethnocentricity*[71], which can lead to *jingoism*[72] in its extremes. But even ethnocentricity needs a standard benchmark to be justified. Efficacy is an excellent place to start.

Reminder: There is no point of neutrality when observing cultures. In other words, no one can stand outside of his own cultural biases when attempting to understand another's culture. The professional coach's challenge is to understand the client's culture and ethnic background without judgment.

When attempting to understand common cultural effects, we cannot automatically assume that everyone from that culture has the same way of being. Cultures simply offer us a rough blueprint to examine for clues to understanding

---

[70] Western European cultures have a long history of "discovering" and subjugating other nations.

[71] Ethnocentrism is judging another culture solely by the values and standards of one's own culture

[72] Jingoism is an extreme patriotism, especially in the form of aggressive or warlike foreign policy.

an individual's self and social perceptions, which gives another dimension to the meaning of their interpretations.

Understanding other cultures allows us to see the repeating patterns that emerge in the individual stories of the people with whom we work.

Even though you cannot be neutral, as an observer of another's culture, you have a unique perspective. Because you do not share its values and logic, you are more able to see another's culture in comparison to your own. This is difficult to do when observing your own culture. Being in our own culture is much like being fish in water. We just don't see it because we swim in it. This is another reason for connections to people from other cultures. It is another way of helping us escape the blindness of our subjective experience by learning to see through another set of lenses.

Meaning is determined by culture.

How do cultures define meaning? If we again look to Wittgenstein for our answer, we would see that the meaning of language is the context within which we are using it.[73] He uses his famous "chess" example to explain his proposition. If a pawn is on the chessboard, we understand what it is and how it is to be used. If we take it off the chessboard, it loses its meaning. How do we understand the statement, *move the pawn two squares forward*? If there are no squares and no game, there is no basis for understanding that a piece of carved material represents a *pawn*. The game of chess constitutes meaning. You might argue that you can recognize a pawn when you see it even though it is out of

---

[73] This is an excellent example of language games as mentioned earlier in this book.

context—not being used in a game of chess. Of course, you can, and that ability depends on your pre-existing linguistic interpretations of a chess game and its components. If you had absolutely no knowledge of a chess game, you could not identify the carved object as a pawn. [lxi]

A humorous example of this phenomenon was well-depicted in a movie titled *"The Gods Must Be Crazy."* Somehow, a Coke bottle fell from an airplane into the possession of a primitive jungle tribe with no previous knowledge of modern civilization. The tribe's various speculations of the meaning of this innocuous Coke bottle were humorous to be sure, but wonderfully instructive on this very point. Culture gives context. Context gives meaning. For instance, it is like the pawn and the Coke bottle. Without a cultural context that is constitutive of meaning, we have no way of understanding others.

Caveat.

A caution here is that the use of cultural information should always be considered additive. In other words, it should only be used to add more to your understanding of the other person. If you use it as a shortcut to assess another, you are using it subtractively. In other words, you depend on it and subtract the individual's uniqueness out of the equation. If you use it subtractively, you will run the risk of distorting your grasp of their unique perspectives and lumping that person into the group. In other words, you can become the bigot we should all be careful not to be when working with cultures.

A final note on culture.

"It is easy to confirm a stereotype. It is more productive to confront one."[74]

---

[74] Although I cannot name the person who made this comment, I know that she was a Minister of Information for the Government of Syria. My efforts to find her name have been unsuccessful. Nonetheless, I cannot take credit for the statement.

Chapter 15 – Untangling Language

"Accuracy of language is one of the bulwarks of truth."

Anna Jameson

Ludwig Wittgenstein and Bertrand Russell[75] agreed that "our language often fails us" when we are faced with complex human problems. They proposed that our language reflects our logic, but our logic doesn't always reflect the affairs of the world. And how well we all know the times when we have had disagreements with others on this very basis. It's evident to the reader that many of our world problems are due to our respective commitments to our own and very different systems of logic. In addition to the differences of the spoken word, it can be argued that the lack of a common logic compounds our efforts to reach agreements and understandings with people from other cultures.

If anything, this problem is becoming more involved, even if we separate language that deals with facts—like objects and things—from language that deals with thoughts or ideology. And if we can't agree on objects, what chance do we have with *thoughts* and *ideology?*

---

[75] 3rd Earl Russell (1872–1970), British philosopher, mathematician, and social reformer; full name Bertrand Arthur William Russell. In Principia Mathematica (1910–13) he and A. N. Whitehead attempted to express all of mathematics in formal logic terms.

Logic is becoming more complicated.

The pre-Socratic philosophers searched for the truth in the physical world. And to some extent until recently, it seemed that language about the physical world could also be grounded with evidence that could be proved or disproved by objective reduction. But now, in the era of quantum physics, we can't use the logic of our language to describe the most fundamental functions of the universe. Recent discoveries make us keenly aware that the universe doesn't function according to our logic.

So, knowing this, we are also beginning to reach the limits of our language. The discovery that light is both a *particle* and *wave* and not either/or put a large crack in that dike.

The problem is that our language and logic is based on our *common sense*. And our common sense doesn't apply in situations that are not *common* to us. In other words, our logic and our language fail us when we are in situations where we have little or no experience. We don't need to experiment in quantum mechanics to understand this problem. It applies in situations where we are in different cultures, where people experience a completely different world. But how many of us can allow that our apparent *facts and evidence* may be insufficient to justify our point of view?

Can we always trust evidence?

Let's go back into our western history to the days of Copernicus and Galileo. The church had all the facts and evidence that they needed to know beyond a doubt that the earth was the center of the universe. One only needed to make a simple observation of the heavens to prove the point.

The sun, moon, and stars revolved around the earth. Anyone could see this *fact*. The church's system of logic was supported by the observable evidence provided by trained observers, who were of course trained by the church.

But Copernicus and Galileo were different and more skilled observers. They discovered a new *truth* and shifted us into a different system of logic. Their *truth* was then enhanced by Newton, and even his *truth* is now incomplete as we begin to understand our universe more accurately. We are becoming increasingly more effective observers. In fact, we are beginning to see that the universe is indeed an incomprehensibly complex place where the act of observation can create the phenomenon that we observe.

The limits seem to be in our logic and not the world around us.

So, do we create the world with our language? Isn't the language of our ideas the basis for our observations? And aren't we now finding that the facts we discover vary with the experiment we design? If our language is so powerful as to create the ideas that generate the experiments that alter our experience of the physical universe, how powerful is it in shaping the social systems that we live in day to day? "We repeatedly create symbolic systems of meaning, i.e., religions, political ideologies, scientific theories and then forget that they are our creations; we have a devilish habit of confusing them with the mysterious nonhuman reality that they were meant to explain."[lxii]

These symbolic systems of meaning become the social structures that guide our interactions with others. These interactions are constituted by our social commitments, i.e., those behaviors we commit to and perform in interactions with others. We create these social commitments through linguistic acts, which hopefully produce coordinated action. Tangled linguistic acts cause tangled and therefore ambiguous social commitments. Tangled and ambiguous social commitments create chaos, a kind of confused sense of reality. Chaos is a breakdown in the transparency[lxiii] of living. So, the process of enhancing our connections at the nexus between our personal experience and that of others is one of untangling the language acts (and games) that create our breakdowns in life.

Using "untangled" language.

Being that language is as powerful as it is, how do we use it healthily to enhance our connections with others? To this end, our language goals should be threefold:

(1) To have a sincere respect for our linguistic acts and their power to create reality because it is within this reality that we live and interact with others.

(2) To ground and validate our assertions and assessments [both public and private] with evidence to assure that they are as accurate as possible within the common meanings of our community.

(3) To keep fully aware of our intentions and assure synonymy between our intentions and our speaking.

Our overarching goal is to create quality interactions with others who we depend on to enrich our subjective limitations.

The immorality of intentional tangled language.

Today, it's an accepted moral principle that it's wrong to lie. A religious authority would say our morality came from divine revelation in one form or another; for instance, the ten commandments. I won't try to confirm or deny this belief in this book. But I do believe that our ancestors knew how lies as a form of tangled language had the power to cause human suffering. That truth didn't need to be revealed in holy texts. They had a keen ability to discern the damage that could be done by the spoken word. I believe the wisdom of their common experiences formed the teachings that have evolved into the moral principles that we adhere to today. These moral standards represented the social practices that were most effective in keeping their communities alive and well.

Tangling in the present.

One need not look further than the business organization to see the chaos that can be caused by tangled language. American corporate history abounds with examples of these kinds of distortions. It is clear when one enters such an organization that reality can change. In fact, one could think of most organizations as having simulated realities that are shaped to be consistent with the accomplishment of a perceived corporate vision. In some instances, their efforts are effective. In others, they are the cause of so much socialized behavior that the individual can lose touch with their authentic self.

The benchmark of any high-performing company is a vision that is commonly understood, a culture that is consistent with the achievement of the vision and people who share both. When the strategy, processes, and structure to achieve it support this, the company has the potential to be a tough competitor and a very successful enterprise. But in many companies, the vision of top management is not owned, shared, or even understood by the people who execute the work. But it doesn't end there. The pressure of conforming to the myths surrounding a *misunderstood* vision creates a *cognitive imperative* that shapes interpretation and permeates the entire organization. This, coupled with communications constrained and distorted by authority, can leave the management team disconnected and alone in its efforts to achieve high performance. In many organizations, no one will dare to offer a different interpretation for fear of the consequences.

Corporate accounting games are now legend. To get a close look, one need only experience one round of budgeting in most companies to find out how distorted reality can become with sales forecasts that are created to meet the dictates of predetermined formulaic annual increases in revenue. Then there are the performance appraisals designed to mirror a normal distribution curve that force a manager to distort reports to match an imaginary bell-shaped curve; forced reductions in expenses that have no relationship to the reality of running the day to day business; distorted activity reports that show conformance to objectives with no substantive activities to support them; and of course, most recently the practice of *off-balance-sheet* accounting that allows management to construct a public picture of a healthy company with continually improved earnings that support inflated stock evaluations and reward those key executives who have stock options that pay rich rewards.

Eventually, everyone becomes a part of a subconscious conspiracy to reinforce the illusion that the company is performing as it should. Most companies can keep from exposing these practices to the public. But the problem can explode when the external community gets a look at this internal hallucination. The market doesn't share the company's illusion and its problems go public.

Companies go out of business because they have lost their connections to external reality.

Remember, "Our language mirrors our logic, but sometimes our logic doesn't mirror the facts."[lxiv] And the most compelling reason to get our language matched up to the facts is that only then can we make progress to correct the real problems that we create. But this can be very dangerous for the individual who takes on the task. In fact, occasionally we read of an executive committing professional suicide rather than face the challenges of cleaning up the mess they contributed to making.

Case in point.

A consumer finance organization in my experience comes to mind. This organization's illusion had been so well formed by a powerful previous CEO that it remained for many years after he had retired. The theme of this illusion was "punishment and rewards" based on nothing but "the numbers." The operations executives had incorporated his views of "how a company should be run" into their style so completely that they could not question their assumptions even though they knew that they didn't seem to be working anymore. Instead, they distorted the facts (numbers) that were being reported daily.

To make it worse, anyone who took the chance of reporting real performance was made to feel like a "loser" in their jargon and punished.[76] So, in this way, the operating management had created a coherent and reinforcing system

---

[76] One example of this management method, was a banquet where those managers who met the numbers we served steaks and those that didn't were served hamburgers.

of logic that distorted the very facts that they needed to make the required improvements.

The pressures on the field management were so great that they had developed methods for restructuring uncollectable loans to create the impression that the company's portfolio was of better quality than it was. They loaned more money to non-payers and reclassified these loans resulting in a reduction in *delinquencies,* which were a significant measurement of successful performance at the field level. So, borrowers who didn't make payments on their loans were loaned more money even though they had a history of non-payment.

Three presidents went through that company in four years. Each one found the problem and each one charged-off millions of dollars. At the end of this four-year period, the parent organization decided that the portfolio was too far-gone to manage and sold it for pennies on the dollar to other financial institutions. They had decided to go out of this business completely. Ironically, the new owners of the portfolio hired the managers who had created this situation. I have wondered many times about what kind of impact they have had on their new organization.

The essence of organizations.

The essence of an organization is a complex blend of ongoing conversations made up of innumerable language acts performed by its people. These language acts, when unconstrained, can open the possibilities that some companies never enjoy because of the mythology that "those in authority know best." At some point, the talented and loyal individual can become a drone who simply repeats the party line to preserve his or her perceived and illusory security.

Finally, the company's performance suffers and in too many instances, those in authority move on to repeat their errors in other organizations because they lived in the cognitive blindness of their own subjective experience. They used their authority to prohibit contact with the objective realities of their previous experiences.

Bertrand Russell was so right when he said that the main reason to untangle language is so that we can know the real facts, and only then can we make the needed corrections.

Clients who are now in or have recently come from these organizations can be some of the most difficult to develop authentic relationships with because they don't have authentic relationships with themselves.

As most organizational change agents know, the introduction of a new and different conversation can often make significant improvements in a company. And, as often, can get you fired. I remember a friend who said family therapy is a confusing area of change work. The troubled family comes into therapy and says, "We are in pain, so please help us get better but don't ask us to do anything different." What they are saying is we know our world is a painful place to be, but it is the one we know and to change it would be too scary. So, make the pain go away but don't ask us to change. The people in Alcoholics Anonymous have a wonderful saying. It goes like this, "Insanity is doing the same things and expecting different results."

Organizational change work is very similar. Organizational resistance has been described as a form of *dynamic conservatism*, and it applies to the individual client as well. We might liken this to the way any complex system works to keep itself in balance. That is, the corporate system works dynamically to conserve the way it sees itself and the world within which it lives. This conservation is held in place by constrained and distorted communications that are delicately balanced to maintain stasis. Another way of saying this is that people can disagree with the prevailing point of view if they do it in an agreeable way. In other words, communications are constrained and distorted by what is and is not acceptable, which is of course based on the organization's illusions. This will be true with clients as well. Their internal ecology is well balanced to maintain stasis. When the breakdown does occur, i.e., stasis is disturbed, the coachable moment is yours.

Sol Alinsky, the social change activist, believed that social change must be "disruptive"[77] because when it becomes normalized, it loses its potency to make any difference. When the new idea is accepted and owned by the authorities in charge, it becomes a part of the status quo and loses its power. The same is true when coaching a client. Something, an event, a crisis, a painfully unfulfilled need, must be disruptive for a client to be emotionally available for effective coaching to happen.

So how do we create that disruption in our clients? "Unconstrained and undistorted communications have the power to find the best possible answers."[lxv] But I have seen no organizations and very few people who can allow *disruption* in the form of unconstrained and undistorted communications. Until the communications match the facts, the same mistakes will be made repeatedly. In most cases, the messenger who brings bad news is beheaded. We haven't made much progress since the Dark Ages in some areas of life.

The Birkman Method® has proven to me that a client's disruption can be seen with a level of accuracy that is simply never disputed. The power of this method to show the client the exact areas where focused attention can bring

---

[77] Disruptive in its ability to challenge and shake up the status quo.

about a new level of satisfaction and contentment is unparalleled. And that accuracy also offers us a clear focus for untangling the language that causes the ineffectiveness that brings our clients to us for relief.

Clarifying the use of language.

The proper use of language is at the root of every effective human action. And, of course, with ineffectiveness, the opposite is true. People create themselves and the world they live in. They themselves produce their realities in interactions with others through their language. So, the first step of re-owning the generative power of language starts with awareness; how we speak, what impact our language has on us and those around us; exactly how we create our connections and disconnection's in life through untangled and tangled language respectively. Only then can we change how we "language" to create a more effective life for ourselves and those around us.

Easy to describe. Much more difficult to do. Wittgenstein said, "We don't need new information. We have what we need.[lxvi] "Statements are, or purport to be, records of facts and by inappropriately interpreting language, we create for ourselves pseudo-problems, and to avoid confusion, we should make statements into a form for which their true function that of picturing facts would be revealed more clearly and readily than ordinary language."[lxvii] So it holds if we are to develop new and more effective ways of relating, we must start with an examination of the assertions and assessments that we make about our world and ourselves. The odds are excellent that when breakdowns happen, the causes are found in the mishandling of assertions and assessments resulting in a problematic declaration.

Remember, breakdown, in this context means, "breakdown in the transparency of living." Your subconscious decision processing is not giving you the answers you need, so your conscious mind is called into action. In other words, something is not working in the areas of our life where things become apparent that most of the time are transparent to us. E.g., the computer software that stops responding. Until that moment, you were not aware of software. It was transparent to you like the declaration that works until it doesn't.

Also keep in mind here, these declarations result in needs that are the adult version of childhood expectations. And as a child, we did an enormous amount of heuristic assessing how the world was, based on our childlike cognitive incompetence. As an adult, we're more prone to treat these assessments as though they are assertions, which is indistinguishable from declaring "this is how the world is." Or in Birkman terms, "this is how I need the world to be." We were damned powerful as children and didn't know it.

Re-claim the power.

A significant step in re-owning the generative power of language starts with this focus; how we speak, what impact our language has on us and those around us as identified by our Needs. The power of these language acts, assertions, and assessments, to create our reality applies to both our private and our public conversations. Even if you don't believe that language creates the objective world it is difficult to deny that it creates the world of interpretations within which our *human beingness* exists. Repeating for emphasis, Needs are more reflective of how we would like our ideal world to be rather than how it might be.

Keep in mind as you read what follows, the central reason for stress is the Need is not being satisfied. The Need comes from our childhood experiences and expectations that were shaped by innocent childhood assessments. Those assessments became expectations in adulthood. And the whole process happens in language.

Origins.

We have known about assertions and assessments for a long time. Early in this book, we saw that out of the speculations of the early Milesian's [500-400 BCE] arose a series of questions that one philosopher addressed. Parmenides of Elea believed that true knowledge rests on nature and is apprehended by speculative reason. [We might call this the origin of an assertion.] He also said that mere opinion is influenced by customs and is perceived by the senses. [We might call this the origin of an assessment.] So, I like to think that this Greek philosopher gave us a clear distinction for the differences between the objective and subjective aspects of our language[lxviii] and a clue to addressing some of our clients' dilemmas.

In getting a real sense of the power of assertions and assessments, we need to understand how we can confuse our subjective assessment [opinions] with an objective assertion [facts] and subsequently create the illusion of what we are talking about, even if it has no basis. And as Dr. Birkman pointed out, these illusions have as much power on our personality as the facts.

As already noted, assertions and assessments are two speech acts, that when confused, can cause a good deal of difficulty in our lives. So, if we can learn the difference and apply them correctly, we can take a step toward grounding our ideal world in the reality of our shared experience. But the task is more difficult than it seems. For instance, our ability to ground a claim with facts about the physical would qualify it as an assertion. As an example, I make the assertion that "I am five feet ten inches tall." I can certainly pull out the tape measure and have some objective party measure my height. But this is sufficient grounding in our culture and may not be in other cultures.

For the sake of our discussion, we will add the qualification that we are speaking of ontological relativity. This means that we recognize the difference between and among different ontological theories of what it means to be. Even in groupings as small as families and among siblings, we know ontologies differ. There is no avoiding the fact that each of us lives within a personal web of beliefs that we weave together based on our continuous interactions with the world around us. Fortunately, the boundary between our web of beliefs and the external world is a permeable one. So, in instances when we have an anomalous experience, we can decide to reconstitute a belief.

In many instances though, we refuse to allow the anomalous experience to change our belief and we continue to act as though the world is the way we perceive it to be. In this case, we remain in a state of subjective blindness building neurotic compensations so we can continue to believe our version of reality. Enough of this and we can add a layer of cynicism that will act as a kind of scar tissue that diminishes the effects of external perturbations (input from the outside) such that we don't even feel them when they happen.

Regarding assertions and assessments, it seems to me that their difference is not as important as the intention of their use. If we treat both as though we are only speaking for our limited view of the world, we are automatically going to keep ourselves out of trouble. Who can discount me if I start all my declarative statements with "in my opinion" or "I think" or "according to how I see things"; allowing others to have equally valid opinions or views of the world?

Is this postmodern relativism? Maybe so! But to this date, I don't know how to be an effective human being in a diverse world but to be ready to accept and learn from those whom I meet from different cultural backgrounds.

It remains my responsibility to treat my language with significant respect for it has the power to affect my life and the lives of others. In fact, it has created the world I live in and how I see myself in that world. And it is equally important to accept the other person's point of view as a valid perspective. The real key to the dilemma between assertions and assessments seems to be in producing mutually beneficial outcomes.

The most important practice is to become aware of what you are about to say before you open your mouth because language not only describes but also creates. Know [and admit to yourself] your intention before you speak. If you don't you might create a world you don't intend.

Observation.

We sometimes propose, "look for yourself," as though others will observe the very same objective attributes or characteristics that we see. But we must respect the fact that *ontological relativity* means that there are many different points of view, and so far, no one has identified any one as being from "God's eye," despite the numerous religions that influence our discourse with their *truth* and over two thousand years of philosophical inquiry.

So, no matter how we may disagree with another person, we must allow space for the fact that disagreement comes from our interpretations, which are biased at best and impoverished at worst.

Korzybski, the father of General Semantics, who in his variously revised lifetime book, *Science and Sanity,*[lxix] told us his reason for much human suffering, and not so surprisingly, it is a certain kind of *built-in* insanity in our language. This coupled with a disregard for the power of what we say and a general lack of respect for what and how we speak and especially its lack of grounding can be devastating. This is especially so when we communicate across cultural boundaries.

Today, we are engaged in tangled discussions with many countries. Our conversations in the Mideast being contaminated with assertions and assessments have so far only made the situation more complex. Yet all the parties to these unfortunate circumstances argue for their assessments as though they were assertions supported by undeniable facts and hold to their linguistic interpretations at the risk of millions of innocent lives.

The importance of synonymy.

Lack of synonymy between the real and apparent intentions of the speaker creates tangled language. When a person is more committed to getting social acceptance from others than he is to use his language with integrity, entanglements are sure to follow. This is a good example of the power of tangled language to create chaos in the process of portraying the *social self.*

There are many instances when people use language to create a private outcome that is different from public appearances. One of the most recognizable forms is "the nice person." The intention of the "nice person" is usually related to our "need for social acceptance." But this public behavior, which is designed to achieve acceptance can mislead and distort. This tangling of language, coupled with its power to generate reality is powerful. The "nice person" probably doesn't try to harm anyone but in many cases creates circumstances that are painful for others anyway. "The nice person" problem doesn't happen in a vacuum. Usually there are social circumstances that set up the conditions.

Case in point.

The following is a case that happened in a business situation, which is one of the more powerful conditions that influence us to act in a socially acceptable way. A consultant friend was hired to work on a project. The client had changed the entire scope of the project on three separate occasions during a four-month period. Each time the consultant informed the sales representative that the changes were not covered in his original contract. Each time he was told to "simply give the client what he wanted." Because the consultant was working on a time-plus materials basis, he worried about his charges becoming more than the client was going to pay for the entire project. He was attempting to avoid a problem later when the total costs would be compared to the quoted price to determine if the project had been profitable. He was certain that he would be asked to justify the fact that he had overrun the budget without formal approvals.

When the fourth change came, he confronted the sales representative and asked why he was not getting change orders and price increases for the additional work. This simple act would have recorded the client's responsibility for these overruns. It became evident that the sales rep needed to sustain his image of *being a nice guy.* When pressed for formal approvals that were documented by amendments to the contract, the sales rep refused to confront the client because the client was very insistent that the work be done for the original price and the sales rep didn't want to upset him. The reason was clear. The client was a social friend of the sales rep's manager.

The sales representative had gained and maintained the client's acceptance and was not going to jeopardize his status. Because of this, the consultant had become the *obstruction*. When a senior executive called to question why he was being such an obstacle for the sales rep and the client, the conversation ended in my friend's resignation. Finally, the situation had become so chaotic that he could not, in clear conscience, continue in his role.

Upon later review of his conversations with the sales representative, there was little doubt in the consultant's mind that his interactions with the client were very different from those had by the sales rep. The sales person's actions were designed to gain and keep the client's acceptance. The consultant's actions were designed to reflect the facts. Who was right? The consultant was no longer employed on the project. The sales representative remained on the project and a *nice guy* in the mind of the client. [Remember that *corroboration* and *connection* are more important than *accuracy* in some language games.]

Biologically, we are primates.

Human beings are linguistic beings. Who we are as individual human beings emerges from language. Our private, as well as our public images, are made up of language. Our self-image or identity is a coherent weave of interpretations of our life experiences. It's our story; our narrative. If that story is to remain coherent and if we want to continue to be effective, we need to guard against tangling, and respect our ability to untangle our lives with language.

Chapter 16 -- Modifying Perceptions and Interpretations

It doesn't work to leap a twenty-foot chasm in two ten-foot jumps.

American Proverb

Let's start this chapter with Nathan, a senior scientist in a Biotech Company. The human resources manager had referred him to me. He was a brilliant researcher with an excellent record of accomplishments in his area of science. But when it came to manage his team, he was having problems. The rapid turnover in his group was an obvious symptom of a breakdown of some sort or another. We used The Birkman Method® assessment and began the process of reflection and inquiry.

As I expected, the report coincided with the complaints that brought him to see "the coach." Given the presenting problem, his *Social Energy* scores were of particular interest. The anecdotal data suggested that he was very impatient with others in his group. The following diagram shows the details as they related to his behavioral construct for Social Energy.

From Nathan's Profile

Behavioral construct	Linguistic construct	Declarative Acts	Performa-tive Acts
Unique orientation in an interaction	*Interpretati on of the interaction* *(Usual Behavior)*	*The world is . . .* *I am . . .* *I will be . . .* *(Needs)*	*If so, I will R, O and P in this way . . .* *(Stress Behavior)*
Social energy - relating to others in groups	Generally pleasant and outgoing. Demons-trates a warm and accepting attitude toward others in social situations.	The world is full of people who would waste my time. I don't have time for them. I need to spend a consider-able amount of time alone or in the company of one or two significant individuals.	If I don't get what I need, I will become withdrawn; I will ignore groups and become impatient with others.

As the reader can see, when Nathan became overloaded with stimulus from the people in his group, his performative language acts flowed from the stress he was feeling from that situation. But it was his declarative acts that set up the world within which he lived and responded.

Our work together focused on reviewing his need for time to be alone. During our work, we began to uncover the assertions and assessments upon which he had based his declarations about the world. When it became clear to him that his view of the world was undoubtedly valid but not the only view, he began to question his assertions and reshape his assessments. This work ended with Nathan's ability to make new declarations that then influenced his performative language acts such that his turnover problems began to improve. Of course, we worked on a whole range of his assertions and assessments that supported this primary script. Remember, we need to see the entire rule-set, as it exists in both the present and the past.

Another case in point.

I was asked to work with a man whom we will call Edward. Edward was the compliance officer and comptroller in a government subcontracting company. His role as comptroller was enough to "agitate him," but his added role of compliance officer gave him an official platform to confront people in the interests of complying with the many government regulations with which these firms must conform. It seems that Edward's problem was that he became aggressive and defensive on too many occasions. His manager called it "becoming exercised" in public forums. This was not appropriate behavior for an officer in this company.

I was very interested in seeing Edward's Assertiveness scores on the Birkman feedback report. The following is what I found:

From Edward's Profile

Behavioral construct	Linguistic construct	Declarative Acts	Performa-tive Acts
Unique orientation in an interaction	*Interpretation of the interaction*	*The world is . . . I am . . . I will be . . .*	*If so, I will R, O and P in this way . . .*
Assertive-ness - directing and controlling.	Tendency to speak up and express opinions openly	The world is a place where you must speak up forcefully to be heard. I will do that when necessary.	If my superiors do not approach me in a pleasant and diplomatic way I will become tense and appear to be aggressive and defensive.

Although this finding was revealing, I found another score that was also helpful. Edward's Self-consciousness score was relevant to understanding his presenting problem. Take a look.

Edward's Profile

Behavioral construct	Linguistic construct	Declarative Acts	Performative Acts
Unique orientation in an interaction	*Interpretation of the interaction*	*The world is . . . I am . . . I will be . . .*	*If so I will R, O & P in this way . . .*
Self-conscious-ness - Sensitivity in relating to individuals.	Use of sensitivity when relating to others.	The world is tough. I'm up to the challenge. I prefer to be direct and straight-forward and base relationships on common interests and activities rather than feelings of general warmth.	If I'm not treated sensitively, I will become defensive and aggressive.

So, when Edward interacted with others, he was very direct and straightforward. They thought that's the way he wanted to be treated and complied. He responded with defensiveness and became aggressive toward them. He didn't get what he wanted, and others felt the effects of his being "exercised."

Edward couldn't or didn't want to make the changes needed to feel better in his job. There were several other personality constructs that kept him acting the way he did, and they were not easily changed, if at all. So, the outcome in this case was a job and career change. He was low on the Extroversion scale which made input from the outside less effective. He needed to be in a situation that was more amenable to his worldview. I spoke to him several months later and he was much happier in his new job and company.

An important reminder.

The fundamental philosophy of The Birkman Method® is there is no ideal style. Each of us needs to create or find the kind of world we enjoy living in and ultimately will be better able to contribute because we have our strengths available to us. Too many people won't face this fact and persevere in situations where they use all their energy managing stress. Edward was able to see this and made a change to have a better life with more possibility for him and his family.

The change process.

There is no magic to the process of assisting others to find their authentic self. Going back to my original proposition, we need each other's perceptions to use as benchmarks to compare and possibly reshape our subjective experience. Without others' perspectives, we are locked into our cognitive blindness and may be doomed to stay there. With the assistance of other caring people, we can borrow their perspective and add it to our own. Another way of saying this is we may become different observers of the same reality. This process adds richness to our mental models and maps such that we have new options that we couldn't see before.

In the case of Nathan, he was limited to his interpretations of the world as a place where he needed to carve out space to be alone and couldn't see any other way of being. But with added perspective, he could question that assessment and make a different declaration for differentiated situations. He will probably always enjoy his private time, but he knows what he needs now and doesn't respond from habit. He is now aware of his declarations, and with awareness, he can make choices.

With Edward, he became a different observer of his own current work life and decided that he would rather shift his world to be more to his liking. Once again, he was empowered with awareness and choice. In the past, he was a prisoner of acting out his ineffective behavior but didn't know what to do about it.

As frightening as choice can be, ultimately, we are empowered by it. In my forty plus years of experience in the field of change work, I found that those who can't or won't choose are the most ineffective people when it comes to managing life's inevitable changes. And we are all there at one point or another.

I can recall a visit to a counselor when I was in the decision process of changing careers. I said to her that I didn't think I had the skills to handle a career change. She said, "Maybe, you don't have the courage." She was right. I realized that skill was not the issue. I would eventually learn new skills. The obstacle was, I was afraid to choose because with that choice came consequences. And what if those consequences were not very pleasant? Who could I hold responsible? Me and no one else, just me.

Reframing experience is an example of becoming a different observer.

The term reframing refers to the process of modifying *our interpretations* of our experiences. This is done by shifting the meaning of the content or the context. For instance, if I say, "I need a light" in a cigar lounge, it means one thing but while sailing my boat at night, it means something entirely different. Same content, different context.

Another example is if I am sailing my boat and I say, "What is the number of that marker buoy on our port side?" It means the same thing as if I say, "What is the number of that can over on our left side?" Same context, different content.

Case in point.

As part of my professional training, I participated in several "T Groups." It was during one of these sessions that I was witness to a wonderful example of reframing. Another participant was working with the group leader and was discussing an incident when he had seriously considered suicide and decided against it. This had happened at a time when he had been ill for several weeks, his recent career change didn't seem to be working, and his marriage was on the rocks. He had returned from a visit to his doctor and pulled into the garage. It was a cold winter day, and as the garage door closed behind him he thought of just sitting there with the engine running until he was dead, and his problems were over.

His interpretation of this incident was troubling him a great deal. The group leader asked him to consider that this may have been the first time that he had decided to live. The leader went on to point out that he hadn't asked to be born and reported no other instances when he had faced the choice to live or die. In this instance, when faced with the choice of living or dying, he had chosen life. At once this man's interpretation of that event was changed or reframed. So, in its simplest form, reframing is the process of changing the meaning of a previous experience. When it is done effectively, one can feel an actual shift in his emotional response to a memory.

A patient often comes to therapy with "emotional issues" that are acting as barriers to his feeling of well-being. Sometimes these "issues" are related to his interpretations and feelings about previous experiences. The therapist can stimulate other interpretations for the patient's consideration. And in this way a connection can be made, resulting in a reframing of the troubling interpretation. This kind of intervention can be as passive as classical Freudian analysis[78] or as directive as the late Virginia Satir's psychodynamics.[79] In either case, the result is a reframe of an existing experience.

To effectively assist by reframing, one needs to understand that all behavior, when seen from the point of view of the person performing it, makes sense. In this way our behavior is always attempting to help, to support us in the maintenance of our point of view. But remember that our

---

[78] The analyst listens while offering few responses and allows the analysand to discover and cure his issues through talking.

[79] Virginia Satir developed a series of directed processes that offered the client ways of dealing with his issues through structured therapeutic activities.

point of view may be the cause of our difficulties. In Nathan's case, he could reframe a particular aspect of his point of view and become more effective in his circumstances. In Edward's case, he chose to maintain his point of view and seek other conditions that would be more consistent with it.

Learning for keeps.

It is curious that most of the managers I know miss the opportunity to reframe another person's experience of a situation. For instance, the late Chris Argyris, well-known professor, author, and organizational theorist, "distinguished between two kinds of organizational learning. Single-loop, the most basic, asks questions about objective facts and is one-dimensional. It focuses on changing tasks and organizational routines. Double-loop learning is longer lasting. It asks questions about the reasons and motives behind the fact. It changes the underlying values and leads to a new framework for learning and to new routines.

Argyris proposed that the only way to have effective, lasting change is at this deeper, personal level. Individuals need to be skilled in productive reasoning and be willing to reset their assumptions and declarations, and in this way, they *frame reality*.[80] Productive reasoning means that people make their premises known and their inferences clear and explicit. Their conclusions are testable by logic other than their own."[lxx]

As Birkman coaches, we can be midwives at the birth of our clients' awareness of their assertions and assessments. And with this new awareness, an ability to test the logic of their decision processes.

---

[80] Emphasis added

Framing and reframing reality is accomplished by sharing more rather than less information about the background for the decisions our clients make. This simple fact can elude them until we make this information available with The Birkman Method® reports.

In my experience, it appears many managers have invested more in conserving formal power and maintaining structural authority than in producing results through others. This seems to be a uniquely Western theme in the art of management. One only needs to read the early experiences of W. Edwards Deming to see this process in action. In the early '50s, he was summarily dismissed by the American auto industry when he attempted to convince management that the people who did the work had something more to add than just their physical effort. He went to Japan and turned their industries around with his approach to statistical process controls that required the active participation of the workers' minds too. It's ironic that one of the most prestigious productivity awards a company can achieve in Japan is named the Deming Prize[81], after an American.

In summary, when we are left to our own subjective experiences to guide our perceptions, we will access past scripts and rules that are similar to the current situation. In

---

[81] The Deming Prize is one of the highest awards on TQM (Total Quality Management) in the world that recognizes both individuals for their contributions to the field of Total Quality Management and businesses that have successfully implemented it. [1] It was established in 1951 to honor W. Edwards Deming who contributed greatly to Japan's proliferation of statistical quality control after World War II. His teachings helped Japan build its foundation by which the level of Japan's product quality has been recognized as the highest in the world, was originally designed to reward Japanese companies for major advances in quality improvement.

most cases, this works well. But in some instances [breakdowns], we need the opportunity and assistance to modify our perceptions. Good coaches provide that safe space.

The External Environment and Our Reality.

Is the objective world the same as our reality? If you answered yes to this question, you have some more work to do. One of the more telling experiments that explain this issue was done by Humberto Maturana and described in his book, *The Tree of Knowledge.*[lxxi]

He surgically rearranged the eye of a frog so that it was upside down. When the frog was then tempted with an insect for lunch it sent its tongue out to the exact opposite space from where the insect was, but the insect wasn't there. The frog was simply responding to external stimulus, you might say. But it responded to it in the wrong place. The external stimulus produced the perturbation to the frog's central nervous system correctly. But the interpretation of the response was dictated by the frog's rearranged optic nerve. In other words, the frog's subjective experience was different from its external reality.

Humans are not very different from this frog except that we are constantly rearranging our CNS to reinforce our subjective experience and very often missing the *meals* that our external surroundings offer us. In other words, we go to the wrong place to get what we want because according to our CNS, that's where it should be. But very often, that's not where our external environment [the world] is serving it up.

It's not very likely that we will have our CNS surgically rearranged, but a closer look suggests that our structure gives us much more flexibility. We have both the advantage and disadvantage of being *re-structured* through conversations.

It's a disadvantage because the lenses of our interpretation distort the incoming information so that it fits within our existing structure. For instance, we know the outside visual stimuli we receive at any moment is augmented with six times more information coming back from our visual cortex. In other words, for every bit of new information, there are another six bits of old information from previous experiences.

Even so, with focused effort, we can modify our maps to create new experiences and interpretations. But we can't do this alone. We need to have contact with others whose subjective experiences are different from ours.

Breaking away from our previous experience.

Can you recall an instance when your interpretations of an event changed over time? As an example, maybe you were distraught over a job you lost. Eventually, you found one in another company with better pay and benefits. There was a subsequent shift in how you interpreted the job loss event that had caused you so much pain in the past. The loss is still an event in your past, but your internal experience of it has changed. So, is your external environment the same as your experience of reality? Not anymore.

As Maturana and Varela claimed, we cannot experience external reality as it is. It is only through the idiosyncratic biological responses of our unique CNS and the filters of our trusted linguistic interpretations that we stay in touch with our external environment and others in it. Another way of saying this is "The map is not the territory," reminding us that the map is an impression upon our internal neurolinguistic structures and the territory is the external world.

So, the external world is rich with possibilities. Our limitations are those that are contained in the linguistic interpretations that we make of the sensations that derive from perturbations to our CNS. Raw sensations need linguistic interpretations to make sense and those interpretations are always based on past experiences. And those past experiences are always based on previous linguistic interpretations. Many of those interpretations come from our childhood experiences. You should be seeing the circularity by now.

The value of our unique interpretations.

Consider this. Although we are limited to our subjective experience, it is unique. It is the only version that has ever been, is now or will ever exist in the history of the universe.

So, our limited experiences can also become our contribution to others. But to fully realize this effect, we must make the authentic connections between our experiences and that of others.

If we are bound up in the certitude of our subjective interpretations, holding that we see the way it *really is*, we rob ourselves and others of a gift that only we can give. That gift is our personal point of view. And we subsequently rob ourselves of the richness of the gifts that others can give us and ultimately the richness of the world within which we live.

A previous professor I knew once told us the story of *the clearing*.[82] In his story, he described a clearing in the forest. The night was dark, and an approaching storm was accompanied by lightning. As the storm got closer, it became apparent that the clearing within which we were standing was rich with detail, but those details could not be seen because it was too dark. Each time the lightning flashed, we could momentarily see the intricacies of our surroundings. Each lightning strike revealed another view of the details. Then darkness. Then lightning. Then darkness again.

A metaphor for life.

We need each other's perspective to have any chance of seeing other details in the forest. Each one of us is a momentary flash of lightning illuminating a perspective on a socially constructed reality. We all need each other's help to see more. Would we argue with the lightning as it lights up another view of the forest? Probably not. But, we humans seem to be inclined to deny and argue with another if their point of view is different from ours. As described in a previous chapter, we often become so convinced that our data is the real data that there is no reasoning beyond that point.

So, if we are faced with a situation where the person we are attempting to assist will not allow another's point of view as valid, how do we help? I have had some success in moving from arguing the validity of the other person's "facts" to the challenge of helping them reassess the meanings related to their "objective data" with the following approach.

---

[82] Personal Notes: Lecture by Rafael Echeverria, Ph.D. 1996

Robert T. De Filippis

Reinterpreting experiences—changing what the data means.

When we read a newspaper, most of us know the difference between a news article and an editorial. The news item is supposed to give us the facts about an event that is deemed newsworthy, who, what, where, when and how. One might argue that even in the best newspapers, it is difficult to find an objective story, but most reasonable people will recognize this distinction.

Then if we want another person's opinion or interpretation of that event, we go to the editorial page. So most good newspapers know that facts *[data]* and interpretations *[meanings]* belong in different places. In this way, they attempt to convince their readers that they are unbiased reporters of the news. Once again, one can argue that there is no such thing as totally unbiased reporting of the news, but it is certainly much easier to recognize than the *reporting* we do to ourselves about the events that happen to us.

Events are just events just as facts in a news story are just facts. They have no meaning without a system of evaluation that is being assessed by an observer. For example, I might read a news item about the discovery of some exotic new plant species. In this story, the facts and data might show that this plant species is related to another but that it is somehow different in a way that botanists are now questioning the boundaries of the previously defined species. This is an interesting news story to me. But its significance is lost on me. Not being a botanist, I cannot truly interpret these facts with the same meaning that a botanist would. To be sure, there would be different meanings made of this story by different readers. So, the story has no essential meaning. It is just an accumulation of facts and data about an event. The meaning comes from the different readers—people.

Does this mean that the universe is indifferent? Are the events that happen all around us void of any value one way or the other? I cannot answer that question with certainty, but from my experience, I have come to believe that this is true. We seem to be the only ones that put the meaning into what happens here. So, it is our interpretations that surround the events that determine what they mean to us. The event itself does not have a meaning of its own.

During my time in the Outplacement and Career Transition business, it became clear to me that we can interpret an event like losing a job as a catastrophe or a blessing. In and of itself, it seems to have no objective meaning.

Personalizing events.

Of course, events don't happen in a vacuum but are they really happening to us or are we simply the observers taking ownership for them and then putting our spin into the interpretation? For example, this book is dedicated to my sister who died at 29 years of age in 1971. It is still difficult to say today that it was just an event. But it was. People die, and that's life. There is no right or better time than another. These are all our interpretations.

My parents could not incorporate this experience into their lives and went to their graves with the belief that God had failed them. It was their interpretation. And I don't mean to diminish the power of the event or its enormity in our lives. But there were many others around us who saw it as unfortunate and untimely but were relatively unaffected.

America is at war with terrorists. And that war includes the conflict of interpretations. How could we observe the events of the disasters on September 11, 2001, without interpreting them as horrendous? Yet, there were people in certain other countries that celebrated in the streets upon learning of our misfortune. Could these acts of terrorism be interpreted in different ways? The answer is yes, of course. To the average American, they were sneak attacks carried out by fanatics on the lunatic fringe. To their compatriots, these acts were courageous displays of faith and martyrdom carried out for their God.

Why is this distinction between events and interpretations so important to us as we go through changes in our lives? Because ever-changing events are out of our control and they will keep coming. But our interpretations are within our control, and we can have some influence on how those events affect us. To quote an anonymous contributor, "When sailing, you can't control the wind, but you can adjust the sails."

But do not be misled with the ease with which I make the statement. Changing interpretations is not easy and the coach who chooses to help is in for a tough time. But with commitment and diligent effort, it is possible. So how does one proceed to reinterpret events? Here's an exercise that worked for me:

Separating facts from interpretations.

Going back to the example of news and editorials, I recommend that coaches use this process personally first and then to assist their clients.

1) Write a story about a change event that has caused difficulty in your life. For instance, if it was a job loss or major financial setback, just write the story.

252

Don't worry about the difference between facts and interpretation yet.

2) Read it and put it away for a few days. Then go back and reread it. Do this several times.

3) After the second or third reading, start a new story. This time write about the event as a news story. For instance, describe who, what, where, when and how. Leave out the interpretations about what it meant. These are your assessments.

4) Now write an editorial about the same event and let it rip. This is where you can give your interpretation of the *wherefores and now whats*.

5) Repeat the process until you begin to truly discern between the facts and your interpretations. The facts shouldn't change but the interpretations will begin to shift.

6) When you can do this, (step 5) keeping the facts the same, rewrite your editorial with different interpretations that you hadn't thought of before. Let your imagination go.

This is where you can create a whole new set of possibilities that you could not see before. Your interpretations are fungible, i.e., they are replaceable by others. They are in Victor Frankl's terms, "the last human freedom. The freedom to choose how you respond to whatever happens to you."

In my coaching work, I have used this exercise effectively to help others absorb, integrate, and move on from events that kept them "stuck" in the past. In all cases, they created new possibilities for themselves and most found a way out of the emotional paralysis that we all get into from time to time when faced with difficult events. So, although we hang on to our interpretations for dear life, they often hamper us. I cannot determine which help, and which hamper for anyone but myself. But I can assist a client to take ownership of his or her responses to the events in their lives.

In summary, we do have the power to change our reality to be more consistent with one that is much more productive for us. We can do it with a few simple exercises if we so desire. But always remember, the old is more comforting because its familiar. Even if it's a painful place to be, it is still familiar and somehow comforting. Our need for certainty is powerful.

Will we ever match our internal experience to external reality? If we are looking for certainty, I don't think we will find it this way. We might just have to settle for personal certitude and the assurances that come with it.

Chapter 17 -- The Affective Being

"Interpreted with the advantage of current hindsight, Spinoza's notion implies that the living organism is constructed so as to maintain the coherence of its structure and functions against numerous life-threatening odds."[lxxii]

Antonio Damasio

The focus of this book is how our cognitive processes work to create and sustain our experience of being human beings and how these very same processes can inhibit us in changing circumstances. Until this chapter, I have only presented cognitive theories of human experience. In this way, I attempted to give coaches another explanation for the unconscious processes that shape observable human behavior. It is my wish that this view will be useful in the process of helping us and others to manage in our complex and changing world.

No such attempt to explore the basis of human behavior can be complete without examining the *affective*[83] aspects of being human. Until recently, science has been slow to explain and connect something as private as emotions and feelings to cognition. Like our cognitive processes, our affective nature is the result of adaptations that have provided a survival advantage for our species. When we examine the exact nature of emotions, we find even the most primitive of living organisms have them. As

---

[83] The emotions, feelings and moods that are shaped by deeper appetites, desires, and motivations.

Damasio[84] points out, emotions are a most fundamental survival mechanism in all living things. Obviously, we share this phenomenon with all other living organisms. But we modern humans have evolved further in the last 150,000 years. We have another advantage that can become a disadvantage. We call them *"feelings."*

Feelings are intricately intertwined with language. Our decision-making processes are near useless without feelings. We depend on a subconscious "gut-level" feeling check to finalize our decisions. Without this mechanism, we would become paralyzed with details instead of able to proceed with decision-making.

Essential elements of affect.

Emotions, feelings, and moods are the essential ingredients for understanding ours and our clients' affective attributes. As most of us know, emotions are relatively easy to observe in a coaching situation. According to Damasio,[lxxiii] what we see are outward behavioral manifestations stimulated by *emotionally competent stimulus*[85] *or ECS*. What we don't see are the feelings that can evolve from the expressions of emotions and interpretive

---

[84]It was my good fortune to hear Dr. Antonio Damasio on NPR one day as he was being interviewed about his most recent book. Dr. Damasio's work is compelling. His findings are very consistent with my observations of people who have been my clients throughout my career as a practitioner. In simple terms, his work explains phenomena I see when coaching and consulting to clients.

[85] The internal or external stimulus that has the power to elicit an emotional response from an organism. Situations, places, objects, thoughts or conversations can cause them.

thoughts. What we also don't see are the related thoughts that come from and with the feelings.

According to Damasio, "Emotions live in the body and feelings live in the mind." So, emotions are created in the deep structures of our central nervous system and can give rise to feelings. Feelings elicit thematic thoughts that are consistent and supportive of the emotions. Emotions usually are apparent, and we can distinguish if a person is happy or sad, angry, or peaceful, effusive, or reticent. Emotions are like the observable surface of a river.[86] We can easily spot the superficial flows and eddies by casual observation. But feelings are the deeper currents that give shape to the surface.

Although moods seem to be observable too, we are observing patterned emotions that persist over time. Moods are different from emotions in a temporal sense. They are created and maintained by patterns of persistent thoughts [private internal narratives] that are shaped by our feelings. They can also become shared phenomenon kept in place by the public discourse within a specific group of people, such as a family, organization, or entire culture. Once in place, prevailing private and public moods can shape our emotional responses to life's events, reinforcing both the private and public discourses. Moods predispose our thoughts and actions.

Discourse and moods.

On an individual level, a disturbing thought could be an internal ECS that triggers an emotional response. When the reaction is triggered, we might enter a loop that proceeds like this:

---

[86] From a lecture by Fernando Flores, Ph.D. 1988

1. An ECS is received – for instance, a disturbing thought
2. Emotional response is triggered
3. Subsequent feeling follows
4. More of the same kind of thoughts follow
5. Reinforced emotional response continues from these thoughts
6. Reinforced feelings happen
7. More similar thoughts occur
8. Etc.

On a public level, if enough people have the above experience as a consistent and pervasive pattern and then engage in public discourse, we have the basis for forming a public mood. Once the mood is in place, it influences the ongoing public discourse even more and will eventually influence other people. Then we have a kind of *mood-loop* as I propose exists in many homogenous communities. Because moods are such strong shapers of our behaviors, we need to understand them to understand another's public identity.

Moods are changeable as are emotions. As an example, if my mood is one of despair, my emotional reactions today and tomorrow will be influenced by it. This is especially true if I live in a culture that reinforces my mood. I might even be able to express emotions that are different from my mood-state for a while but ultimately, my mood will reveal itself as a consistent pattern in my life.

Cases in point.

Some segments of the African Americans in this country are influenced by a mood of despair about their opportunities for a better quality of life. Each day, anyone in those segments might experience emotions of elation caused by a series of positive events. And an individual member's feelings might range from happiness and satisfaction to sadness and despair as a balancing mechanism in response to any given event or circumstance. But the generalized mood doesn't change until some level of critical mass is reached that shifts the public discourse.

It was only most recently that Civil Rights laws have been enforced such that this mood of despair can someday dissipate. And this will take a good deal of time to affect large segments of an entire subculture. Yet there remain whole segments of this culture that will live in this mood for their entire lifetimes. Emotions will be expressed in response to daily events. They will shift and change in response to recurring patterns of events that promise new opportunities. But it will take a whole new public discourse within this community[87] to change the mood.

Another interesting case is the white supremacy subculture. This culture thrives on a mood of fear, i.e., that control of America can be regained by removing some of the more recent immigrants with darker skins, disempowering Jews from their imagined control of everything and taking supposedly lost white power back to its previous levels. It promotes the belief that white people are superior to all others and should control America for whites only. Those who consider themselves white supremacists reinforce this mood with their ongoing discourse.

---

[87] When referring to African Americans as a community it should be noted that there is no single community and like any other ethnic group there are many varied segments.

The power of mood.

Public mood as a major external factor that predisposes an individual's emotions, thoughts, and feelings, shaping the behavior of whole groups like those cited above. It's most important impact is the way it shapes one's anticipation of what the future will hold. Most often, it is grounded in a person's cultural and familial history and can make the future be very much like the past. For those in the black culture mentioned above, it's despair. For those whites mentioned above, it's fear.

Taking hold.

How do moods take such a strong hold on people and cultures? Beyond the obvious reinforcing loop that was described above, some emotionally competent stimuli seem to be able to subvert our reasoning processes. When this happens, our normal regulatory ability, that of reasoning, is diminished. For instance, certain fear stimuli, like that experienced by white supremacists, provoke emotional responses that come directly from more primitive parts of our brains. In these cases, reasoning is of no use.

Personal case in point.

A personal case in point, although somewhat old, was the three weeks of sniper shootings in the Washington, D.C. area in October of 2002. In the first week, I was able to resist the mood of fear by reasoning that the odds were very high against being shot. As the attacks continued, and I was in increasingly more conversations about the possibilities, my mood began to shift to one more consistent with the overall public mood. I began to fear the possibility that I could be in the line of fire. I was also being bombarded with constant news releases and press conferences that added more and reinforced my existing emotional status. So, the fear that I was feeling was being reinforced in almost every conversation I had for three weeks. My internal conversation shifted to worrisome thoughts and I was completely hooked into the public mood.

I noticed even after two suspects were captured and the shooting stopped I remained in a cautious mood for several days. At some level, I was still entertaining "what if" thoughts. What if these are the wrong guys? What if there is a copycat out there? What if the real sniper is waiting in the bushes to make a major move just to embarrass the authorities? Etc.

How do we work with moods?

Freud said, "Dreams are the royal road to the unconscious." Moods can be the royal road to understanding a client. Moods influence emotions and feelings, but they differ mainly in temporality. Moods show up in the present, stimulated by some consistent and persistent ECS from the past but predispose a person to future actions.

Another way of looking at prevailing moods is that they inform our emotional and feeling responses to present events even though they come from the past. The key question for the coach is, "Which mood does this person demonstrate now and how it will affect their ability to be successful in our work together?"

The coach should not give present emotions too much emphasis. They are highly transient. The real message is the prevailing mood. For instance, I have seen people whose emotions were mixed and varied in type and intensity, but as a competent observer of mood, I learned to "capture" the pattern that exists and shapes these emotions.

Understanding mood will allow you to assess your client's Openness to new experiences.[88] Individuals with high Openness tend to be more matter of fact about the present and more ambitious about the future. Conversely, those with low Openness can be resentful and resigned allowing no possibilities for change—sometimes even to the point of being dogmatic about their position. Some disagreement remains about how to interpret and contextualize the Openness factor. Although I didn't do a formal factor analysis, I found it to be loosely related to a client's level of Extraversion. This might have to do with the fact that Extraversion tends to be a measure of a client's orientation to their external or internal stimuli. I'm offering this because it seemed to be simple yet revealing in my coaching work.

Client's orientation	To the present	To the possibilities
Closed Mood	Resentment	Resignation
Open Mood	Acceptance	Ambition

How much resistance should you expect?

Consider these scores too:

- **Challenge** -- the need for external vs. internal challenge.
- **Freedom** -- the need to be and individual or not.

---

[88] The source of this diagram is Rafael Echeverria, Ph.D. Newfield Group.

The *Freedom* and *Challenge* scores[89] are made up of items from the other Components and are therefore composites. These two constructs are essential in understanding how a person will respond to coaching. While the *Challenge* construct is vital to understanding how a person will receive feedback and coaching, the *Freedom* construct fills out our understanding of a person's willingness to take the initiative to do something productive with the coaching being received.

If a clients' orientation is open, their mood will be one of acceptance of the facts and ambition about possibilities in the future. Your work with them will be relatively trouble-free. But conversely, if the person's orientation is closed, and the mood is resentful and resigned, you are sure to encounter constant resistance to anything new.[90] The coach is left with the question, "What mood seems to be possessing this person and how do we help to either reinforce it or reconstruct it to his or her benefit?

Case in point.

A case in point was a young executive I worked with whose emotional responses indicated that he was possessed by a mood of extreme ambition and his possibilities for the future. In fact, his emotions were so pronounced and overly intense I suspected them from the first session. They also seemed forced and too consistent. In this case, it would appear on the surface this would be an easy case with which to work. The presenting problem was he had difficulties working with his peers. So, his prevailing mood seemed to be getting in his way of seeing his difficulties more clearly.

---

[89] Reported in the Birkman Signature Suite
[90] From a lecture by Fernando Flores, Ph.D. 1988

And without a clear view of himself, he would not be able to develop the commitment to the change that he needed. He was not motivated to do anything different. He was seeing me at the insistence of his boss, which is the worst way to begin a coaching relationship for the coach.

He agreed to his manager's interpretation that he was *isolated from and indifferent to* his peers. But he had convinced himself that it was a problem created by them. He couldn't see his part. He felt superior to the others, and he concluded that they were jealous of him and his thought patterns were consistent with that assessment. As you can imagine, this was a self-reinforcing "mood-loop."

After some feedback and discussion about how his Birkman scores described a person whose usual behavior hid his real needs, he began to talk more openly. We had struck a resonant chord. It seemed to me that I needed to create a *breakdown*[91] for this client. His mood was so transparent that he couldn't observe it on his own and because of this, in his isolation, his beliefs seemed to be the way the world was to him. In fact, he had accomplished a great deal by getting into a highly regarded Eastern business school and earned his MBA, which surprised his friends and family who did not expect him to achieve much in his life.

He had developed his mood over many years of fighting his basic feelings of inferiority in highly competitive situations. He perfected it in his graduate program. With some work on our part, he was eventually able to see that whatever assertions, assessments, and declarations he had made while in the competitive world of MBA candidates in

---

[91] Remember, "breakdown" refers to the breakdown in the transparency of life. In other words, to make the transparent apparent can be useful in helping another person see what he/she does not yet see.

tough Eastern schools could and should be questioned now that he was working with others whose cooperation he needed to accomplish his job requirements.

His was a powerful learning experience for both of us. He went on to become a slight bit more sensitive in his relationships with others. But our main accomplishment was that he had new tools to work with in the future. And with new tools, he had new possibilities. I learned how even seemingly positive moods can sometimes work to a person's disadvantage given the context of the specific situation.

What does our affective nature do for us?

Beyond the obvious answer that "it helped us survive on the savanna," we now live in circumstances that don't require us to be affectively motivated to either fight or take flight from foraging predators. Having our external world change does not necessarily mean that we will readapt internally to adjust to it. Evolutionary adaptation is not a process that senses the external world and then adjusts. It's quite the opposite. Our adaptations are random mutations that are genetically conserved if they provide advantages. If one mutation doesn't provide a survival advantage over another it can be lost in the process of reproduction. In the meantime, we continue to conserve those genetic adaptations that provided the advantages to our ancestors. And they are still activated when we perceive a threat.

A good deal of this book has referred to the human motivation to have our point of view, as well as our bodies, survive. So, we can see all our survival instincts come into play when and if our point of view is being seriously threatened. [Think terrorists here.] Although this is usually done linguistically in a language game, our response is as real and intense as if we were standing in the presence of a hungry saber-toothed tiger.

Feelings.

While working with clients, I saw that most of them were not aware of their feelings or their moods, for that matter. I would ask, "How do you feel about your boss treating you this way?" They responded with something like, "I feel that . . ." [and then they gave me a thought]. Feelings are not something that people can quickly articulate.

What they seemed to be telling me was a *thought-fragment* of the consonant pattern of thoughts that accompany their feelings, but not the feelings themselves. Although a thought-fragment can be useful, it is only a snapshot of one detail of an entire landscape. It is like having a person show you a single photograph from a vacation to the Grand Canyon as evidence for its beauty. There is no way you can get a grasp of that beautiful place from one photo. And there is no way that you can get a grasp of how a person is feeling from a thought-fragment.

So how do you get into the pattern of thoughts that accompany feelings? And why do we need to know more anyway? To answer these questions, we need to understand feelings and how they are interconnected to our cognitive functioning.

I think of feelings as being related to our private conversations. Damasio proposes that to have feelings, we need to have neural maps of our body states that represent them. The term, "neural maps" indicate related internal conversations to me. In many instances, these conversations are so deeply private that even the client might not have access to them. So, when clients offer a thought-fragment, we might use it to dig deeper into their internal conversations to help them come to conscious awareness.

A common theory about feelings is that they have their own logic and don't respond to rational methods. In my experience, this is a dependable theory. I've coached people in instances when feelings were so intense that we could accomplish nothing until the intensity of their feelings subsided.

How do we defuse feelings if they do not respond to rational methods? The theory goes on to say, "feelings need to be acknowledged, felt, and expressed." And I have also found this to be true to some extent.

Now as a better observer of how feelings function, I am a more critical witness to what seems to work in these cases. Although the above process may be the first steps, there appears to be another important process that must follow. And that is until we can consciously participate in the inner conversation that accompanies the neural maps, we cannot affect a person's feeling state. So once again, we see how language can be such a powerful tool for assisting others.

We cannot separate feelings from language.

The neural maps that underlie feelings and give them their shape consist of a (linguistic) narrative that provides coherency. At the core of this whole process is interpretation. And as we know, interpretations can be modified. As we also know, interpretations are what we do with the neutral events that happen in our lives. Building on Damasio's logic, feelings are the result of how we linguistically interpret our body states as structured in our neural maps.

Subsequently, giving vent to our feelings allows us to begin talking openly about the private conversations, which contain the interpretations, and which shape the feelings. Language is the tool to break the cycle once reason can be restored enough to use it effectively.

By now, the reader can see that I am very enthused about the work and discoveries being done in the cognitive sciences with regard to our neurolinguistic structures. The most important reason is that we can now examine the relationship of the cognitive process of language in the context of how it is related to feelings, emotions, and moods. And we can do it with the confidence that comes from legitimate scientific inquiry. As practitioners, we depend on those who can make these kinds of discoveries to improve our methods of practice.

In summary, coaches shouldn't underestimate the power of our cognitive-affective nature. When emotions are in charge, reason takes a vacation. Reasoning while in an intense feeling state comes from the logic of the patterned thoughts that accompany those feelings. These are always past tense and probably don't reflect current events very accurately. Further, we know interpretations can create declarations and declarations do not require evidence or grounding. So, a person in an intense feeling state may be caught up in a summary declaration that has no basis in the reality of the moment. People in these states can be completely disconnected from reality in the most extreme cases.

Once again, we get back to the idea of staying connected to others in our world because it is with this connection that we ground ourselves and have access to our innate tools for coaching effectively. The knowledge of and skill to assist when working with human affect is a powerful lever for helping another person manage change. In the hands of a skillful coach, it is unsurpassed.

Chapter 18 -- On Coaching:
The broad strokes

Treat people as if they were what they ought to be and you help them to become what they are capable of being.

Johann W. von Goethe

It was a bright spring day, and the Little League Baseball coach was hitting practice grounders to his infield kids. The little boy at shortstop was missing almost every ball that came to him. Finally, the coach had enough and told the child to stand aside and watch him play the position correctly. The coach had another boy hit a few to him as he took the shortstop position. The first one went through the coach's legs. The second to his right. The third to his left. The coach had enough. He turned to the little boy who had been playing shortstop and said, "see, you've got this position so screwed up, even I can't play it."

The moral of the story is coaches are not players. We stand on the sidelines and offer our observations. We create awarenesses that our clients can use or ignore. That decision belongs exclusively to the client.

NO tips and techniques.

Never do anything that distracts or disconnects you from your client. While coaching other coaches, I found too many instances when the attempt to use a model, tip, or technique, interfered and distracted them causing them to miss the opportunity to assist.

So instead, this chapter offers some broad strokes to use as rough guidelines as you coach. The next chapter will delve much deeper as a kind of review that brings the whole book together.

It has been a long trip, but I make no apology for the distance. As coaches, we need to have a comprehensive understanding of human beings. That means we need to know ourselves as well as those we hope to assist. You might think that this book contains a lot of extra information. Maybe you would have preferred a straightforward model to follow: Do step 1 and then step 2, etc. The problem with that approach to coaching, besides the fact that it really doesn't work, is that people are not machines. Consequently, algorithms don't apply. For instance, if you have ever programmed an Excel spreadsheet, you can put formulae into the cells, and they will perform the same functions every time you input new data. The result is predictable and immediate. They handle different data the same way, over and over. We, humans, are heuristic decision makers. Different data gets various treatments almost every time.

So, you know working with human beings is more challenging. You have already figured out every time you "input data," the result is unpredictable, and it may or may not happen at all, let alone immediately or in your presence. When working with people, as opposed to machines, we don't know when we will get a response, if we do, or what it will be.

We human beings are complex systems made up of complex systems made up of more complex systems. We can choose lots of different reactions and when, where, and if our chosen responses will take place. And here's the icing on the cake: those different reactions are being decided upon subconsciously. Yes, we usually have a conscious explanation, but it's nano-seconds after the decision is made by our huge subconscious thinking complexes that govern 95 percent of what we do.

Being a human being, and a complex system myself, I chose to write a book about coaching that attempts to build a solid foundation for understanding how human beings function cognitively below the consciousness level, how our affective nature works, and how they work together to make us who we are. But it all depends on the committed professional to make his or her unique "sense" of it. In this way, this material can only get better as you make it your own.

Linguistics as the tool.

By now you understand how our neurolinguistic structure processes, creates, and maintains our points of views . You also understand how that process works in the client's themselves and the world within which they create and live. You know how The Birkman Method® identifies the precise areas of personality at work when, as Dr. Birkman articulated, "behavior is not determined so much by objective facts as by the particular meanings the individual attaches to those facts. [...] The perceptions of some individuals about "most people" and/or "self" may be illusory, irrational, or unreal. Nevertheless, these perceptions are real and reasonable to the individuals, and so, influential on their behaviors."

This is the precise opportunity to assist as a coach and the reason to use The Birkman Method® as an aid.

Breakdowns, another review.

Why another review of breakdowns? Because breakdowns are the coachable moments.

The process of understanding and assisting others begins with identifying and deconstructing the declarations and system of scripts and rules that do not seem to be working. But to do so in any reasonable time span requires that we become very focused in our process. Most people are relatively effective in some domains of action and ineffective in others. It makes sense that we should look to those domains of ineffective action for clues as to where the *breakdowns* are happening. The Birkman Method® offers clues by identifying Stress Behaviors and related Needs.

A reminder here: a *breakdown*[lxxiv] is a disruption in the normal transparency of living; i.e., the 95 percent of our cognitive functioning where the majority of our decisions are made. In other words, in our normal state of living, the *tools* of life are "ready to hand" and out of our awareness, or consciousness, until they don't work. For instance, the computer I am using to write this book is for the most part transparent to me except when it fails to work. Then I become very aware of it. At all other times, I use it without thinking about it.

Breakdowns in rules are the same. When they work, we aren't aware of them. They are transparent. When they don't work, we become aware of something vague or missing. Their transparency breaks down. Our conscious mind, about five percent of our cognitive processes, is called upon to assist. *Breakdown* is not a pejorative term. Remember, it means "breakdown in the transparency of life," and it is usually an excellent opportunity to address a specific need.

An obvious caution.

Declarations, scripts, and their embedded rules are very different from tangible objects. I can easily see that a computer is not working. But a declaration is much more elusive, and most of us need help to find and fix the problem. We know something is not working, but we are not sure of what it is.

In my experience, these breakdowns seem to fall into categories, described below. As you will see, each of these breakdowns has past, or retrogressional, and future, or projectional qualities, to it. In other words, we use old and familiar information to negotiate the unknown future, but we don't know if it's going to work.

These breakdowns are another aspect of our gift of human consciousness. This is what Korzybski refers to as *time-binding* when he said that humans are "time-binding beings."[lxxv] He meant there is an exponential quality to how we learn from the experience of previous generations. We can also learn from our personal previous experiences. Human knowledge is exponentially advanced with each new generation, but for some reason, we often don't advance from the knowledge of our personal past experiences. Some of us, like other animals, need to relearn the same things over and over. And many of our breakdowns come from old lessons that don't apply today.

Some categories of breakdowns.

- **Cultural** -- Social perceptions based on "a priori" structures that are no longer appropriate or applicable in new situations. This is especially probable when transitioning from one culture to another.
- **Historical** -- Self-perceptions based on historical or familial narratives that may have been effective in the past but are no longer appropriate such as a first-

generation person living in the interpretations of his immigrant family.

- **Situational** -- Use of rules of engagement that are effective in one domain and not effective in another such as trying to manage people with the same rules being used to perform technical tasks.
- **Factual** -- Ungrounded or invalid assessments such as having strong opinions about a group of people without ever having direct personal experience with them.
- **Adaptational** -- Converting assessments to assertions without evidence such as forming and holding a belief when faced with factual evidence to the contrary.

The retrogressional-projectional qualities of these breakdowns strongly suggest the need for temporal examination. If you will recall, I identified my presuppositions at the beginning of this book. Among them was the belief that certain external structures shape who we are. These are the historical, familial, and cultural narratives. That means we must be aware of how our behavioral and linguistic constructs and the scripts that hold them together are determined from both diachronic [past – future] and synchronic [present] perspectives.

Our challenge is to uncover the patterns that underlie the individual's scripts that are causing the breakdown. To observe a single script as it is being applied in the present is like trying to describe all Western history based on a single skirmish in the War of 1812. But to begin the process of discovery, deconstruction and reconstruction require that we understand scripts two ways: (1) in the context of time and (2) their relationship to each other in the present. In other words, it is important to see not only the individual script but also the *script-set* to which a person adheres, not only in the present but also in the past and how likely they are to be followed in the future given no compelling or unusual reasons for change.

To summarize this point, we should examine the past, present, and potential future of a given script as well as the relationship of all the scripts to each other. And we do this by discussing the past, present, and future of how the Needs of each Birkman personality component affects our clients lives. Although this requires considerable analysis, the reward is that we begin to see the underlying patterns of interpretations that shape a person's self and social perceptions and ultimately their ability to be effective in life and the ever-present need to manage change. In this way, The Birkman Method® provides an understandable and useful framework that can guide focused feedback sessions and practical discussions.

Causing breakdowns.

It is not unusual for a coach to need to cause a *breakdown* using Heidegger's definition. In other words, we may need to break the transparency of their common assumptions which are built on their past histories. It is breaking down this transparency that allows them to utilize their generative powers to reinvent themselves for the future. A well-designed breakdown can be the first healthy step, as it was in the case of the young executive described in a previous chapter on our affective nature. On more than one occasion I had to confront his assumptions so unequivocally that he could not continue to hold the position that kept him in pain. This is particularly useful in career coaching situations when clients have lost several jobs due to some unconscious declaration or ungrounded perspective that prohibits them from holding a position long enough to reach full potential.

Then we need to quickly establish a process of correction before the other's emotional responses to the breakdown becomes a pervasive mood of resignation using the coach as a negative ECS. (emotionally competent stimulus)

Breakdowns are not a terrible thing. We have all experienced them when somewhere in our life we were not able to cope with a situation that caused us to develop another point of view. And this is where the coach gets his or her power to assist.

Of course, coaches must act ethically with respect to causing breakdowns. The single purpose must be that the client can see their past actions, their self-imposed limitations, and their possibilities for more effective efforts in the future. In the hands of an ethical coach, the knowledge of and skill to work with moods to create breakdowns are powerful levers for helping another make change.

We coach best from our wounds.[92]

There is nothing quite so effective at building trust as the feeling that the other person has empathy for your circumstances. And to have authentic empathy, we need to have experienced the same pain as the other person.

Think about who you relate to more closely, a very successful person whose life seems charmed or an average Joe or Jennie whose life has been a series of difficulties, successes and failures, losses, and gains? Joe and Jennie are like the rest of us. Their lives are real, and we have more

---

[92] From a lecture by Julio Olalla, 1990

empathy for them because our lives are more like theirs. Which brings us to the issue of the ethics of coaching.

Ethics.

Anyone who has ever coached another person knows that when trust is established, the productive work can begin. Without trust, no amount of time, effort, tips, or techniques will achieve a positive result. So, what is it that builds and maintains trust? The only way to build this vital component in a relationship is by rigorously applying an ethical process that follows a few fundamental guidelines. They are as follows:

- Respectfully accept your clients as independent of you and having equally valid perceptions and experiences, unconditionally respecting their legitimacy to see the world as they do.
- Proceed only with the clients' permission and when and if this permission is retracted, stop the process until it is restored. The reason for the retraction is sometimes the coachable issue.
- Be sincere, reliable, and competent. Continue to work at learning and improving your current skills.
- Be authentic by expressing the empathy and compassion that comes from your own wounds and weaknesses.
- Do not attempt to take a superior position in the relationship. Remember that there are only *participants* in the process of enlightenment.
- Coach for the singular purpose of generating new possibilities for your clients without attempting to influence them with your values or those of others.

Who's the client when an employer is paying?

A common question that gets asked when discussing the ethics of coaching is, "Who is the client when an employer is paying for the work?" Based on my experience, the only way a coach can work ethically is to have one client and one client only in any coaching engagement. And that is the person sitting in the room. This makes the engagement more complicated and difficult for the coach to remain objective. This may seem like a dilemma to some, and if it does, I would advise them to reconsider their choice to be a coach.

Coaching is not a good career choice for everyone. In fact, there are more people who should not attempt it than those who should. This is a serious career choice, and like any other, one can use the information provided throughout this text to assist in a decision. And this includes enlisting the assistance of a qualified career coach.

Did you say learn to love your clients?

Mother Theresa said, "If you judge people, you have no time to love them." Does this mean we should love our clients? Yes, but a different definition of love applies here. Dr. Humberto Maturana says, "love is the unconditional legitimization of the independence of the other." In other words, if you love someone, you may not agree with their every action, but you do unconditionally accept them as different and independent of you, having equally valid experiences and points of view. We have romanticized this word *love* in our culture, so we don't often think of it in this context.

On a broader level, it is the glue that holds our species together. With the advent of postmodernity and its traveling companion, cynicism, we seem to have lost sight of the phenomena of love in this fundamental context and what remains are fragments of its real meaning. A coach cannot do an ethical job without *loving* his or her clients in Maturana's terms.

Can we love everyone in this way?

I do *love* some people who do not fit into our culture's rules about who we should love, but I fail with others. It is a difficult task, but it can be done most of the time. When I apply Maturana's definition, I can even love the person who calls and interrupts my quiet, peaceful evenings with a political message or a request for a donation. I don't need to like their actions, but they are legitimate other persons doing what they think is an ethical job. I'm virtually never interested in their offers, and I tell them that from the beginning. But they are real live human beings and deserve my respect for that if for no other reason. This is the only way I can ask for respect from others. Do I love them? In Maturana's terms, yes, I guess I do, most of the time but not always.

If we are to ever have personal peace, it must start with some form of this acceptance Maturana calls love. Will I ever love everyone in our species? That's a tall order that I have not been able to deliver, and I truly don't think I will ever accomplish. So, what do I do if I want to be a professional coach? I don't coach those whom I cannot *love* in this way. So far, I've only declined a few people.

Conversations as tools.

Many years ago, I took my son who was ten years old at the time, to work for a day as a part of his school-sponsored program designed to show children the world of work from their father's and mother's perspective. Of course, I asked permission from my clients for my son to sit in on my meetings with them. During one session, I looked over and saw him nodding off to sleep. He was obviously bored. As we left and got into my car, I asked why he was not enjoying these sessions. He said, "All you do is talk."

To the untrained eye, a coaching discussion would look like a conversation—and it is. My son was a pretty good ten-year-old observer, but he missed an important point. And that was the use of conversations as tools for assisting others. In fact, conversations are a skillful coach's most potent tool.

If we apply the concept of games as frames of meaning, we can more quickly get to the power of conversations to make change. Because the conversation is usually reflective of the frame of meaning within which the other person is operating. Our challenge becomes knowing exactly *what game is being played* as we interact with another. This knowledge can guide us to use the right conversation.

Gaining access to and influencing another's perceptions to add new possibilities can be accomplished best if we understand the kind of conversations that we can have and design them properly and with forethought. The following list describes those conversations that can be very helpful.

Types of conversations.[93]

- Open or social -- the objective is simply contained in the process of talking to another. The purpose is

---

[93] From a lecture by Fernando Flores, Ph.D. 1986

human contact. These are good for breaking the ice and required in some cultures if we want to produce some action.

- Stories and assessments -- do not produce action but help us understand the other's point of view, self, and social perceptions
- Creating possibilities -- free-ranging discussion about the different ways to perceive a situation that allows the participants to consider and choose a set of possible actions.
- Planning actions -- focused on the decision process where the participants take a possibility and begin to set a course for applying it to get results.

It is most important to be aware of these kinds of conversations as you meet with your client. Misapplying a conversation type causes many mistakes. For instance, if the client is not ready for a conversation about *planning actions,* it is futile to discuss choosing to take the next steps. Once again, good listening skills will be of invaluable assistance here.

Public and private conversations.

Did you ever notice during a conversation that the other person might be having his private conversation in his head? And it doesn't include you. By the way, have you noticed your personal private conversation; the one going on in your head?

If you have ever taken professional listening training, you have probably learned to quiet or filter your own private conversation. If it was an advanced course, you probably even know how to "listen for" the other's private conversation. So, when you go into a coaching situation, you are now empowered to listen professionally, right? Right. So why does it usually take a long time to truly understand the other person? And then, even when we think we do, we often make serious mistakes in "listening" to what we need to discern.

Well, there a conversation that is even more hidden. It's not only hidden from you but is sometimes also hidden from the speaker because our *consciousness window* is a proportionately tiny spot in our total mind.[lxxvi] While our speaking is representative of what is in the conscious window of our minds, there is a whole lot more going on in the background. In fact, a good deal of what we are consciously thinking and saying at any moment is meta-thinking[94] as opposed to object thinking[95].

Although I call this background conversation the subtext, it often contains the real information that is necessary to better understand our client. As a well-trained professional listener, I can catch a glimpse of it from time to time. But without assistance, I need a long time to get the stories that are often hidden between, under and around the lines of the speaker's subtext.

Listening for your client's thinking.

Dr. Birkman pointed up the differences between our social [or public] and private behaviors: the social behavior

---

[94] Meta-thinking is thinking about our object thinking and it is shaped by our categorical and hypothetical imperatives. In other words, it is a process of judging our object thinking.

[95] Object thinking is our basic thinking process that seems to run uninterrupted from thought to thought and represents the content that we think about.

being more driven by conventions and the private being shaped by our real needs. He went on to point out that we can become so wrapped up in the social that we forget the authentic self. We can forget who we are. Our public conversations tend to be about meta-thoughts that are shaped by the social circumstances within which they occur. Our object thinking is a more reliable representation of our authentic self but is being moderated for public approval.

This awareness has been invaluable in helping my clients and me to explore this deeper hidden conversation that eludes us all. As an illustration, the following dialog demonstrates this process. I was coaching an executive when this happened.

- *Me:(In italics)*

- *"Why do you believe that the people in your department can't be trusted to carry out their jobs without your close supervision?"*

- **Him: (In bold)**
- **"They can, but they don't seem to do it. They don't seem to follow through and get it done."**

- *"Can you give me an example?"*

- **"Well, there is nothing that comes to my mind at this point."**

- *"Try to think of something."*

- **"It's just that there's a constant inability to do what I ask them to do."**

- *"That's not very helpful. I can't get a grasp of what you're talking about without an example."*

- **"Why are you pushing me so hard?"**

- *"Am I pushing you too hard?"*

- **"I don't think that you understand my circumstances."**

- *"I am trying my best."*

- **"You are missing the mark . . . The problem is with my people. If they did their jobs, I wouldn't need to be so hard on them."**

- *"I understand that. Do you think that most people are like that, or is it your people?"*

- **"I think that most people need close management to do their best. A good leader is the one who stays on top of them and monitors their moves and isn't afraid to correct them when they need it."**

- *"I see, and when did you first discover this fact?"*

- **"In the military, of course."**

- *"Of course."*

Here is a diagrammatical look at this conversation with imaginary private and hidden conversations made explicit. Keep in mind that my comments are italicized, and his are not.

Public	Private	Hidden
"Why do you believe that the people in your department can't be trusted to carry out their jobs without your close supervision?"	*I need to find out the basis for his management style.*	*Need clear-cut reasons for people's actions.*
"They can, but they don't seem to do it. They don't seem to follow through and get it done."	He doesn't understand the situation and will blame it on me.	Don't accept blame.
"Can you give me an example?"	*Pin him down.*	*Get the facts.*
"Well, there is nothing that comes to my mind at this point."	He's going down the wrong road with this line of questioning.	I don't trust consultants.
"Try to think of something."	*I need to force him to get*	*Don't trust authority*

	specific.	*figures.*
"It's just that there is a constant inability to do what I ask them to do."	I'm not going to get trapped into this conversation. I know what the problem is and where he is going with this.	Maintain control.
"That's not very helpful. I can't get a grasp of what you're talking about without an example."	*This is going to be difficult. He's avoiding my inquiries. He may not trust me.*	*Don't trust him.*
"Why are you pushing me so hard?"	I need to push back, or he will get the upper hand.	Stay in charge.
"Am I pushing you too hard?"	*I need to find out exactly what his limits are.*	*Don't trust authority figures.*
"I don't think that you really understand my circumstances."	He needs to be straightened out early in this process or he will be trying to fix me.	Remain in control.
"I am trying my best."	*Maybe I can get him to reveal a*	*Negotiate but don't*

	bit more by being less confronting.	*compromise.*
"You are missing the mark . . .the problem is with my people. If they would do their jobs I wouldn't need to be so hard on them."	I don't want to let him focus on me. The problem is with them.	Stay in charge.
"I understand that. Do you think that most people are like that, or is it your people?"	*This will give me a look at how deep this belief system is.*	*Don't trust authority figures.*
"I think that most people need strong management to do their best. A good leader is the one who stays on top of them and monitors their moves and isn't afraid to correct	He should know this by now if he is worth his fees.	Stay in charge.

them when they need it."		
"I see, and when did you first discover this fact?"	*How far back does this crap go?*	*Don't trust authority figures.*
"In the military, of course."	That was my best time as a manager. I told, and people listened.	Be proud.
"Of course."	*I should have known that . . . his bearing is that of an arrogant person.*	*I don't trust military officers...more than any other authority figure.*

As we can readily see, having access to the private and hidden conversations would have created an entirely different dialogue. It may not have concluded in a more effective outcome but would have certainly been more authentic.

It's doubtful that anyone would agree to major surgery if a physician lacked skill with a scalpel. Most of us would want to know that he/she was a master of its use. How then can we coaches do anything less with our most important tool—the conversation?

Recognizing natural dynamics.

We seem to live in a suspended state between what are called the *transformative* and *conservative* forces. The transformative is that which creates our interest in the possibilities. The conservative wants us to stay where we are. We probably feel the transformative force mostly when we are experiencing a *breakdown* in our everyday life. This is the time when we are aware that something isn't working for us and we look for new possibilities. But then comes the conservative force. We might say, "But wait, give it some time. I'll hold off changing my actions or point of view for a while. Things will change."

It is in this instant that we can make new choices that can be mutually discovered in effective coaching relationships. This is precisely when all our stories and assessments, self and social perceptions, and our worldviews come into question, and without the aid of a trusting relationship, we are left to fall back on our subjective blindness and submit to the conservative force. Once again, this is another dynamic at work in the *coachable moment*.

I've seen many examples of this tension between the two forces while working with others. The transformative force pushes us to make changes to improve our overall quality of life, and the conservative force tells us to stay where we are. On the one hand, we can see the possibilities, and on the other, we enjoy our current personal certitude. When we can discern this tension and use it, we will assist others to make breakthroughs in our coaching relationships. We have the greatest opportunities to assist others when they sit in the vice-like jaws of this dilemma.

Coach or therapist?

In general, coaches work with people who are "emotionally healthy" and therapists work with people who have "emotional problems." With the disclaimer that most of us are neurotic in varying degrees, this can be a pretty good formula to explain the difference between the two areas of practice.

I also suspect that the operative distinction between coaches and therapists is to some extent a linguistic phenomenon. In other words, I know that I have coached people with emotional problems. My challenge was to recognize that fact and not attempt to treat the emotional problem. And I can say that in some cases it was not possible to be effective without touching on the issues that were at cause.

Yes, there are educational and licensing issues at stake, but I have known as many coaches as therapists who offer value very effectively. Short of prescribing medications for serious emotional disturbances or focusing on the treatment of major emotional illnesses, the coach may be of assistance if he or she does not claim to be a therapist. The secret is in the relationship. A trusting relationship, in either case, is the basic reason for successful work together.

Remember that one of the basic premises of this book is that the core challenge of helping others is that of knowing and accepting the unique personal experience of another. If we don't have answers to the great philosophical questions, maybe all we have are each other's subjective experiences upon which to depend.

There is more than just a little bit of evidence for an eventual total shift in the practice of clinical psychology. Each day we seem to find more evidence toward determining which cognitive processes need help, identifying what physiological systems are involved and learning how to give that help with biological interventions. We have come a long way toward understanding the physiological causes of mental illnesses such as depression and schizophrenia and then treating them with chemicals designed to help us back into a somewhat normal state.

The growing science of behavioral genetics is giving us new insights into how we function at both the physical and psychological levels. And most importantly, we are beginning to understand how the interactions between these two levels work to develop our personalities and influence the quality of our lives.

I don't mean to propose that therapy is dead. In fact, we also know that even if we find that the causes of our psychological problems are fully physical, we still need the help of trained professionals to adjust maladaptive thinking and behaviors that have developed because of these primary causes.

I don't mean that coaches should pass themselves off as licensed therapists. I do mean that, with or without a license, we can help or hurt. It can be difficult to distinguish between what some coaches do and what a licensed therapist does once they close the door and begin the session.

Either as a coach or a therapist, to do this work, one must learn to become an excellent observer of oneself and others. This does not only refer to our outward behaviors but also being able to see the *observers* that we and the clients are.

Case in point.

A good case in point was a recent discussion I had with a business colleague. We had just witnessed an outburst of rather unexpected behavior from a business acquaintance in a meeting. This behavior was not explainable upon examination of the events that preceded the outburst. It seemed totally out of place. Neither of us knew the person well, and we speculated about his motivations. We both observed the same behavior. My colleague speculated that a practical financial motive was the cause of this person's actions. I speculated that his motivation was coming from a threat to his professional self-esteem. It is not important in this case as to who was right or wrong. The teaching point is that both of us were different observers of the same event and we came up with ideas that reflected our unique perspective. My colleague is far more business-oriented than I am. And I am far more behaviorally oriented than he is.

If we had been exacting in our observation of the other person, we would have described merely his behavior and said that we didn't know what his motivations were. But we jumped quickly from a simple observation of an event to a complex set of interpretations and explanations for his behavior.

Coaching requires that we can separate the events that are being experienced by another from explanations and interpretations. Being able to observe in this way allows us an opening to explore. We must put a wedge between the two or we might enter the other's interpretive world and get lost in unknown territory. The question then for the coach is, "Where does this opening show up, so we can observe it more accurately?"

I propose that it shows up in two places: (1) the person's language and (2) the person's body. Do not confuse another's body with his biology. A person's biological processes are not necessarily open to us. But the physiological organization of the person's body is sometimes a very potent clue to their interpretations. It is not very difficult to see a person who fidgets in the chair or shows up looking disheveled. Or the individual who interrupts at the exact time that you are about to say something they need to hear. And then there is the person who will not allow feedback and keeps the conversation going on unrelated topics, changing its direction every time you get close to helping.

To me, the mind is a derivative of these two basic functions, our language, and our bodies. In this way of looking at behavior, there is no need to worry too much about who the authentic person is in front of you. You will soon know them well enough because they will show themselves by the observable actions they take. We not only *act* according to who we *are,* but we *are* according to how we *act.*

Good news and bad news. The bad news: What you usually see is socialized behavior. The good news: We have The Birkman Method® to quickly get to the authentic self.

Coaching requires openness to continuous learning.

People often ask questions in coaching sessions that require answers that keep them from learning. For instance, a seemingly logical question might be, "Who should I vote for . . . a Democrat or a Republican?" But the question comes from an existing system of logic, and the answer usually keeps the person in that system. If we answer that kind of question, we may just be filling their need to feel comfortable within their worldview and as a result, pander to the pressures of the conservative force.

To assist our clients, the coach needs to resist giving a pat answer to this kind of question. When we offer the client a different worldview, we add new possibilities by answering this kind of question wisely. So maybe another way of answering this question to introduce new possibilities would be, "What are your concerns and what candidate might best represent those interests in government? It just might be that there is a candidate, regardless of party affiliation, who is more available to your point of view."

If we sit by while clients stay in the comfort of their existing systems of logic, they will usually wind up with no new options. We need to learn how to ask the questions that cannot be answered from within their systems of logic. Missing this opportunity is a surefire way to keep the client stuck in subjective blindness.

Make no mistake that the partner of change is new learning. A question formed to get a predetermined answer is a method that some people use to resist the need to keep learning for the future. As adults, we have built-in prejudices to overcome when we attempt to learn. The first thing we must do is be able to say *we don't know*. Subjective certitude is a major block to learning.

Case in point.

I had a friend who was a flight instructor. His job was risky as one can imagine so he was very particular about whom he would accept as a student. Based on his past experiences, he had decided to never attempt to teach a medical doctor how to fly a plane again. His reason, "They already know everything." [This is not an indictment of all physicians but a real story.] If learners are to learn, they need to declare incompetence in a domain and find a teacher or coach.[lxxvii] My friend would not have assumed to teach surgical techniques any more than he would take instructions for instrument flight from a physician who had never been at the controls.

Barriers to learning in coaching relationships.[lxxviii]

The greatest enemy to learning is the rational self-concept. In other words, the self-concept that holds that one is made up of fixed attributes and the process of learning is the discovery of one's innate abilities. Do not confuse *innate abilities* with temperament and the behavioral constructs previously described, which are relatively fixed personality orientations. And do not confuse innate abilities with the core intuitive learning faculties that we are born with. They are empty slots that require experience to fill. And although personality orientation does predispose us to learning certain kinds of skills those skills are not innate in any way.

The adult learner is particularly prone to the inhibitors of continuous learning because of this belief. Why? Because as adults, we are supposed to know it all already or at least we need to act as though we do to avoid embarrassment. Beware of this process in yourself and those you coach. These are a few other barriers that you might watch for:[96]

- Inability to recognize what you don't know and admit it.
- Need for continual clarity, all the time, even during learning. "If it's not clear, it's someone's fault: the student or the teacher…so stop the class."
- Fear of making mistakes and losing face.
- Lack of desire or feeling of necessity for new learning.
- Frustration.

---

[96] Julio Olalla, from a lecture, 1990

- Adversarial positioning of the teacher or coach. Remember Habermas who said, "There are only participants in the process of enlightenment.

Continuous learning is a way to recreate our identities such that we are better able to experience our authentic self.

The future of coaching.

I've spent a good deal of time discussing our entry into postmodernity. This is an era that is recognized by the shift in the definition of reality. The *constructivists* seem to be winning. We now see reality as a linguistic creation characterized by the social constructions within which we all live. It's not all bad news. This era brings with it a new awareness of how we socially construct our realities together. In this way of thinking, we can continue to create and recreate ourselves progressively. This is good news for the coaches in these times. With the right intentions, we can recreate how the whole human race behaves in ways that we can make the world work for everyone.

This point is important for coaches because it claims that people are the inventors of themselves and their futures. If this were not valid, coaching would have far fewer possibilities. But being valid, now people can help each other by coaching to generate new possibilities for more effective social actions. The main opportunity in coaching is that of helping others realize their creative capacities. Coaches have an obligation to see the vast human potential for designing social realities that improve the overall effectiveness of our lives and the accomplishment of our dreams for the future. And we can only do it together.

Chapter 19 – Bringing it all together

I am not proposing a static coaching model. Instead, that you have expert command of a body of knowledge that makes you free to create a coaching approach that adds value to your clients' lives. This approach should be based on reliable diagnostic information, so you can produce the outcomes you and they desire. The Birkman Method® provides some of the most reliable and valid diagnostic information available for coaching. It also gives us excellent access to a range of tactical steps that can be used to hit the target every time we coach.

The Nine Components are the heart of The Birkman Method®.

To grasp them is to understand the power that differentiates the Birkman from other assessment methods. This chapter is designed to give the reader a review and deeper understanding of the nine behavioral components and how to use them to coach. Throughout it, I have indicated essential learning elements as **Key Points**. They are reminders of certain principles in this book as they apply to any coaching approach you may use.

Why does coaching work?

I once believed in the old saying that "seeing is believing" but after several years of coaching experience I've come to agree with those who say, "believing is seeing." Unfortunately for me, and lots of others, often the things we believe are based on erroneous perceptions about others and ourselves; consequently, any action we take can magnify the error. And helping others to correct these misperceptions is one of the core opportunities in coaching. In fact, it is the reason coaching works.

This is not new news, but how well do we really understand it? We will deconstruct it a bit more here to get a closer look at how it works. Most importantly we will also explore how The Birkman Method® gives us a special look and becomes an excellent tool for working with this phenomenon.

Are there common misperceptions that coaches face?

The Birkman Method® give us a good deal of help here. It has such practical application in coaching because it deals with the six common **misperceptions**[97] that skew our **interpretations**[98] and they are:

- We're normal- it's the other people who have the problem.
- The best way to do it, is my way.
- The way people act is the way they want to be treated by others.
- Most people feel the way I do.

---

[97] The word misperception needs to be defined. It suggests that there is a proper perception and that someone is making a mistake when they have a misperception. For my purposes it means that that person's perception is not shared by others. In other words it is not intersubjectively verifiable. Or that the misperception is causing a client problems or troubles in his or her life.

[98] The same is true for the word interpretation. When an interpretation is causing a client to have difficulties we have a reason to work with it. Until then it is really not our place to try to change it. We are better advised to just try to understand it.

- There is an ideal behavioral style.

Key Point: *Deconstructing Misperceptions*

One, some or all these six common misperceptions are usually at work when coaching is needed. The information on personality traits found in the Birkman report become the map to understanding our clients.

Birkman refers to the ***Components*** in the report as the *nine windows on behavior*. To fully appreciate the power of these Components, we will look at how misperceptions *and* erroneous interpretations shape them.

Until now we have referred to misperceptions as though they are singular when in fact they have two parts. Perception is a physiological process that begins when we are still in the womb. But we cannot interpret our perceptions until we develop cognitive abilities. As we do, our families, cultures, religions, and historical circumstances teach us the rest. For the sake of review:

"Our earliest perceptions don't mean much to us until we develop the cognitive competence to interpret them. This requires language and a native culture. In any event, we still come with these genetically conserved faculties in place. We depend on these cognitive structures to make sense of our perceptions. But these innate faculties bring biases with them that have evolved out of our need to survive in the distant past. Our subjective experience is then mediated by these cognitive processes and resides in the structures of our nervous system. So, in order to really understand subjective experience, we need to recognize that the human neurophysiological structure represents evolutionary biases that cannot be overlooked.[99] Our *fight or flight* response is a good example of such an evolutionary influence. When we interpret a situation that threatens us, we automatically respond just as we did 100,000 or more years ago. This is *wired* into the more primitive structures of our brains for our protection against the dangers of the jungle. We can still experience this primitive response in a present-day confrontation with a business associate. In this case, this response does not require language but the moderating influence of our cortex and comes directly from the primitive amygdala. Language was a later evolutionary development and resides in this newer part of our brain but is no less a natural and innate ability that comes with our unique human neurophysiology." [100]

Our language faculty.

"As stated previously, Noam Chomsky is noted for his theory that we come into the world with a deep generative language structure that allows a young child to learn language.[lxxix] We can think of this deep structure as a pre-linguistic universal human grammar. It is like a bio-program that allows us to take on the difficult task of learning our native language. To repeat myself for emphasis, I liken it to our species non-linguistic language that facilitates learning a functional language. Steven Pinker calls it mentalese.[lxxx]

---

[99] An excellent book to read to become familiar with these biases is Steven Pinker's The Blank Slate, a modern denial of human nature.
[100] This excerpt is from my first book, You, Your SELF and the 21st Century: Coaching your self and others in postmodern times. (pages 51-52)

"Mentalese is not a public language per se. It is another kind of language that might be thought of as belonging to the pre-conscious mind where raw human meaning resides. This is the storehouse of universal human experience and is why we can communicate and connect with other people across cultures and language differences.

"The research of other cognitive scientists has also identified additional structures that allow us to make sense of our experience of the objective world. Although they may differ, the overwhelming evidence is that we come genetically prepared to live and learn in this physical world, but it seems to be the world to which our ancestors were adapted at the time of the emergence of what we can refer to as modern human beings.

"So perception is shaped by our unique neurophysiology and our interpretations are taught to us by our surroundings. I paraphrase professor Rick Roderick; "we don't learn our ethics by reading the classics. We learn them by getting our bottoms spanked by our mothers".[101]

Key Point

We have two significant variables to work with:

- *Our physiology and how it shapes our perceptions. (Internal structures)*
- *Our socialization and how it shapes our interpretations. (External structures)*

These have been referred to as *nature* and *nurture* in the past and more recently we are finding that nature has a good deal more to do with our unique personalities than was once thought. Although the focus is the socialization process

---

[101] Rick Roderick, Ph.D. National University

that creates the interpretations that we will be exposed to when reading the Components in a Birkman report, we cannot ignore the fact that temperament is physiologically *hard-wired,* and no amount of coaching is going to change it. In addition, cognitive scientists are showing us that each of us has a unique way of perceiving even though we are generally species-bound in that ability.

As you will remember, the Birkman Components are presented considering three different perspectives, and when we examine them together we begin to get a better understanding of how our behavioral styles impact our relationships. In addition we begin to get a sense of our clients' rules for engaging their worlds. This multilevel presentation makes the Birkman a unique and powerful tool.

Key Point
To understand the concept of components is to grasp the most crucial part of The Birkman Method®

- "The components combine to provide a revealing picture of the way a person relates to *self and others.*"[102] In other words, their scripts, and *rules of engagement.*

- Coaching is the art of offering the choice of another observer to a person being coached. In this way that person can see another view of how he or she relates to *self and others.* By doing so we can give them the opportunity to examine their *rules of engagement* to produce more effective outcomes.

---

[102] Birkman certification training manual, emphasis added, page 3-1

A Quick Review of the Three Perspectives of Components

The three perspectives are: **Usual Behaviors, Needs and Stress Behaviors.**

- **Usual Behavior** is just that. How we usually behave, given that our needs are satisfied.

- **Needs** are the most important part of each person's personality. They describe what we really want from our environment. This is the non-negotiable part of our personality and when satisfied allow us access to our usual behaviors, which is where our strength lies.

- **Stress Behavior** is what happens when our needs are not met. Oftentimes, we then resort to these less effective and usually non-productive behaviors.

Key Point

*We can easily see that **Needs** are at the center of understanding human behavior. They are somewhat like a children's playground ride called a "teeter -totter" with **Needs** being the fulcrum point. If **Needs** are satisfied we have access to our effective behaviors and if **Needs** are not satisfied, we may access our stress or ineffective behaviors. This three-pointed multi-perspective makes up a linguistic construct that contains a person's **scripts** and **rules of engagement**.*

- *Scripts and Rules of engagement are constructed like this: "I usually act this way and speak like this if*

> *the world is as I need it to be but when it's not I can speak and act this way. "*

- *For example: I am usually **frank and direct** as a long as others treat me the same way. If they do not, I can become **suspicious and withdrawn.***

Why do we need rules of engagement?

Society establishes rules of engagement to maintain order. These are what we can consider to be *categorical* in nature. That is if we want to remain a member in good standing we need to follow them. These change from *era* to *era*. For instance, I remember watching TV sitcoms in the 50's when a bedroom scene always had twin beds; even for married couples. I needn't say much more about how that set of rules has changed in the last sixty-plus years.

In order to live in a society we must conform to its rules but also set up a set of rules of our own as individuals. We can consider these to be *hypothetical*. That is, we try them out and if they seem to work we keep them. We also revise them as we grow in living experience. But sometimes we hang on to them as though they are also *categorical*. And sometimes this happens when they are clearly not working. (that is, clearly to those around us but not us.) When this happens, we create *psychological turmoil* or in Birkman terms, **Stress**.

How Do We Develop Needs?

Let's separate physical and psychological needs at this point. We are only examining the latter. Physical needs such as food, shelter, and warmth must all be satisfied before we ever get to the issue of psychological needs. Abraham Maslow taught us that fact a long time ago.

I think that it's safe to say most of us will work with people whose physical needs are satisfied. So, we won't spend any more time on that issue. But the issue of satisfied psychological needs leaves us with a good deal of space to explore.

"The Needs provide us a sense of *inner self* through which we see the whole world. The visions provided by this set of inner eyes is a way of translating our own understanding of the world into a set of expectations that although seldom seen impact every relationship in our lives".[103]

Our needs are really expectations that we have from the world around us. We need to have the world be the way we want it to be for us to feel fulfilled and able to function at peak capacity. And where did we learn how the world should be? From our parents of course. And their parents before them. And their parents before them. Even our unchangeable physiologically based needs come from them when you consider that they gave us our neurophysiology.

How are Needs Constructed?

Needs are expectations. Where do expectations come from? They come from our familial, cultural[104] and historical backgrounds. Let's examine this statement using a very present topic, politics. Political candidates promise to fulfill expectations. Some people want the government to be more involved in everyday life and some people want it to get the heck out of the way. One could show a direct

---

[103] Birkman certification manual, Page 3-2.

[104] I consider religious influencers to be a part of both familial and cultural. With the advent of the ethical relativism of Postmodern times we might consider it a part of historical too.

relationship from our historical and economic circumstances to our choice of representatives to fulfill our expectations. And we call these groupings of people with similar expectations *political parties*. Ask a politically active individual what they *need* from the government and you'll hear all their expectations.

Key Point

"How we perceive ourselves and others will motivate how we act and how we behave. This means that our perceptions and misperceptions assume critical importance in how we live our lives".[105]

Looking at a more granular level, expectations come out of the common cares and concerns that families, cultures and historical times transmit to us.

"Caring" is the cultural bridge.

"Heidegger proposed that the core of our being human is care. That means that to be human is to care or be concerned about something. The concept of caring is a species phenomenon. What we care or concern ourselves with are reflective of the culture from which we come. It follows that culture is what provides the background for our care at a personal level—about what we will care or be concerned with in our individual lives. One can travel to other countries to see evidence of these cultural phenomena."[106]

If we consider that a core attribute of needs is what we care about, and if care is shaped in families, cultures, and

---

[105] Roger Birkman, Ph.D.
[106] My first book, "You, Your Self and the 21st Century."

historical times, we must understand Needs and consider all these externals and the impact they have on those we coach?

Can We Deconstruct Needs While Coaching?

First let's consider how Needs were transmitted to us. One could argue that they come to us in a variety of ways, which is true. But the main way we understand them, sort them out, organize them, contextualize them, and apply them is through language. Language, then becomes the tool we use to address the question of *can we deconstruct them while coaching*.

Of course, the first question that should come up in a coach's mind is, "Why"? And the only reason to even consider attempting to deconstruct a Need is to help the client see possibilities that they could not see before. To do this, we should have a more thorough understanding of how language constructs a Need.

Early in our lives people begin to make declarations around us. They may be positive or negative. They may be made without spoken language by actions or body language. But they begin to shape what we believe about the world and ourselves.

As we begin to understand language we also begin to hear assertions and assessments about us and the world we live in. "You are a smart little girl". You are a clumsy little boy". "Those people can't be trusted." "These people are good." As we grow up we are accumulating a good deal of knowledge of what the world is all about, who we are in it, and what we should expect to get from it. And we are beginning to find evidence for *what we now believe* so we can add a good deal of our own experiences to the data.

Key Point

> *"We don't see things as <u>they are</u>. We see them as <u>we are</u>."*[107]

We are shaping our Needs. By an early age we have constructed cognitive maps of our world and then they filter our direct experience of it. So now we **need** to have our experiences with the external world fit our cognitive maps. And when we have an anomalous experience we can either deflect or deny it or if it's powerful enough we might reconstruct something in our maps. That's the only way we can grow and develop.

How then can the coach assist to have useful but anomalous experiences be powerful enough to create reconstructions and not be deflected or denied? This is the coaching challenge. The answer is that we can use the same tools that were used to construct the cognitive maps to begin with.

Cognitive maps are constructed with three basic language acts: *assertions, assessments* and *declarations.*

Guided by the formation of our early family-based cognitive maps of the world, we begin to use other language acts to interact with them and to keep them coherent and intact. We **request, offer,** and **promise** according to the worldview that we have built.

As you will remember, these six basic linguistic moves in **bold** are in the two paragraphs above. These speech acts are sometimes found in the literature on variations on ***Speech Act Theory***. Theorists and linguistic

---

[107] A quote from Anais Nin found in the Birkman certification manual.

philosophers don't always agree on nomenclature but nonetheless they do agree that language not only describes but also creates the social worlds we live in.

Key Point

*We declare how the world is with the first three language acts. We **perform** actions consistent with our proclamations by using the second three language acts. This is how we construct and maintain our cognitive maps even in the face of overwhelming evidence to the contrary.*

Now that we know how we construct our world linguistically and we also know where needs come from we can look at how we can use The Birkman Method® for the mutual discovery of a client's *rules of engagement* which derive from the interplay of the three perspectives given to us in the Component report.[lxxxi]

Although the Usual Behavior scores can show the themes and patterns of the client's social interactions, (i.e., the expected or socialized behavior), the clues to a client's authentic self are to be found in the relationships of the Needs and Stress Behaviors scores. You can infer from this relationship which needs are not being fulfilled and which rules of engagement may be failing.

Key Point

Once aware of this information, you can then begin to work with the client to produce a linguistic deconstruction and reconstruction process culminating in:

(1) The ability to discern the needs-driven rule set that is at work

(2) New choices that come with discernment and/or

(3) The revision and/or enrichment of our needs-driven rules

(4) *The creation of additional rules with the potential for more effective needs satisfaction.*

The Birkman Method® reports nine Components. Some of the behaviors described in them are more changeable than others. Temperament, which is the stem from which the flower of personality grows, is fixed for practical purposes. It is well-advised for a coach to consider personality traits as fixed too. The reason is straight forward. Even if a client's personality trait-driven behavior is somewhat changeable, you usually don't have time to change it.

If a change in personality-driven behavior is not the goal, what can you expect when you take on a coaching client. The objective of change should be the client's actions and not their personalities. It is in creating a safe place for your client to stop, reflect and inquire that actions can be changed.

How much resistance should you expect?

As noted in the previous chapter, the *Freedom* and *Challenge* construct scores available in the Signature and Signature Suite levels are made up of items from the other Components and are therefore composites. These two constructs are essential in understanding how a person will respond to coaching. While the *Challenge* construct is vital in understanding how a person will receive feedback and coaching, the *Freedom* construct fills out our understanding of a person's willingness to take the initiative to do something productive with the coaching engagement.

Coaching Strategies.

Like any other important endeavor, we need to develop a set of objectives before we establish a strategy. Objectives and strategy will keep us moving in the right direction. Objectives say, "this is where we're going." Strategy says, "this is how we'll get there." If one strategy doesn't work, then we can choose another but only if we have the objectives clearly in mind to determine if the new way keeps us on the right track.

When using The Birkman Method® Components in coaching there are three fundamental strategies:

Key Point
Three Major Coaching Strategies:

*(1) Calibrate your coaching method to work with clients whose **Challenge** and **Freedom** scores indicate potential difficulties in listening to and accepting your coaching.*
(2) Assist with changes in those rules that are open to change.
(3) Assist in creating awareness and acceptance of those that are not.

Before we go deeper into coaching strategies it is important that we review how a rule of engagement looks when viewing a specific Component. The following matrix gives an example of how a client might construct a rule given the use of **declarative** and **performative** language acts.

This matrix illustrates the process further.

Behavioral Construct	Linguistic Construct	Declarative Acts	Performative Acts
Physiological orientation in an interaction	Linguistic interpretation of the interaction	The world is . . . I am . . . I will be . . .	If so, I will R, O & P[108] in this way . . .

Person A – High Needs scores

Assertiveness	Tendency to speak up and express opinions openly and forcefully	The world is a place where people need to speak their minds. I am a confident and capable person in it. I will be forceful and confident.	My requests will be firm and directive. My offers will be seriously delivered. My promises will be kept without fail.

---

[108] R,O & P refer to requests, offers and promises.

Person B – Low Needs scores.

Assertiveness	Tendency to speak up and express opinions openly and forcefully	The world is a place where speaking out is easy and informal. I am an easygoing person who doesn't care much about dominating. I will be pleasant and agreeable.	My requests will be pleasant and more like suggestions. My offers will be simple, easy and open to suggestion. My promises will always be open ended and deferential.

This example should give us ideas about where and how to begin deconstruction and reconstruction of this rule set. For instance, we might challenge the belief that the world is the way the client perceives it, offering other observations. Or we might point out how a client's performative acts are inconsistent with producing his outcomes. The entry point for any coaching discussion is the Component and a review of all three perspectives, Usual, Needs and Stress.

As I've noted throughout this book, The Birkman Method® is seemingly custom made for coaching. The latest version gives the coach several new reports with additional information tailormade for our purposes. 1. Coaching Page, 2. Coaching to Needs, and 3. Coaching Report, all offer specific information vital to a Birkman coach. In addition, considering the Challenge and Freedom scores as part of a planning strategy is an excellent way to prepare.

Finally, our very *self* is created and maintained in interaction with others. You will remember, Heidegger uses the concept of *Dasein* to uncover the nature of "Being" (Ontology). We are always a *being* engaged in the world. We're not our internal or external structures alone, but the coherence of "being-in-the-world."

Coaching then, is a tool to assist in the full development of the client as a "being in the world"—a continual process of involvement with the world as mediated through the development of the authentic self.

The self depends on context and context depends on human interaction. Developing, changing, and re-finding our authentic *self,* by its very nature, requires others. It requires grounding that cannot be fully realized in the blindness of our subjective experience. To discover ourselves, we need each other. This is the role of the coach: To be midwife to the birth of that discovery. Happy coaching.

Bibliography

[i] Neisser, 1967; Gregory, 1980, Michael W. Eysenck, ed. The Blackwell Dictionary of Cognitive Psychology (Oxford / Cambridge: 1990)

[ii] Peter Senge, The 5th Discipline, The Art and Practice of the Learning Organization (New York: 1994) p.235

[iii] Steven Pinker, The Blank Slate, The Modern Denial of Human Nature (Penguin Books LTD, registered offices: Harmondsworth, Middlesex, England: 2002)

[iv] Ibid.

[v] Martin Heidegger, Being and Time, translated by Joan Stambaugh (New York: 1997)

[vi] Connie Zweig and Jeremiah Abrams, Meeting the Shadow, the Hidden Power of the Dark Side of Human Nature (New York: 1991)

[vii] Laura Pappano, The Connection Gap, Why Americans Feel So Alone, (Rutgers University Press, New Brunswick, NJ and London, 2001) p.20

[viii] Bruce Bridgeman, Psychology & Evolution, the origins of mind. (Sage Publications, Thousand Oaks, CA: 2003)

[ix] Noam Avram Chomsky, Syntactic Structures, (1957)

[x] Karen Armstrong, The Battle for God (New York: 2000) p.64

[xi] Alisdair MacIntyre, Whose Justice? Which Rationality, (South Bend, IN: 1984)

[xii] Immanuel Kant, The Critique of Pure Reason, translated by Norman Kemp Smith (New York: 1965)

[xiii] J. L. Austin, How to Do Things with Words (Oxford, 1961).

[xiv] Ludwig Wittgenstein, Ludwig. 1953. Philosophical Investigation,. Translated by G.E.M. Anscombe (New York: 1953)

[xv] J. R. Searle, Intrinsic Intentionality, Behavioral and Brain Sciences (1980).

[xvi] Ferdinand de Saussure, Course in General Linguistics, translated by Wade Baskin (New York: 1966)

[xvii] Connie Zweig and Jeremiah Abrams, Meeting the Shadow, the Hidden Power of the Dark side of Human Nature (New York: 1991)

[xviii] Douglas Kellner, Editor, Baudrillard: A Critical Reader (Cambridge, MA: 1994)

[xix] Ibid.

[xx] Viktor Frankl, Man's Search for Meaning, an introduction to Logotherapy, (Simon and Schuster, revised New York:1977)

[xxi] Humberto Maturana & Francisco Varela, The Tree of Knowledge, (Boston / London: 1988)

[xxii] Michael W. Eysenck, ed. The Blackwell Dictionary of Cognitive Psychology (Oxford / Cambridge: 1990) p.262

[xxiii] Ibid.

[xxiv] Steven Pinker, The Blank Slate, The Modern Denial of Human Nature (Penguin Books LTD, registered offices: Harmondsworth, Middlesex, England: 2002)

[xxv] Noam Avram Chomsky, Syntactic Structures, (1957)

[xxvi] Steven Pinker, Blank Slate, a Modern Denial of Human Nature (Penguin Books LTD, registered offices: Harmondsworth, Middlesex, England: 2002

[xxvii]https://straightlinelogic.com/2016/05/25/the-empty-brain-by-robert-epstein/

[xxviii] William H. Calvin, How Brains Think (Basic Books, A division of HarperCollins, 1966) p.21

[xxix] Ibid.

[xxx] ibid.

[xxxi] ibid.

[xxxii] Humberto Maturana & Francisco Varela, The Tree of Knowledge, (Boston / London: 1988)

[xxxiii] Ibid

[xxxiv] Ibid.

[xxxv] William H. Calvin, How Brains Think (Basic Books, A division of HarperCollins, 1966) p.64

[xxxvi] J. R. Searle, Intrinsic Intentionality, Behavioral and Brain Sciences (1980).

[xxxvii] Michael W. Eysenck, ed. The Blackwell Dictionary of Cognitive Psychology (Oxford / Cambridge: 1990)

[xxxviii] Ibid.

[xxxix] Carl Rogers, On Becoming a Person, (Houghton Mifflin, New York:1961)

[xl] Martin Heidegger, Being and Time, translated by Joan Stambaugh (New York: 1997)

[xli] Immanuel Kant, The Critique of Pure Reason, translated by Norman Kemp Smith (New York: 1965)

[xlii] Eric Fromm, Marx's Concept of Man, (New York: 1969)

[xliii] Sigmund Freud, Civilization and Its Discontents, (New York: 1961)

[xliv] Immanuel Kant, The Critique of Pure Reason, translated by Norman Kemp Smith (New York: 1965)

[xlv] Ibid.

[xlvi] Ibid.

[xlvii] Martin Heidegger, Being and Time, translated by Joan Stambaugh (New York: 1997)

[xlviii] Immanuel Kant, The Critique of Pure Reason, translated by Norman Kemp Smith (New York: 1965)

[xlix] Humberto Maturana and Francisco Varela, The Tree of Knowledge, (Boston / London: 1988)

[l] Thomas Hobbes, Leviathan (New York: 1968)

[li] Humberto Maturana and Francisco Varela, The Tree of Knowledge, (Boston / London: 1988)

[lii] Peter Senge, The 5th Discipline, The Art and Practice of the Learning Organization (New York: 1994) p. 237

[liii] ibid. p.242

[liv] Roger Birkman, Ph.D., True Colors, (Nashville: 1995) Pgs. 14-15

[lv] Martin Heidegger, Being and Time,

[lvi lvi] Martin Heidegger, Being and Time,

[lvii] Jared Diamond, Guns, Germs, and Steel, the Fates of Human Societies, (W.W. Norton & Company / New York:1999)

[lviii] Philip Carey, Ph.D. From lecture series - Great Minds of Western Intellectual Tradition, The Teaching Company

[lix] Ibid.

[lx] Ibid.

[lxi] Rick Roderick, Ph.D. from a lecture "the Siege of the Self in modernity," The Teaching Company

[lxii] Ibid.

[lxiii] Martin Heidegger, Being and Time, translated by Joan Stambaugh (New York: 1997)

[lxiv] Ludwig Wittgenstein, Tractatus Logico-Philosophicus, translated by D. F. Pears and B. F. McGuiness. (London: 1961)

[lxv] Jurgen Habermas, Toward a Rational Society, (Boston: 1970)

[lxvi] Ludwig Wittgenstein, Ludwig. 1953. Philosophical Investigation,. translated by G.E.M. Anscombe (New York: 1953)

[lxvii] Ludwig Wittgenstein, Tractatus Logico-Philosophicus, translated by D. F. Pears and B. F. McGuiness. (London: 1961)

[lxviii] Philip Wheelwright, The Presocratics (New York: 1986)

[lxix] Alfred Korzybski, Science and Sanity, An Introduction to Non-Aristotelian Systems and General Semantics. (Lakeville, CT: 1924)

[lxx] Bente Elkjaer, Associate professor Department of Informatics, reference from Internet with no other information available for credit.

[lxxi] Humberto Maturana and Francisco Varela, The Tree of Knowledge, (Boston / London: 1988)

[lxxii] Antonio Damasio, Looking for Spinoza, Joy, Sorrow and the Feeling Brain (Harcourt Inc / New York: 2003)

[lxxiii] Ibid.

[lxxiv] Martin Heidegger, Being and Time, translated by Joan Stambaugh (New York: 1997)

[lxxv] Alfred Korzybski, Science and Sanity, An Introduction to Non-Aristotelian Systems and General Semantics. (Lakeville, CT: 1924)

[lxxvi] Daniel M. Wegner, White Bears and other Unwanted Thoughts, Penguin Books (New York: 1989)

[lxxvii] Ibid.

[lxxviii] Ibid.

[lxxix] Noam Avram Chomsky, Syntactic Structures, (1957)

[lxxx] Steven Pinker, Blank Slate, a Modern Denial of Human Nature (Penguin Books LTD, registered offices: Harmondsworth, Middlesex, England: 2002